Asia.com

The Internet is developing quicker in Asia than in any other region of the world. This book is the first comprehensive analysis of the information society in an Asian context, and the impact of these technologies in Asia. The contributors examine why these impacts are inevitably uneven and how they are conditioned by issues of telecommunications infrastructure, government policies, cultural and social values, and economic realities.

The first half of the book examines such core issues as:

- the extent of Internet usage in Asia
- who is using the Internet and why
- the digital divide in the Asian context
- state attempts to enforce censorship, and resistance to this
- surveillance of web usage
- the challenges of piracy and intellectual property law

The second half of the book draws upon case studies from Japan, China, Singapore, Malaysia, India, and Indonesia to demonstrate how Internet use by different groups allows for interaction at both international and national scales, as well as between real and virtual worlds, and its impact on politics, community, and economy.

The combination of original research, theoretical innovation, and detailed case studies make this an important book for scholars and students in Asian studies, media studies, communication studies, and sociology.

K.C. Ho is Associate Professor at the National University of Singapore.

Randolph Kluver is Associate Professor at the School of Communication and Information, Nanyang Technological University, Singapore.

Kenneth C.C. Yang is Associate Professor, Department of Communication, The University of Texas at El Paso.

Asia's transformations
Edited by Mark Selden
Binghamton University and Cornell University, USA

The books in this series explore the political, social, economic and cultural consequences of Asia's transformations in the twentieth and twenty-first centuries. The series emphasizes the tumultuous interplay of local, national, regional and global forces as Asia bids to become the hub of the world economy. While focusing on the contemporary, it also looks back to analyze the antecedents of Asia's contested rise.

This series comprises several strands:

Asia's Transformations aims to address the needs of students and teachers, and the titles will be published in hardback and paperback. Titles include:

Critical Asian Scholarship is a series intended to showcase the most important individual contributions to scholarship in Asian studies. Each of the volumes presents a leading Asian scholar addressing themes that are central to his or her most significant and lasting contribution to Asian studies. The series is committed to the rich variety of research and writing on Asia, and is not restricted to any particular discipline, theoretical approach or geographical expertise.

China's Past, China's Future
Energy, food, environment
Vaclav Smil

China Unbound
Evolving perspectives on the Chinese past
Paul A. Cohen

Women and the Family in Chinese History
Patricia Buckley Ebrey

Southeast Asia
A testament
George McT. Kahin

Asia.com

Asia encounters the Internet

Edited by K.C. Ho, Randolph Kluver, and Kenneth C.C. Yang

RoutledgeCurzon
Taylor & Francis Group

LONDON AND NEW YORK

First published 2003
by RoutledgeCurzon
2 Park Square, Milton Park, Abingdon, Oxon, OX14 4RN

Simultaneously published in the USA and Canada
by RoutledgeCurzon
270 Madison Ave, New York NY 10016

RoutledgeCurzon is an imprint of the Taylor & Francis Group

Transferred to Digital Printing 2005

Typeset in Sabon by Wearset Ltd, Boldon, Tyne and Wear

British Library Cataloguing in Publication Data
A catalogue record for this book is available from the British Library

Library of Congress Cataloging in Publication Data
Asia.com : Asia encounters the Internet / edited by K.C. Ho,
Randolph Kluver, and Kenneth C.C. Yang.
    p. cm. – (RoutledgeCurzon studies in Asia's transformations)
(Asia's transformations)
Includes bibliographical references and index.
    1. Telecommunication–Asia. 2. Information society–Asia.
3. Internet–Asia. 4. Information technology–Asia. I. Ho, Kong-
Chong, 1955– II. Kluver, Randy. III. Yang, Kenneth C.C. IV. Series.
V. Series: Asia's transformations
    HE8342.A8 2003
    384.3'3'095–dc21
                                                    2003004072

ISBN 0–415–31503–4 (hbk)
ISBN 0–415–31504–2 (pbk)

Contents

Illustrations

Tables

Contributors

Tim Beal (tim.beal@vuw.ac.nz) is a senior lecturer in the School of Marketing and International Business at Victoria University of Wellington, New Zealand, where he teaches international marketing and Internet marketing. He is an Asia specialist with an interest in a wide range of contemporary issues. He is currently involved in an international research project examining the use of the Internet by small and medium enterprises. Details are on his homepage at http://www.vuw.ac.nz/~caplabtb/beal.html

Brenda Chan (PS7344964B@ntu.edu.sg) is a doctoral student at the School of Communication and Information, Nanyang Technological University, Singapore. She graduated from the National University of Singapore with First Class Honours in Mass Communication and obtained her MA in Social and Political Thought from the University of Warwick, UK. Ms Chan's research focuses on the Internet and cultural identity.

James Chin (JChin@upgn.ac.pg) is Deputy Dean, School of Humanities and Social Sciences, University of Papua New Guinea. He has published extensively on Malaysian, Singaporean, and Papua New Guinean politics. His recent publications include *The Chinese of South East Asia* (Minority Rights Group International). Prior to an academic career, he worked as a journalist in Singapore and Malaysia.

Anthony P. D'Costa (dcosta@u.washington.edu) is an Associate Professor of Comparative International Development, University of Washington in Tacoma. He is affiliated with the International Studies and South Asia Programs at the Jackson School of International Studies at the University of Washington, Seattle. As a political economist, he researches how developing countries negotiate structural barriers to industrial development, innovations, and the opportunities offered and constraints imposed by globalization. He has published widely on the steel, auto, and software industries. Some of his recent publications are "Uneven and Combined Development: Understanding India's

Software Exports," *World Development* (2003); "Institutions and Industrial Governance in India: Learning to Cooperate the Japanese Way," *Asian Business & Management Journal* (2003). He is currently co-editing *India in the Global Software Industry: Innovation, Firm Strategies and Development* (Palgrave). He serves on the Board of Trustees of the American Institute of Indian Studies, Chicago, and on the editorial board of the *Asian Business and Management Journal.*

Karsten Giese (karsten@uniterra.net) is a research fellow at the Institute of Asian Affairs, Hamburg, Germany. Dr. Giese studied modern China studies, sociology, and political science in Berlin (Germany). His research interests include social and cultural change, Internet development, and migration in China, as well as Chinese foreign and security politics. Currently he is head of a German–Chinese research project on "virtual identity workshops and identity construction in the Chinese Internet." Recent publications include, in 2003, "Internet Growth and the Digital Divide – Implications for Spatial Development" in Christopher R. Hughes and Gudrun Wacker (eds), *China and the Internet: Politics of the Digital Leap Forward* (Routledge), and in 2001, "Internet and E-Business in China" in Benno Engels and Olaf Nielinger (eds), *Elektronischer Handel in Afrika, Asien, Lateinamerika und Nahost* (Schriften des Deutschen Überseeinstituts).

Debora Halbert (DHalbert@otterbein.edu) is an Associate Professor of Political Science at Otterbein College. She has published numerous articles on the subject of copyright law and is the author of *Intellectual Property in the Information Age: The Politics of Expanding Property Rights* (Quorum).

K.C. Ho (sochokc@nus.edu.sg) is an Associate Professor at the National University of Singapore. He was founder coordinator of the Information and Communications Management Programme (1999–2002) and Chair of Sociology (2000–3) at the National University of Singapore. His research interests lie in globalization and inter-city competition, economic restructuring, and the political economy of Internet development. Further details are available at: http://www.fas.nus.edu.sg/staff/home/sochokc

Randolph Kluver (TRKluver@ntu.edu.sg) is an Associate Professor at the School of Communication and Information, Nanyang Technological University, Singapore. Dr. Kluver conducts research on Asian political communication, technology, and cultural and social change in Asia. He is the author of *Legitimating the Chinese Economic Reforms: A Rhetoric of Myth and Orthodoxy* (State University of New York Press), and co-edited the volume *Civic Discourse, Civil Society, and Chinese Communities* (Ablex Press). He is co-founder of the Chinese Internet Research Network and has recently participated in a comprehensive analysis of the Internet and democracy in Asia, sponsored by the Konrad Adenauer Foundation and the Asian Media Information and Communication Center.

Waipeng Lee (twplee@ntu.edu.sg) is an Assistant Professor at the School of Communication and Information, Nanyang Technological University, Singapore. She is a member of the Singapore Internet Project Research Team. Her Internet-related publications include: "Internet and Displacement Effect: Children's Media Use and Activities in Singapore" (in vol. 9, issue 2 (2001) of the online *Journal of Computer-Mediated Communication*), and "Internet in Singapore" in *Internet in Asia*, edited by Sankaran Ramanathan and Jorg Becker (Asian Media Information and Communication Centre). Besides the Internet, she is interested in persuasion and public opinion, and has written both journal and conference papers on the inoculation and spiral of silence theories.

Xiguang Li (xiguang@public.bta.net.cn) is Professor and Director of the Center for International Communication Studies, and Academic Dean of the School of Journalism and Communication, Tsinghua University, Beijing, China. He is a former fellow at the Joan Shorenstein Center at Harvard University and the senior editor and director of the political desk of Xinhua News Agency (New China News Agency). He is the author of a number of books on Chinese media, including the recently published *Media Power* (Southern Daily Press) and *Essential Journalism* (Southern Daily Press). Professor Li has won a number of journalism awards for his news writing and has published a number of academic articles on the press in China.

Merlyna Lim (limmerlyna@hotmail.com and merlyna@bdg.centrin.net.id) has a degree in architecture, and is presently a doctoral candidate in technology and society studies, University of Twente, Enschede, the Netherlands, and is a research fellow with the Social Construction of Technology Research Group in Bandung, Indonesia. Her doctoral research explores the socio-political dimensions of Internet technology in the Indonesian-global context, with a focus on relationships between the Internet, identity politics, and democratization.

David Lyon (lyond@post.queensu.ca) is Professor of Sociology at Queen's University, Canada, where his research and writing is in communication and information technologies, religion, and social theory. His most recent books are *Surveillance Society: Monitoring Everyday Life* (Open University Press), *Surveillance as Social Sorting: Privacy, Risk, and Digital Discrimination* (Routledge 2003), and *Surveillance after September 11* (Polity). His current work is on a sociology of cyberspace and the globalization of personal data.

Junko R. Onosaka (jo604@hotmail.com) is a Ph.D. candidate in the history of women's education in the Graduate School of Education at the State University of New York at Buffalo. She has written "Joseigaku no Shōrai (The Future of Women's Studies)," *Josei Shigaku* (*The Annuals of Women's History*), No. 11 (2001), "Marilyn Boxer's *When Women Ask the Questions: Creating Women's Studies in America*," *Joseigaku* (*Journal of Women's Studies Association of Japan*, No. 9 (2001), "American Women Who Created Their Own Educational Space," Kokuritsu Fujin Kyōiku Kaikan Kenkyū Kiyō (*Journal of National Women's Education Center of Japan*), No. 6 (2002), and (forthcoming) "Challenging Society through the Grid of Information" in *Japanese Cyberculture* (Routledge).

Carolyn Penfold (c.penfold@unsw.edu.au) is a lecturer in the Faculty of Law at the University of New South Wales, and is a Research Associate of the Baker and McKenzie Cyberspace Law and Policy Centre, UNSW. She has published a number of papers relating to Internet content control in both Australia and the UK.

K.S. Arul Maragatha Muthu Selvan (arulselvan@vasnet.co.in) is a doctoral student at the Manipal Institute of Communication, Manipal, India. His interests include computer-mediated communication, ICT for development, and new media production. He moderates two listserv newsletters, ICERNET and MORGUE, that deal with Indian communication education and research respectively.

Shyam Tekwani (TSRTekwani@ntu.edu.sg) teaches in the School of Communication and Information at Nanyang Technological University, Singapore. He is a photojournalist turned academic who spent over a decade covering conflict and terrorism from the front lines in South Asia. His world-exclusive photo reportage of the separatist war in Sri Lanka has been published in *The New York Times Magazine*, *Newsweek*, and *India Today*, among other publications. His dissertation and current work focuses on the adaptability of new media technologies by and communication strategies of terrorist and dissident groups around the world.

Leslie M. Tkach-Kawasaki (tkach@japan.email.ne.jp) is a Ph.D. candidate in the International Political Economy Program, University of Tsukuba, Japan. Her research focuses on how Japanese political actors are using new media technologies during election and non-election periods, and comparing their use of the Internet with political actors in other countries. Ms. Tkach-Kawasaki's publications to date include a research report in *Party Politics* (2003) and papers in various conference proceedings.

Qin Xuan is a research assistant at the Center for International Communication Studies, Tsinghua University, Beijing, China.

Kenneth C.C. Yang (**kq43210@yahoo.com**) is Associate Professor, Department of Communication, The University of Texas at El Paso. Dr. Yang's research interests are the social implications of new information and communication technologies (ICTs). Past research involves the analyses of the impacts of ICTs and convergence on universal service policy, the study of bypassing activities on telecommunications policy, and marketing strategies on the World Wide Web. His current research project focuses on the impact of emerging global computer network on transborder information flow and freedom of speech policy in South and Southeast Asian countries. Dr. Yang's works may be found in the *Journal of Information, Communication, & Society, Human Communication, On the Internet, Journal of Marketing Communications*, and *Journal of Mass Communication Studies.*

Preface

Since the advent of the Internet in the early 1990s, analysts, policy makers, and academics have generated an impressive amount of research examining the role of the emerging technology in human life, and, perhaps more importantly, the impact of the Internet in the personal, social, and political realms. So much of this analysis, however, has examined the role of the Internet in the advanced Western nations, where technological development and diffusion are common, the mass media are privatized or semi-privatized and competitive, and assumptions of personal liberty are taken for granted. Even with the tremendous amount of cultural overlap between advanced Western nations, the Internet has had widely varying impacts, and netizens have deployed the technology to vastly different uses.

The purpose of this book is to begin the process of examining the encounter of the Internet with Asian cultures, Asian nations, and Asian netizens. The significance of this interaction cannot be understated, as the expectations for information technology began to impinge on almost all of the significant policy decisions faced by Asian governments, including funding priorities, educational priorities, military priorities, and so on. In many ways, the questions from which we find ourselves working boil down to this: Does the Internet transform Asia, or does Asia transform the Internet? Or are there a host of more complex cultural and social factors that make answering any version of these questions impossible?

On September 14–15, 2001, the university members of the Internet Political Economy Forum held a conference entitled "the Internet and Development in Asia" at the campus of the National University of Singapore. Nearly 150 participants attended from many nations with dozens of papers presented that provided in-depth examination of the economic, social, and political implications of the Internet, as well as the role of intellectual property in Asia. Although participants from North America were prevented from coming due to the tragic events of September 11, the conference was a meaningful effort to begin to consolidate and synthesize the findings of researchers from around the world.

This volume is a collection of some of the most significant of the papers presented at that conference. All of the papers have been significantly revised since that conference, taking into account not only new developments, but also the fruit of discussions at the conference. The editors wish to express their deep appreciation for all of the participants at the conference, including the paper presenters whose work is not represented in this volume. We deeply appreciate the sacrifices involved for those who came from many nations to participate, as the conference was a success only because of the rich dialogue and debate that occurred during the few days together.

Research grant R-124-000-001-112 from the National University of Singapore provided the seed funds for the conference. The editors would like especially to thank the Microsoft Corporation and the Lee Foundation, whose generous donations to the conference enabled them to provide a higher quality of debate on many difficult issues. We would also like to thank the Dean of the Faculty of Arts at the National University of Singapore, Professor Lily Kong, whose support enabled us to host this event. We would be remiss if we failed to thank all of those whose help enabled us to host the conference with a minimum of disruption, particularly the conference administrative staff: Jane Ong, Maggie Chee, and Hannah Lim.

We must also highlight the role that Mark Selden played in this book, as his personal interest in this project and his high quality of review and analysis undoubtedly made the volume a stronger book than it would have been without his attention and scholarly care. We would like to thank Craig Fowlie and Zoë Botterill for their encouragement in the preparation of this volume. The production of the manuscript owed much of its success to the patience and care that Sue-ann Soon gave to the project. Finally, we must thank the contributors, who endured seemingly endless emails and revision requests, and often impossible deadlines. Without your cheerful willingness to work with us to help craft the very diverse perspectives and topics into a coherent whole, it would have been impossible to produce a work with the scope that this volume represents. K.C. Ho was on sabbatical during the final stages of the production. He thanks Ying-Hwa Chang and Vipan Prachuabmoh, Directors of the Institute of Sociology, Academia Sinica and Center for Population Studies, Chulalongkorn University, respectively, for the warm reception and generous use of facilities and resources for the production of the manuscript.

The love and concern of our families sustain us in numerous ways. We would like to thank them for their encouragement and support of this project.

K.C. Ho, Randolph Kluver, and Ken C.C. Yang
February, 2003

1 Asia encounters the Internet

K.C. Ho, Randolph Kluver, and Kenneth C.C. Yang

For some years, leaders in Asia have argued that Information Communications Technologies (ICTs) would play a significant role in economic, political, and social developments in Asia. There is some compelling evidence of the truth of this judgment, although the outcomes have frequently defied the hopes and dreams of planners. Of all the benefits promised by ICT proponents, the one which seemed to hold the greatest promise within Asia was that of economic development. These benefits may be viewed directly in terms of the creation of a booming market in information and communications equipment and networks, and indirectly in terms of the growing business applications that are linked to ICTs (e.g. online commerce, accounting, and communications). They may also be observed in the proliferation of Internet access, websites, and bulletin boards reaching millions of people, not only in the urban centers of Asia, but also in rural areas. Such developments have also led governments to see an efficient telecommunications infrastructure as a crucial element in the attraction of investments, becoming a priority investment alongside transportation and manpower in the basket of items essential to the building of a country's economic competitiveness.

In order to gather a sort of "mid-term assessment" of the impact of these developments in Asia, the Internet Political Economy Forum and the Information and Communication Management Program at the National University of Singapore convened a conference of scholars and analysts on September 14 and 15, 2001 in Singapore. Dozens of papers were presented which examined a variety of issues associated with Asia's encounter with the Internet, and the economic, political, and social consequences of this encounter. Although the events of September 11 grounded many of our North American participants, the conference was a success in helping us to understand the impact of the Internet in Asia. The goal of this book is to provide a representative sample of some of the issues with which individuals, businesses, and governments across Asia are grappling. The chapters presented in this book are broadly representative not just of the theoretical and policy-oriented issues that have come to the fore, but also of the very different regional and geographic diversity of Asia, and help to illustrate the very different ways in which Asians are encountering the Internet.

INTERNET AND DEVELOPMENT IN ASIA: A BRIEF SURVEY

The rapidly increasing global economic importance of the Internet is clearly demonstrated by the realization and application that the Internet can facilitate the discovery, publication, and dissemination of knowledge through its seamless global information infrastructure (OECD, 2000a). The Internet is particularly well suited to support and facilitate the creation and formation of a knowledge-based economy that emphasizes the acquisition, generalization, utilization, and diffusion of knowledge in all activities to create wealth (Latifah, 1999).

The economic promise of ICT has led many Asian countries to focus on information technology as a critical component of national development plans. Several statistical indicators may be used to represent and illustrate state-sponsored efforts at ICT developments (see Table 1.1). The share of GDP attributed to ICT has been on the rise in the past five years (between 1995 and 2000) for many Asian countries, most prominently in the developed economies in this region. For example, in Japan, the increase is from 5.3 percent in 1995 to 9.6 percent in 2000, while in China, the percentage increased from 2.9 percent to 5.7 percent during the same period. The relationship between economic development and the importance of ICT is clear, since most developed economies in this region show a high ratio of ICT to the overall GDP in 2000 (i.e. Hong Kong, SAR (8.7 percent), Japan (9.6 percent), Korea (7.4 percent), and Singapore (9.9 percent)). Even the lesser developed countries have seen some striking increase, such as in Vietnam, as the percentage has increased from 3.6 percent to 6.7 percent, and in the Philippines, where it increased from 2.6 percent to 4.2 percent.

As in the advanced economies of the West, the use of ICT has revolutionalized the modes of production and directions of economic development in Asia. In many cases, ICT has also dramatically changed Asian societies. In developed economies such as Hong Kong, Japan, Korea, Singapore, and Taiwan, the number of personal computers per 1000 persons doubled between 1995 and 2000. For developing economies such as China, Malaysia, Sri Lanka, and Vietnam, where the absolute number of personal computers has been much lower, the growth rate has been even more phenomenal. For example, in Vietnam, the number of personal computers almost doubled, from 4.6 percent in 1997 to 8.8 percent in 2000.

Many governments in this region have seen the adoption of ICT as a central part of strategic planning in the informationalization of their societies. The Internet is especially emphasized, since as it has relatively low

Table 1.1 ICT development in Asia

Country	Personal computer (per 1000 people)		Internet users (thousands)		ICT as % of GDP	
	1995	2000	1995	2000	1995	2000
Bangladesh	N/a	1.5	N/a	100	N/a	N/a
Brunei	38.7	70.1	3	30	N/a	N/a
Cambodia	0.5	1.1	N/a	6	N/a	N/a
China	2.3	15.9	60	22,500	2.9	5.7
Hong Kong, China	154.3	350.6	200	2601	6.1	8.7
Indonesia	5.0	9.9	50	2000	2.1	2.2
Japan	120.3	315.2	2000	47,080	5.3	9.6
Korea, Rep.	107.7	237.9	366	19,040	4.7	7.4
Lao PDR	N/a	2.6	N/a	6	N/a	N/a
Macao, China	N/a	159.9	1	60	N/a	N/a
Malaysia	37.3	103.1	40	3700	5.0	6.6
Myanmar	N/a	1.1	N/a	7	N/a	N/a
Pakistan	3.5	4.2	0	134	N/a	N/a
Philippines	9.6	19.3	20	2000	2.6	4.2
Singapore	201.9	483.1	100	1200	6.9	9.9
Sri Lanka	1.1	7.1	1	122	N/a	N/a
Taiwan*	98	196	250	4540	N/a	N/a
Thailand	14.1	24.3	55	2300	2.7	3.7
Vietnam	1.4	8.8	N/a	200	3.6	6.7

Sources: Data are compiled from ITU (2000), *Yearbook of Statistics: Telecommunications Service 1990–1999*, Geneva: International Telecommunications Union, and World Bank, Development Data Group [online]. Available: http://www.worldbank.org/data/countrydata/countrydata.html

Note:
*The year 2000 data are not available. The 1999 data are used instead. The World Bank does not have a separate section on Taiwan due to its ambiguous political status.

technical and economic requirements and is thus suited for rapid deployment, allowing Asian countries to leap-frog into the Information Age. Most countries in this region have employed a combination of telecommunications policy deregulation, market liberalization, private and foreign investment, and government initiatives to expedite the diffusion of the Internet among their countries, with the result that within five years, the growth of the Internet population has grown dramatically across the region. For example, in China, the number of Internet users increased 325-fold in the years from 1995 to 2000. Japan and Korea have also witnessed rapid growth in the number of Internet users, with Hong Kong and a number of Southeast Asian countries (Singapore, Malaysia, Thailand, and Indonesia) experiencing more modest but nevertheless significant increases. The most dramatic improvements, however, have been in poorer countries, which started at very low levels. Thus the number of users in Japan increased by a ratio of 20, whereas in the Philippines the rate increased by 100 times and in Sri Lanka 122 times.

There are a number of governmental plans and policies in various countries that demonstrate how IT expenditures are justified by those advocating them. For example, the Chinese government identified the growth of ICTs as a sector in which the nation could potentially become internationally competitive, and by the late 1990s the government was clearly focused on enhancing the infrastructure so as to prepare the way for greater economic expansion (Kraemer and Dedrick, 2001). Likewise in Japan, where the government promises that it remains committed to the growth of this sector, in spite of criticisms that it has fallen behind in this sector (Kuroda, 2000). In Southeast Asia, Malaysia's commitment to ICTs is integrated into a broader national development master plan called *Vision 2020*, which is designed to transform Malaysia into a "fully developed nation" by 2020 (Huff, 2001), a goal remarkable in its aspirations, and where formidable hurdles will have to be overcome if the status is to be achieved within the time frame. In Singapore, a plan called *InfoComm 21* also aims to harness information communication technologies for national competitiveness and "improving the quality of life," and moving Singapore into "the ranks of 'first world economies' of the Net age" (IDA, 2000). These policies, although selective, demonstrate the ways in which governments across Asia aspire to participate in the digital revolution. In fact, as in so many instances in the past, national goals were expected to be accomplished by the private sector. For example, a number of national telecommunications incumbents rushed to take advantage of the commercial potential of the Internet either by setting up a separate Internet service provider entity or strengthening existing communication infrastructure for leasing to private information service providers (Valingra, 1997).

The importance of the Internet, as well as other ICTs, in assisting developing countries has also been articulated by the development community for over twenty years. In some ways this is an article of faith and there are a number of practical difficulties in assessing whether or not it is attainable. In 1980, the UNESCO General Conference initiated the International Programme for Development of Communications, and in 1982, the International Telecommunications Union's Plenipotentiary Conference established an independent commission to investigate the relationship between telecommunications and development. In 1994, then US Vice President Al Gore laid out his vision of the Global Information Infrastructure (GII) as "an essential prerequisite to sustainable development for all members of the human family" (Cukor and McKnight, 2000). Largely as a result of these expectations and the policies that have issued forth from them, the Internet has diffused at a far faster speed than past generations of communications technologies. In less than a decade, the Internet has reached fifty million users worldwide, a level which took the telephone seventy-four years, the radio thirty-eight years, the personal computer sixteen years, and television thirteen years to reach (Goldstein and O'Connor, 2000).

The promise of ICTs is enticing, not only for national governments, but also for regional groupings. For example, an e-ASEAN Task Force was established in late 1999 "to develop a broad and comprehensive action plan for an ASEAN e-space and to develop competencies within ASEAN to compete in the global information economy" (E-ASEAN, 2000). Many within the region argue that human development, through narrowing the digital divide, is a critical issue for ASEAN nations (Karnjanatawe, 2001). One critical argument is that income disparity and inequality lead to greater political instability; thus it becomes urgent for regional and international bodies to cooperate to promote ICTs, so as to guarantee that all nations and people share in the digital dividends, an approach affirmed in the 2001 United Nations Development Program Report (UNDP, 2001a and 2001b).

Besides the economic, political, and geopolitical considerations, personal interaction with information technologies is seen as critical for facilitating national integration into an information society. For example, China mapped out plans to establish a nationwide network linking every urban family and rural village (Wu, 1996). Likewise, the Malaysian government has adopted the PCFAIR Fund and USP Fund measures to boost computer and Internet literacy (Yang, 2001). The government of Singapore launched a National IT Literacy Programme (NITLP) to promote 350,000 Singaporeans' IT skills in the workforce (IDA, 2001). IT literacy within the nation is also closely monitored and published annually as the InfoComm Literacy Report (IDA, 2001). Taiwan's National Information Infrastructure Task Force also aggressively promotes computer and Internet literacy to increase the Internet population (Taiwan NII Task Force).

In the US and OECD nations, the Internet, along with other ICTs, has increased productivity, efficiency, and individual wealth as documented in numerous empirical reports (US Department of Commerce, 2000; Goldstein and O'Connor, 2000). Six major economic studies published in the US have concluded that the production and application of information technologies contributed to more than 50 percent of US productivity growth in the second half of the 1990s (US Department of Commerce, 2000). It was with this promise that many argued that the Internet and other information technologies will give poorer nations expanded access to markets, information, and other resources that were previously inaccessible, due to geographic and linguistic barriers, the lack of efficient logistics, and poor infrastructure.

It is clear, however, that the ability of the Internet to create new jobs, new business models, new industry sectors, and indeed, to quickly metamorphize the entire nation is often exaggerated. Hollywood movies, novels, and advertisements envision a world where consumers can sit in front of the computer and order whatever they want without leaving their "electronic cottage" linked by broadband fiber-optic networks. At this point, it is still too early to tell what the ultimate economic impact of the Internet will be, but it has become clear that the easy developmental models which accompanied the marketing of ICTs are hampered by a number of factors in the region, including excessive or inadequate policies, other infrastructural issues, bureaucratic morass, and the all too real digital divide. Along with these issues, the economic downturn of 2000 to 2002 also deflated many of the hopes of ICT promoters. For example, Goldstein and O'Connor (2000) point out that many governments in Asia will need to undergo massive regulatory and institutional changes if they are to eliminate market inefficiencies in their countries and take full advantage of ICT; at the same time, in this view, these steps are essential to make their local businesses competitive to survive fierce foreign competition.

Moreover, since the Internet offers this potential for economic expansion, inevitable political pressures arise. For example, in order to allow entrepreneurs to take full advantage of the flexibility and dynamism promised by the Internet, telecommunications markets must be liberalized, but this in itself can endanger national industries. Likewise, rebuilding telecommunications infrastructures to meet the capacity requirements and price developments for electronic commerce can divert shrinking national revenues from other critical tasks, such as education, healthcare, and other infrastructural investment. Moreover, laws and regulations pertaining to trade and competition, taxation, and consumer protection are often revised to create a friction-free environment for electronic commerce, which can endanger local tax revenues. How these issues are addressed will inevitably have an impact on the existing political systems, regulatory regimes, and social developments within Asian nations.

Due to their economic dependence on the US economy, and what seemed to be a compelling model in the US economy, many Asian countries also attempted to follow the "New Economy" development model that so many saw as the standard for achieving "higher, sustainable economic growth and higher, sustainable productivity gains" in the past decade (US Department of Commerce, 2000). With the global economic slowdown and the technology collapse, which for Asia lasted from 1997 until at least 2002, many of these hopes have been dashed. However, it remains an open question whether ICT can be an effective tool of economic development for Asian countries, including the deployment of up-to-date information infrastructure, the penetration of consumer premise equipment for Internet access, computer and network literacy programs, and narrowing the digital divide (OECD, 1999).

At the time of writing, many parts of Asia have indeed been able to harness effectively the information technologies for commercial and social reasons, while other parts remain almost hopelessly left behind. Singapore, South Korea, China, Taiwan, and Japan are at the forefront of the development of new technologies, including mobile technologies, while at the other end of the spectrum, Laos, North Korea, and Burma, and Vietnam remain virtually isolated from the World Wide Web. Some Asian nations have become significant manufacturers of digital technologies and leading producers of software, and several Asian companies have become global competitors in the new economy. However, penetration rates for information technologies vary widely across Asia. While Singapore and South Korea have very high penetration rates, even within these nations there are significant pockets, often defined by ethnicity, social class, and rural–urban differences, where few of the benefits of the Internet have appeared.

In fact, contrary to the earlier promises of the equalizing effects of ICTs, and in line with the impact of all new technologies, the Internet has reinforced certain existing income and wealth inequalities with and between countries, and within different strata of a given society, a phenomenon fashionably termed as the "digital divide." Hargittai (1998), in a study of the "international stratification" caused by the Internet, argued that the "Internet connectivity of a country depends on its overall position in the world system, thus on its development level, its financial and technical resources, and its culture." Studies found that the Internet may yield smaller benefits in more rigidly regulated economies with tight labor and product markets and inefficient capital markets (Cohen *et al.*, 2000; OECD, 2000b). In addition, nations with high-development-level status have the highest level of network connectivity while nations with low-development-level status have the lowest level of connectivity (Hargittai, 1998). In Cambodia and Vietnam, fewer than two in 10,000 people have access to the Internet (Romulo, 2000). On the contrary, more developed nations have Internet penetration rates comparable to Western Europe, the USA, and Canada. For example, 47 percent of Singaporeans use the Internet (IDA, 2001). In Taiwan, the Internet penetration rate is 32.8 percent as of November, 2001 (FIND, 2001). The inequalities within the Asian region both in economic terms as well as Internet development between Asian nations is likely to widen. These developments have profound impacts upon the social, cultural, economic, and political structures of the region. These impacts, however, are likely to be uneven, modified, and conditioned by issues of telecommunications infrastructure, government policies, cultural and social values, and economic realities.

ORGANIZATION OF THE BOOK

Part I Perspectives on the Internet and development in Asia: critical orientations

Part I provides a pan-Asian perspective on the trends that will most likely accompany the emergence and growth of the Internet. The five chapters guide the reader through the different stages of development with regard to Internet penetration to issues of digital divide as well as various issues of regulation concerning the Internet.

Tim Beal provides a statistical overview of the development of the Internet in Asia and assesses the current state of the digital divide in Asia. He argues that such disparity is likely to worsen, at least in the short term, given that social, political, and economic situations continue to widen between developing and developed nations in this region. In the same vein, Anthony D'Costa explores the dynamics of selective benefits of information technologies in Asia, and argues that heavy investment in IT furthers the opportunities of elites within developing nations, who thereby gain the ability to emigrate. He proposes a hypothesis positing that the relationship between the digital divide and Asia's role in the global information technology economy arises both from the generalized processes of global integration and pre-existing local social structures and processes of inequality.

As noted above, in spite of the fact that the Internet is valued chiefly by governments for its economic potential, the technology itself can catalyze and accelerate a variety of changes within a nation or region, including political and social changes. Of course, the pressure on every government to "get it right" in terms of Internet regulation and policy, as well as the processes of globalization, have led to a conflict between the perceived social value of the Internet and the unique particularities of every nation. The standards and laws of the front-runner nations have in some ways led to a *de facto* reliance on those standards as nations enter the wired world, in areas such as content regulation and access. For example, Lessig (1999) argues that for fifty years, the US used diplomatic, economic, and military means to attempt to export the ideology of free speech. And yet, almost overnight, closed nations have been wired with an architecture of communication that embodies the "First Amendment *in code* more extreme than our own First Amendment *in law*" (p. 167, emphasis in original). If the technology of the Internet implies certain social and political values, is it possible, then, for Asian nations to re-create the Internet in a manner more conducive to their own traditions, political cultures, and values?

For example, in most Asian nations there is little concern for the ethic of privacy that undergirds much discussion of policy within the West, a situation made more threatening by the war on terrorism. In this volume, David Lyon's assumption that there is little popular or governmental concern for privacy rights in most Asian nations is widely shared, given the political cultures prevalent in Asian nations, where communitarian ideologies have had far greater influence than individualistic political philosophies, as well as assumptions about the importance of national or communal sovereignty over the lives of individuals. After reviewing the multiple legal regimes that govern surveillance within Asia, Lyon asks for a critical reappraisal of the entire process of surveillance, and raises the possibility of shifting the frames of the debate away from an assumption of the legitimacy of surveillance by arguing that Asian nations have the most to lose by assuming the legitimacy of the practice, as it is they who are most likely to lose out in the economic and social sorting that will follow.

Another perceived threat to Asian nations, most of which have achieved their independence only in recent decades, is that of the loss of national sovereignty, particularly their ability to enforce laws prohibiting certain kinds of socially or politically volatile material. The Internet, along with the globalization of capital and economic forces, has introduced new political and moral pressures into sometimes delicate social fabrics. Many Asian nations have fought long battles to regulate the sexual and political content of the Internet, although China and Singapore are probably the most public. Carolyn Penfold examines one specific arena of national sovereignty, the ways in which many Asian nations have attempted to maintain their sovereignty by taking action at the most objectionable of content: that of pornography. Besides the technical barriers to devising effective controls over content, nations often face political pressures and international criticism when they attempt to maintain control over this most global of media. Penfold reviews some of the policies that arose within Asia, and raises significant questions concerning the implications of technologies designed to reassert state control. Penfold's chapter suggests that there are interesting and important questions at the level of state sovereignty, especially the clash between an international culture of the Internet and the values of nations and peoples of Asia.

Besides these political issues, Asian nations face significant economic questions associated with information technology policy. For example, Debora Halbert raises the issue of intellectual property regimes, and argues that these regimes are designed expressly to guarantee the future economic dominance of the West. She examines one specific example of this phenomenon, that of proprietary versus open source software, and argues that Asian nations must be able to selectively participate in or opt out of global IP regimes in order to guarantee their own economic sovereignty.

In Part II of this volume, we present individual case studies that arise from specific nations, to develop further some of the critical issues associated with Asia's embrace of the Internet.

Part II Issues and impacts: case studies

Internet and political development: mobilization and transformation

Since the early 1990s, scholars have generated an impressive body of research examining the impact of information and communication technologies on political processes and configurations. There have been a significant number of books and articles that critically examine the power of information technologies to increase political participation, civic society, and democracy (Hague and Loader, 1999; Kamarck and Nye, 2000; Loader, 1997; Locke, 1999; Splichal, Calabrese, and Sparks, 1994). Of particular interest has been the extent to which ICTs either empower citizen activism and democracy (Dahlberg, 2001; Giddens, 2000; Kedzie, 1997; Locke, 1999), or rather facilitate state control and surveillance (Agre and Rotenberg, 1997; Gandy, 1993). Much recent analysis, countering the cyber-utopianism that characterized earlier research, argues that the Internet can actually demean political discourse (Applbaum, 1999; Blumler and Gurevitch, 2001; Moore, 1999; Wilhelm, 1999).

This literature has greatly increased understanding of the political implications of emerging communication technologies, particularly in the context of the mature democratic systems of North America and Europe, and, to a lesser extent, the emerging democracies of Eastern Europe. However, there has been very little sustained research on the political issues that arise from widely varying political systems and philosophical foundations, although there is an emerging body of literature examining the larger social issues that surround the introduction of information technologies in diverse cultures (see e.g. Ess and Sudweeks, 2001). However, scholarship that assumes a uniform impact of information technologies across all cultural boundaries is not only wrong-headed; it could have disastrous policy implications. As Docter and Dutton (1999, p. 223) argue, "it is equally important to examine how electronic communications have been shaped by the producers and users of technologies. The design and use of technology, and the policies governing its use, will shape its political implications." This is especially true when we attempt to understand the political impact of ICTs in disparate cultural settings.

The nations of East, Southeast, and South Asia provide a marked contrast to the political systems of Europe and North America. Asian political regimes represent a mix of political philosophies, policies, and structures, cultural systems, depth of political engagement, and histories. These various forces can lead to dramatically different political configurations within the various nation-states of Asia (Pye, 1985). Japan, with its well-developed industrial infrastructure, and more than half a century of peace, bears perhaps the most striking similarity to the nations of the West in terms of technological and economic status, in spite of the fact that Japan's industrial and information policies have been markedly different from those of most Western nations.

The question many nations face, then, is how to embrace the economic promise of the Internet while minimizing the potential for political unrest. Nations such as Taiwan, Singapore, Malaysia, and South Korea have deliberately made huge infrastructural investments in electronics and information technologies as part of their commitment to achieve economic growth, with various responses to the political threats and opportunities engendered by ICTs. The People's Republic of China has invested a huge sum of capital to develop the information technology sector to transform its economic potential, but with much more ambivalence concerning the political ramifications. Finally, some Asian nations, such as North Korea, Cambodia, Burma, and Laos, due to both political and economic factors, remain "unwired," allowing, or unable to prevent, the global flow of capital – economic, political, and ideological – to bypass them.

A variety of new issues are introduced by considering the questions of political action, mobilization, practice, and regulation via information technologies within the Asian context. Asian political systems, arising from philosophical and religious traditions vastly different from those of the West, are also influenced by historical experiences of colonialism and ethnic issues that are more subdued than in the West. Moreover, the social systems within some Asian nations are less influenced by the individualist models of personal identity, expression, and political affiliation than are Americans and Europeans.

The list of systemic and cultural distinctions to be drawn between the Western nations, where most research on the social and political impact of ICTs has been generated thus far, and those of Asia, could grow much longer. Within Asia, though, the differences between nations, regions, and localities may be even more dramatic. The bureaucratic systems which predominate in Singapore and China are conceptually and experientially quite different from the charismatic traditions of leadership in Indonesia, Thailand, and the Philippines (Pye, 1985). The religious-philosophical traditions of Islam, Buddhism, Hinduism, Christianity, and, indeed, Marxism, as well as numerous indigenous religions, have influenced different Asian nations in different ways, leading to very different understandings of the nature of governance, the role of government, and the rights and duties of citizens.

Since the late 1980s, ICTs have been used within the political realm in Asia, beginning, perhaps, with the extensive use of email and fax by Chinese students in North America and Europe to gather and transmit information concerning the pro-democracy movement of 1989 centered on Tiananmen Square, both facilitating the growth of the movement within China as well as serving to mobilize sympathizers in countries around the world. This event and others like it, such as the use of SMS (short messaging systems) on mobile phones in mass movements in the Philippines and Indonesia, has led many to conclude that information technology is inherently "democratizing" (Kedzie, 1997). Even when claims about the impact of ICTs are not quite so dramatic, academic opinion seems to echo a conviction that the new technologies will strengthen civil society, empower individuals through increased access to information, and ultimately, create greater transparency on the part of governments.

Although it is clear that there is potential for greater political openness and empowerment with ICTs, there is also potential for greater state control. Although the ongoing battles between government censors and the Internet in nations such as China and Singapore are often reported in the

world press, the role of information technologies for purposes of state surveillance and control are rarely mentioned in these same media outlets.

Perhaps one of the most considered questions in discussions of the political potential of the Internet is its ability to provide an alternative institution of civil society in nations that lack a tradition of an accessible public
sphere. Merlyna Lim's chapter examines the emergence of civil society in
Indonesia through the phenomenon of *Warnet*, an Internet café chain that
provides online access across the nation to provide a means for participation in purely online sites of civil society, including chatrooms and forums,
as well as in offline versions of civil society. Lim argues that ultimately,
civil society must emerge from a sense of identity that is forged through
political struggles. Moreover, the Indonesian case, although it demonstrates the potential for the emergence of civil society in an authoritarian
regime, also demonstrates the ways in which discussion of "democratization" is perhaps an empty term when it comes to these societies, since
the emerging political activists and classes are drawn largely from a new
digital elite. Moreover, in a society divided by political, ethnic, and religious factions, the Internet can also create a space for greater mobilization
of factional warfare.

James Chin examines the way in which an online news service,
Malaysiakini.com, exploits the gap created by the Malaysian government's
commitment not to censor cyberspace, a pledge that contrasts sharply with
that nation's tightly controlled newspaper and broadcast outlets. This
opportunity provides an online space for a press free from the kinds of
governmental restrictions that have limited print and broadcast journalism, and its relative freedom to report dissenting perspectives during incidents such as the Anwar Ibrahim trial has enabled Malaysiakini.com to
achieve readership levels that are almost on a par with the larger news
outlets. However, as this example demonstrates, the development of cyberspace, including an online civil society, requires money, as well as political
openness. The irony of the case is that although there is not a political
threat to the site, the economics of maintaining a website threaten the viability of an online civil society. After this essay was written, in early 2003,
the offices of Malaysiakini were raided by authorities attempting to track
down the author of a letter the site had published, and a number of computers seized (Malaysiakini.com, February 10, 2003). Thus, in spite of a
technical promise of autonomy for the cyber sector in Malaysia, this incident illustrates the precarious status of online news sites in politically
authoritarian states.

China's relationship with the Internet is perhaps one of the most thoroughly documented in the world press. Regular stories in major newspapers highlight the arrest of "Internet dissidents," the closure of cyber
cafés, or net censorship. The relationship between the government of
China and the Internet is far more complex than commonly portrayed.
China has made a huge investment in ICTs, including launching one of the

world's most ambitious e-government programs. However, the control of information and the rise of chatrooms has created pressures on China's official propaganda mechanisms, including the national press. Li Xiguang, Qin Xuan, and Randolph Kluver examine the way in which online chatrooms are forcing China's media outlets to respond to a larger universe of news than that generated by Xinhua, the government-sanctioned news agency, and presented in the influential *People's Daily* newspaper. Their chapter examines a particularly influential chatroom hosted by the *People's Daily* newspaper, and finds that participants in that forum used it to post foreign news items and commentary that often undermined the government's position during the April, 2001 spy plane stand-off with the United States. In spite of diligent efforts to censor the chatroom, the technology itself created opportunities to introduce new ideas into influential forums. They conclude that although the Internet might not directly undermine authoritarian regimes, it certainly introduces information that forces authoritarian governments to respond to and account for more outside sources, thus increasing the transparency and professionalism of the Chinese sources themselves. If the government chooses to ignore the new information sphere brought by ICTs, China's governing mechanisms are likely to lose their capacity to influence public opinion.

It is not only individuals who have benefitted from the rise in information technology, but traditional political actors, such as parties, have also found ways to deploy the technology. Leslie Tkach-Kawasaki looks at how the Internet, as a broadcast and communication medium, has affected political campaigns in Japan, one of Asia's most technologically advanced nations. Tkach-Kawasaki's chapter explores the ways in which Japanese political parties have deployed the Internet in order to bolster party organizational and electoral power, as well as to garner greater input into policies and practices. She also demonstrates how media policies, formulated for more traditional media formats, often inhibit the dynamic use of emerging communication technologies.

Finally, Shyam Tekwani examines another side of the way in which the Internet provides greater organizational mobility to new or disaffected political actors, namely the role of the Internet in mobilizing diasporic communities for political action, including militant action. Tekwani, who, as a photojournalist, observed firsthand the techniques of the Tamil Tigers in Sri Lanka, documents the ways in which cyberspace has provided new opportunities for information dissemination, recruiting, mobilization, and fund-raising among militant and terrorist organizations. These issues become all the more pressing in the light of the events of September 11, 2001, when terrorists attacked New York and Washington, DC, as it has become clear that information technology has become a major factor in the abilities of "super-empowered" individuals to influence global events (Friedman, 1999).

Internet and social development: community and identity

Among the most interesting questions arising from the widespread dif-fusion of the Internet concerns the social use made of it, or the ways in which communities and individuals form and revise identity. With its open architecture, can the Net empower communities which have been margin-alized in society and reinforce the solidarities of existing social groupings based on mutual interests, values, and shared identities through its ability to communicate information and coordinate action among geographically dispersed users? Answers to this complex question come from different directions. Some studies have highlighted the technical and instrumental abilities of the Net. This involves reducing the friction of space by over-coming the need for a physical place to meet (Ayres, 1999; Klein, 1999), as well as reducing time costs by allowing for asynchronous communication to occur (Klein, 1999). Other studies have identified the specific functions of the Net. In terms of the provision of information, websites function to provide information and act as information clearing houses (Ayres, 1999). The capacity of the Net to serve as a technology for organization and mobilization is demonstrated by the presence of online protests and online drives (Hurwitz, 1999). Online forums function as a space for discussion and re-education of citizens about participation in public affairs (Klein, 1999). Summarizing the capabilities of the Net, Tambini (1999) specifies four functions: information provision, measure preferences (through e-surveys, expression of opinions in forums), deliberation (through online forums), and will formation (via online protests, online drives).

Apart from technical and instrumental functions of the Internet, other writers have pointed to the social and psychological needs that can be met through affiliations developed over the Internet. Rheingold (1994) points to the basic human need for community which may be expressed over the Web as informal physical spaces disappear. The growing literature on the Internet provides ample evidence for the motivational bases for identifying with virtual communities. Denzin (1998) highlights the growth of the online self-help industry where a participant who asks for help can receive advice from countless, faceless persons who inhabit these sites. Groups of different religious beliefs create sites in the hope of linking and drawing in persons of similar persuasions or of securing converts (e.g. Bunt, 1999; Lal, 1999). The same energies for strengthening ties may be found among ethnic groups (e.g. Lal, 1999; Zhang and Hao, 1999). McKenna and Bargh (1998) have also argued that the Internet has provided "those with stigmatized identities an opportunity to share in the benefits of group membership." In leisure, the playing of textual computer role-playing games on the Internet has also spawned their own virtual communities where key users are committed to defining the norms governing their virtual worlds (Coe, 1998). Through their study of Netville, Wellman and Hampton (1999) have shown the tendency for users to simply transfer the communication, social obligations, and needs from actual relationships online. The Internet, as a communications technology, helps to support real networked communities by providing a function similar to that of the telephone, thereby allowing for social relationships to be maintained.

For all these reasons, Net users who are part of cyber communities are likely to invest significant amounts of time and energy being part of such virtual groups. They do so because such involvements are intricately linked to identities. From a psychological perspective, Wallace (1999) has argued that the natural tendency to conform and a desire to be a member of cohesive groups are the foundations of vibrant virtual communities.

To the extent that virtual communities involve organization and mobilization, and incorporate shared meanings, identities, values, and commitment, discussions have moved to whether our understanding of the term *community* may be used to describe associations that form over the Net. Two recent papers addressing this issue have arrived at similar conclusions; namely, that it is more productive to get on with the task of exploring online/virtual/electronic communities rather than to worry about whether these possess particular attributes of "real" communities (Fox and Roberts, 1999; Komito, 1998). Komito (1998) concludes by suggesting that "a community is not fixed in form or function, but is a mixed bag of possible options whose meanings and concreteness are always being negotiated by individuals, in the context of changing external constraints."

In Asia, as elsewhere, the continuing importance of ethnicity, nationality, religion, education, social status, and gender as the basis for social divisions as well as identity provides an ongoing basis for the organization of interests, and potentially rich material for the study of how technologies such as the Internet act as a new medium for existing communities to maintain solidarity and cultural and religious identities as well as work as an empowering tool, enabling new forms of association among marginalized individuals. Economic development in certain parts of Asia has also resulted in a growing middle class which is educated, rights-conscious, mobile, and open to causes of different kinds. As Ebo (1998) points out, "access to cyberspace becomes even more important as new notions of social identities develop, and the measurement of a good life assumes new dimensions." These become important motive forces for virtual communities in Asia.

For example, Karsten Giese's analysis of several Mainland Chinese bulletin board services on issues of love, marriage, and sexuality shows how the Internet allows its users to discuss, venture, and form opinions. His study also shows how virtual groups replicate the processes of real or offline groups, where inclusionary and exclusionary devices are practiced and collective identities evolve out of long-term active participation. Likewise, Junko Onosaka demonstrates how the development of women's websites in Japan has opened up opportunities for women, who have found both space and voice on the Net. Onosaka shows how such sites allow women both to express their problems, and to find emotional support and solutions. She argues that while such efforts do not necessarily result in political activism, it shows the ongoing and sustained attempts by Japanese women to effect social change.

If the Internet is normally considered as a positive space as individuals find reinforcement and emotional commitment, it can also provide a context for opposition and hostility. Arul Selvan examines several Hindu newsgroup to demonstrate that these groups not only enable geographic-ally dispersed members of a religious community to affirm their religiosity and to allow for the socialization of novices, but also attract radical criti-cism of Hinduism and India.

As a small city-state, Singapore is one of the most open nations to glob-alizing influences, no doubt in part helped by the widespread availability of the Internet. In what ways has the Internet shaped the sociability of Sin-gaporean youths? Waipeng Lee and Brenda Chan's study examines Singa-porean youths' use of the Internet, and argues that the Internet provides a platform for youth to achieve new forms of social competence. Their data indicate that contrary to popular opinion, the youths do not use the Inter-net to supplant existing relationships; rather, they use it both to expand their circle of friends and maintain existing friendships.

CONCLUSION

In summary, Asian governments, businesses, and individuals have embraced the Internet for primarily economic reasons, and, in so doing, have opened the gates to a wide variety of unanticipated consequences. The chapters in this book illustrate only a few of the myriad issues that arise when Asia encounters the Internet. The Asian experience draws to light several issues that are often not encountered in Western experiences with the Internet, due either to the results of modernization, economic cir-cumstances, or cultural contexts. For example, in Asia, to a much greater extent than in the developed West, investment in information technology does indeed have real economic benefits, but often comes with hidden costs, such as a growing inequality between social classes and nations, as well as the acceleration of brain drains. Moreover, Asian governments, while following the lead of many advanced Western governments in the formation of policies to govern the new information society, have also addressed a host of policy issues in very different ways, and in some cases quite inadequately. The significance of these very different policy orienta-tions is yet to be fully explored. Similarly, the assumptions of political mobilization, action, and empowerment that accompanied the Internet in the West were matched by suspicion within Asia, and subsequent experience has demonstrated that the technologically deterministic nature of much of this discussion was misplaced. In the Asian context, the Internet is seen as likely to incite unrest and discord as much as to bring political empowerment. Finally, the Internet has indeed opened up new opportunities for social interaction and support in the Asian context, but it has also been adapted for uses by Asians that are often distinctly different from those in the West.

As Asia encounters the Internet, then, both Asia and the Internet are changed. Asia's long history, unique socio-political configurations, and, yes, Asia's values, will ultimately help to shape the technological phenomenon known as the Internet, through the evolving of a set of regulatory mechanisms and policies surrounding the Internet, as the chapters in this volume will demonstrate, but also in terms of how existing religious and cultural values shape virtual group formation, collective identity, and the participation of individuals.

BIBLIOGRAPHY

Agre, P.E. and Rotenberg, M. (eds) (1997) *Technology and Privacy: The New Landscape*, Cambridge, MA: MIT Press.

Applbaum, A. (1999) "Failure in the cybermarketplace of ideas," in E. Kamarck and J. Nye, Jr. (eds) *Democracy.com? Governance in a Networked World*, Hollis, NH: Hollis Publishing.

Ayres, J.M. (1999) "From the streets to the Internet: the cyber-diffusion of contention," *Annals, AAPSS*, 566: 132–43.

Blumler, J. and Gurevitch, M. (2001) "The new media and our political communication discontents," *Information, Communication, and Society*, 4, 1. Online. Available HTTP: http://www.infosoc.co.uk/ (current as of February 11, 2003).

Bunt, G.R. (1999) "Islam@britain.net: 'British-Muslim' identities in cyberspace," *Islam and Christian Muslim Relations*, 10, 3: 353–62.

Coe, C. (1998) "Defending community: difference and utopia online," *International Journal of Cultural Studies*, 1, 3: 391–414.

Cohen, S., Bradford DeLong, J., and Zysman, J. (2000) "Tools for thought: what is new and important about the 'E-conomy,'" BRIE Working Paper No. 138, Berkeley, CA.

Cukor, P. and McKnight, L.W. (2000) "Knowledge networks, the Internet, and development," paper presented at the 28th Annual TPRC Conference.

D'Costa, A.P. (2001) "Asia, Asia diaspora, and the digital divide," paper presented at the Internet Political Economy Forum Conference: Internet and Development in Asia, September 14–15, National University of Singapore.

Dahlberg, L. (2001) "Democracy via cyberspace: mapping the rhetorics and practices of three prominent camps," *New Media and Society*, 3, 2: 157–77.

Denzin, N.K. (1998) "In search of the inner child: co-dependency and gender in a cyberspace community," in G. Bendelow and S.J. Williams (eds) *Emotions in Social Life*, London: Routledge.

Docter, S. and Dutton, W. (1999) "The social shaping of the democracy network (Dnet)," in B. Loader (ed.) *Digital Democracy: Discourse and Decision Making in the Information Age*, London: Routledge.

Drake, W. (1998) "The distributed information revolution and the global information society," in W. Drake (ed.) *Telecommunications in an Information Age*, Washington, DC: United States Information Agency. Online. Available HTTP: http://usinfo.state.gov/products/pubs/archive/telecomm/drake.htm (current as of February 11, 2003).

E-ASEAN Task Force (2000) *An overview*. Online. Available HTTP: http://www.e-aseantf.org/about.html (accessed on November 12, 2001).

Ebo, B. (1998) "Internet or outernet," in B. Ebo (ed.) *Cyberghetto or Cybertopia*, Westport, CT: Praeger.

Ess, C. and Sudweeks, F. (eds) (2001) *Culture, Technology, Communication: Towards an Intercultural Global Village*, Albany, NY: State University of New York Press.

FIND (2001) "Internet users reach 7.55 million in Taiwan." Online. Available HTTP: http://www.find.org.tw/0105/howmany/20011107.asp (accessed on November 12, 2001).

Fox, N. and Roberts, C. (1999) "GPs in cyberspace: the sociology of a virtual community," *Sociological Review*, 47, 4: 643–71.

Friedman, T. (1999) *The Lexus and the Olive Tree: Understanding Globalization*, New York: Farrar Straus Giroux.

Gandy, O.H., Jr. (1993) *The Panoptic Sort: A Political Economy of Personal Information*, Boulder, CO: Westview Press.

Giddens, A. (2000) *Runaway World: How Globalization is Reshaping our Lives*, New York: Routledge.

Goldstein, A. and O'Connor, D. (2000) *E-Commerce for Development: Prospects and Policy Issues*, Paris: OECD Development Center.

Hague, B. and Loader, B. (eds) (1999) *Digital Democracy: Discourse and Decision Making in the Information Age*, London: Routledge.

Hargittai, E. (1998) "Holes in the Net: the Internet and international stratification," paper presented at the INET98 Conference. Online. Available HTTP: http://www.isoc.org/isoc/conferences/inet/98/proceedings/5d/5d_l.htm (accessed on November 12, 2001).

Huff, T. (2001) "The Web & national systems of innovation: Malaysia's multimedia super corridor," paper presented at the Third Annual Conference of the Internet Political Economy Conference 2001, September 14–15, National University of Singapore.

Hurwitz, R. (1999) "Who needs politics? Who needs people? The ironies of democracy in cyberspace," *Contemporary Sociology*, 28, 6: 655–61.

InfoComm Development Authority of Singapore (IDA) (2000) *InfoComm 21: Overview*. Online. Available HTTP: http://www.ida.gov.sg/Website/IDAhome.nsf/Home?OpenForm (current as of February 11, 2003).

—— (2001) *National IT Literacy Programme (NITLP)*. Online. Available HTTP: http://www.ida.gov.sg/Website/IDAhome.nsf/Home?OpenForm (current as of February 11, 2003).

—— (2001) *2000 InfoComm literacy survey*. Online. Available HTTP: http://www.ida.gov.sg/Website/IDAhome.nsf/Home?OpenForm (current as of February 11, 2003).

—— (2001) *Survey of Infocomm Usage in Households*. Online. Available HTTP: http://www.ida.gov.sg/Website/IDAhome.nsf/Home?OpenForm (current as of February 11, 2003).

Kamarck, E. and Nye, J., Jr. (eds) (1999) *Democracy.com? Governance in a Networked World*, Hollis, NH: Hollis Publishing.

Karnjanatawe, K. (2001) "E-ASEAN group to address regional digital divide." Online. Available HTTP: http//www.newsbytes.com/news/01/167092.htm (accessed on November 12, 2001).

Kedzie, C. (1997) "A brave new world or a new world order?" in S. Kiesler (ed.) *Culture of the Internet*, Mahwah, NJ: Lawrence Earlbaum Associates.

Klein, H.K. (1999) "Tocqueville in cyberspace: using the Internet for citizen associations," *The Information Society*, 15: 213–20.

Komito, L. (1998) "The Net as a foraging society: flexible communities," *The Information Society*, 14: 97–106.

Kraemer, K. and Dedrick, J. (2001) *Creating a Computer Industry Giant: China's Industrial Policies and Outcomes in the 1990s*, Irvine, CA: Center for Research on Information Technology and Organizations. Online. Available HTTP: http://www.crito.uci.edu/git/publications/pdf/china-jun-01.pdf (current as of February 11, 2003).

Kuroda, H. (2000) "Information technology, globalization, and international financial architecture: Japan's views on the main topics of the Fukuoka finance ministers' meeting," speech to the Foreign Correspondents Club of Japan, Ministry of Finance, Japan. Online. Available HTTP: http://www.mof.go.jp/english/if/if018.htm (current as of February 11, 2003).

Lal, V. (1999) "The politics of history on the Internet: cyber-diasporic Hinduism and the North American Hindu diaspora," *Diaspora*, 8, 2: 137–72.

Latifah, W. (1999) *The NITC/MIMOS Berhad K-Economy Advanced Paper*, Kuala Lumpur, Malaysia: NITC/MIMOS BERHAD.

Lessig, L. (1999) *Code and Other Laws of Cyberspace*, New York: Basic Books.

Locke, T. (1999) "Participation, inclusion, exclusion, and netactivism: how the Internet invents new forms of democratic activity," in B. Hague and B. Loader (eds) *Digital Democracy: Discourse and Decision Making in the Information Age*, London: Routledge.

McKenna, K.Y.A. and Bargh, J.A. (1998) "Coming out in the age of the Internet: identity 'demarginalization' through virtual group participation," *Journal of Personality and Social Psychology*, 75, 3: 681–94.

Malaysiakini.com (2003) "Police raid Malaysiakini," January 20. Available HTTP: http://www.malaysiakini.com/news/200301200018962.php (accessed 10 February 2003).

Moore, R. (1999) "Democracy and cyberspace," in B. Hague and B. Loader (eds) *Digital Democracy: Discourse and Decision Making in the Information Age*, London: Routledge.

Organization of Economic Cooperation and Development (OECD) (1999) *Building Infrastructure Capacity for Electronic Commerce: Leased Line Developments and Pricing*, Working Party on Telecommunication and Information Service Policies, Paris: OECD.

—— (2000a) *Information Technology Outlook 2000*, Paris: OECD.

—— (2000b) *OECD Economic Outlook*, Paris: OECD.

Pye, L. (1985) *Asian Power and Politics: The Cultural Dimensions of Authority*, Cambridge, MA: Harvard University Press.

Rheingold, H. (1994) *The Virtual Community*, London: Minerva.

Romulo, R.R. (2000) "Bridging the digital divide in Southeast Asia," in *Inter-*

national Herald Tribute: The IHT Online. Online. Available HTTP: http://www.iht.com/cgi-bin/generic.cgi?template=articleprint.timlh&ArtcileId =2323 (accessed on November 12, 2001).

Splichal, S., Calabrese, A. and Sparks, C. (eds) (1994) *Information Society and Civil Society*, West Lafayette, IN: Purdue University Press.

Taiwan NII Task Force website (2001) Online. Available HTTP: http://www.nii.gov.tw/ (accessed on November 12, 2001).

Tambini, D. (1999) "New media and democracy: the civic networking movement," *New Media and Society*, 1, 3: 305–29.

United Nations Development Programme (UNDP) (2001a) *Creating a Development Dynamic: Final Report of the Digital Opportunity Initiative*, New York: United Nations.

—— (2001b) *Human Development Report 2001: Making New Technologies Work for Human Development*, New York: Oxford University Press.

US Department of Commerce (2000) *Digital Economy 2000*, Washington, DC.

Valingra, L. (1997) "Internet fever hits Asia," *Telephony*, 30–5.

Wallace, P. (1999) *The Psychology of the Internet*, Cambridge: Cambridge University Press.

Wellman, B. and Hampton K. (1999) "Living networked on and offline," *Contemporary Sociology*, 28, 6: 648–54.

Wilhelm, A. (1999) "Virtual sounding boards: how deliberative is online political discussion?" in B. Hague and B. Loader (eds) *Digital Democracy: Discourse and Decision-making in the Information Age*, London: Routledge.

Wu, W. (1996) "Great leap or long march: some policy issues of the development of the Internet in China," *Telecommunications Policy*, 20, 9: 699–711.

Yang, K.C.C. (2001) "Alleviating the digital divide in Malaysia," paper presented at the RIAP (Research Institute of Asia and Pacific), October 18–19, University of Sydney, Sydney, Australia.

Zhang, K. and Hao, X. (1999) "The Internet and the ethnic press: a study of electronic Chinese publications," *The Information Society*, 15: 21–30.

Part I

Perspectives on Internet and development in Asia

Critical orientations

2 The state of Internet use in Asia

Tim Beal

INTRODUCTION

It has become clear that the global "digital divide," between those who have access to the Internet and those who do not, is widening. Asian governments need to provide support and to create an environment which facilitates Internet usage among business, customers, and citizens, but which offers them some protection against the economic and cultural hegemony of the Western developed nations. This chapter will examine Internet usage in Asia within the global context. Asia is as diverse in terms of Internet penetration as it is in other social and cultural indicators. Some parts of Asia, notably Singapore, Hong Kong, Taiwan, and South Korea, have rates of per capita Internet access at leading international levels. In other parts, such as North Korea, there is very little access. In China, high access in the major coastal cities stands in stark contrast to minimal access in the rural areas. This inequality is mirrored to a lesser degree in India which, while in general it has very low rates of Internet access, is a major international provider of software expertise (see D'Costa, Chapter 3, this volume). Moreover, although Japan currently has the most Internet users in Asia, its per capita rate is not commensurate with its Gross Domestic Product.

The linkage between technology, economic and employment growth, social factors, and government policies is complex and the evidence inconclusive. For instance, the variation of Internet access rate among European countries of comparable wealth suggests that language is a factor in terms of penetration. Scandinavian countries and the Netherlands, which have high levels of English competency, as well as Britain, have appreciably higher Internet access rates than Germany and France. In Asia, Singapore's high English competency helps its access to the international Internet while the Chinese economies have the advantage of a large common language area. Thailand, on the other hand, has neither of these advantages and this may be a reason for its low Internet rate.

This chapter comprises two sections. The first looks at the political economy of the global digital divide. The second section is an exploration of the global digital divide itself, looking principally at the configuration of world Internet use, again with a focus on Asia. The Internet environment is volatile and fast changing but has to be understood within the context of the wider political and social framework, and I will address this complex issue first.

GLOBAL DIGITAL DIVIDE

The phrase "digital divide" has become a generally recognizable term, and for good reason. Some people have access to, and are able to harness the benefits of digital resources, revolving mainly around information and communications technologies (ICT). Others are cut off from this and are deprived not merely of the immediate benefits of digital technology but also, by extension, many of the fruits of the modern economy. Although the phrase was coined in the United States to refer to domestic disparities in access to the digital economy (especially on ethnic and class lines) it may, of course, be applied globally. The world may either be divided regionally (Figure 2.1) or by country (Figure 2.2) into digital "haves" and "have-nots." Moreover, according to the International Labor Organization, there is a widening digital divide within countries and between countries (International Labor Organization, 2001).

Thinking of the "global digital divide" in terms of regions, as illustrated in Figure 2.1, is a good starting point because it graphically illustrates the disparities. However, definitions of "region" are somewhat problematic

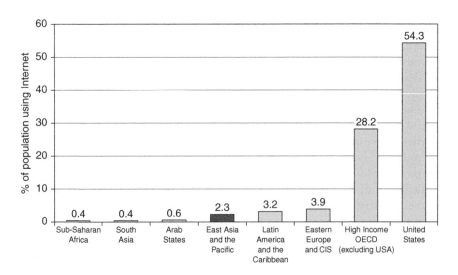

Figure 2.1 Internet users by region

Source: UNDP *Annual Report* (2001): 13

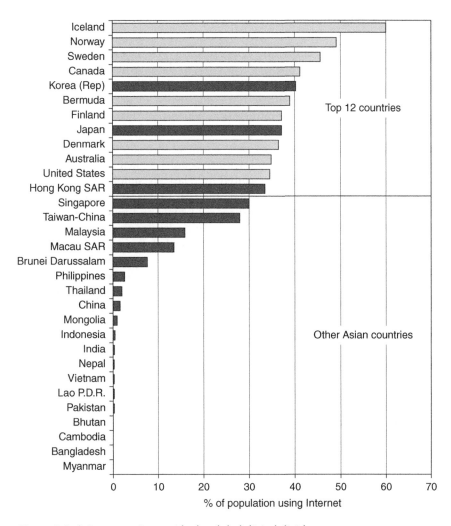

Figure 2.2 Asian countries astride the global digital divide

Source: International Telecommunications Union, Internet Indicators (2000)

and, in most cases, there is wide disparity within the various regions. Figure 2.2, from the International Telecommunications Union, shows the percentage of the population who are "Internet users," and demonstrates that Asia, defined here as South Asia and East Asia, spans the range of the digital divide. Some Asian economies, notably the Republic of Korea, Japan, and the Hong Kong SAR are in the top twelve worldwide. Others, such as Singapore (16), and Taiwan (19), are in the top twenty. China (100) and India (136), though they have large numbers of Internet users (as discussed below), rank lower because they have only a small proportion of their population online. However, many Asian nations rank at the lower ends of the scale, such as Cambodia (189), Bangladesh (192), and Myanmar (203). Not shown here, because the ITU has no data, is North Korea which is in the process of connecting to the Internet (Beal, 2002).

However, the phrase "global digital divide," while it focuses attention on the socio-political implications of disparities in access to ICT, also implies a simple and definite bifurcation between a "first world" which is linked to the digital revolution, and a "third world" which is not. The situation is far more complex than that. From both a global perspective, in terms of regions, countries, and within countries themselves, there is a wide range of ICT access, as measured by relatively simple metrics such as "Internet connectivity." Beyond that, the real utilization of ICT, and the degree to which its potential is realized by people and by organizations, is unclear, but the plethora of fragmentary and often contradictory information does suggest there is a wide range. Nevertheless, it is useful to focus on the division between those who have no access to ICT, no experience of it and perhaps, though this is increasingly less likely, no expectations of it, and those who have, however partially, used ICT. "Barely 6 per cent of the world's people have ever logged onto the Internet" (International Labor Organization, 2001).

The poor are excluded from prosperity by a variety of mechanisms – lack of political and social power, lack of education, religious, ethnic, and sexual discrimination, and most basically, by lack of capital. Being excluded from digital technologies is of course a result of this deeper deprivation, and is one aspect of it. It is similar perhaps to education. Lack of education is usually the result of fairly evident social and economic factors – for instance, female illiteracy is usually much higher than male illiteracy – so it cannot be solved without tackling the underlying causes. However, lack of education is in turn a barrier to getting a reasonably well-paying job. A familiar vicious circle of deprivation sets in, and is usually passed on to the next generation.

"Digital illiteracy" is similar, but with significant differences. It is less closely correlated with general deprivation and is relatively easy to eradicate or ameliorate. For instance, in developed countries, "digital illiteracy" may be as much correlated with age as with poverty. Many older, middle-class people do not use the Internet because of unfamiliarity with, or even fear of, the technology. The remedy here is not simply more financial resources but quite modest training and support. In some countries, such as China, the barrier to access to the Internet for a substantial number of people is not so much lack of disposable income, but the inadequacy of the current land-based telecommunications system. A potential remedy might be wireless-based technologies, a technology leap-frogging which may provide access at relatively low cost. Given that the productivity and efficiency gains from ICT are potentially so considerable over a wide range of business and social activities, it may be argued that smart investment in removing barriers to the Internet, and facilitating its efficient and effective use, delivers more value for money than most other investments. This is not to unduly privilege such investment over conflicting claims – basic education, clean water, basic health service, and so on – but merely to suggest that the "digital divide" is one of the most productive places to address more general issues of deprivation, rather than a peripheral and indulgent frittering of scarce resources. As the UNDP argues, "The information revolution is changing everything about the world we live in, including the practice of development ... ICT is now a basic component of development, not a luxury" (UNDP, 2001). Thus it is as true in Asia, as anywhere else, that crossing the digital divide and development go hand-in-hand.

McConnell International (2001: 20), in a recent report on the digital divide in India, notes that "connectivity remains the biggest hurdle," a phenomenon that applies to many countries. The report, which attempts to measure "E-readiness," or the "capacity of nations to participate in the digital economy" (McConnell, 2001: 20), gives a telling vignette:

> Bullock carts overloaded with sugar cane still creep past the telephone access shops that have sprung up in every congested village, the drivers and shop operators both unaware of the valuable information about crop markets that lies just beyond their reach in cyberspace.

"Beyond their reach" begs many questions but does lead to the vital question of the political and economic framework which might enable the sugar cane growers to link more effectively with the market. Having access to information in cyberspace is no panacea of course; it is no protection against a slump in the price of sugar or the social and political structures that impoverish the many and enrich the few. The democratizing potential of the Internet should not be overlooked however (see Lim, Chapter 7, this volume).

ASIA AND INTERNET GROWTH

Data on Internet usage are subject to great uncertainty and limitations (Foley, 2001). For instance, there was a debate in China at the beginning of 2001 about whether there were 15.2 million online, or 20 million (Nairne, 2001). The data used here for China derive from a survey conducted in January, 2002 and give a figure of 33.7 million; however, in April, 2002 another survey claimed that "China has around 56.6 million households with access to the Internet" (Nua Ltd, April 22, 2002). Perhaps the best global source has been the Irish Internet company Nua Ltd which compiles results of surveys of numbers of Internet users from around the world. A note on Nua's methodology is provided in the Appendix to this chapter. Survey techniques vary, of course, as does the reliability of surveys. This means that data, especially across countries, are not rigorously comparable. Moreover, since Internet usage is increasing very fast in most of the main countries, the date of the survey is of great importance.

The Internet is but one part of the bundle of information and communication technologies (ICT) that construct the digital world. The International Labor Organization *World Employment Report 2001* has a useful Statistical Annex which among other things tabulates data on the following ICT indicators:

1   Internet hosts
2   Internet users
3   Estimated PCs
4   Main telephone lines
5   Mobile cellular subscriber
6   Digital cellular subscriber
7   Television receivers
8   Cable TV subscribers

The International Labor Organization gives Internet data for only seventy countries (out of 220) and this is appreciably smaller than the Nua dataset (198). Although the International Labor Organization data capture the major Internet countries, there are surprising omissions, such as Poland and Russia. The International Labor Organization data, though smaller in some respects than the Nua surveys, are broader in scope. They complement the Nua data and are broadly consistent with it. The Nua data remain the most comprehensive and most up to date (the most recent survey as of this writing was February, 2002), and are used to describe the pattern of global Internet use, but the limitations should be borne in mind. In addition, although there is no space to discuss the broader ICT environment, it should be remembered that companies and people do not operate in one technology alone.

NUMBERS ONLINE

The simplest and most basic statistic on the Internet is the number of people online. Clearly this is a very approximate measure and leaves out much crucial information, such as who the "persons" are (large companies, SMEs, individuals), where they are (apart from on a country basis), their characteristics (class, sex, age, ethnicity), what they use the Internet for (e-commerce, email to friends), or how often they use it. Nevertheless, it does give a rough indication of the Internet environment. Bearing in mind that the value of a computer network varies exponentially with the number of computers attached to it, numbers are important, though not all-important. It should also be borne in mind that the main business use of the Internet in the USA and Europe is Business-to-Business (B2B) (Beal, 2000) rather than Business-to-Consumer (B2C) and this is likely to be the case in Asia (Nua Ltd, October 20, 2000 and January 2, 2001). It may be assumed that B2B e-commerce is more intensive than B2C. In other words, numbers may be less of an issue as long as the key entities, especially other businesses in the supply chain, are connected. However, B2C should not be neglected and we may expect to see it rapidly growing in Asia, though, as elsewhere, many goods and services researched online are ultimately bought offline (Nua Ltd, November 17, 2000).

GLOBAL GROWTH AND REGIONAL DISTRIBUTION

First, we know that the Internet as a mass phenomenon is very recent, and is still growing very fast, except in countries where it is more mature (see Figure 2.2). The first survey given by Nua dates from December, 1995, and gave a figure of 16 million people, just 0.39 percent of the world's population. Some seven years later, in February, 2002, that had grown to 544.2 million, representing 8.96 percent of the global population.

Although the Internet is, by definition, a global network, the location of these users is important. As Figure 2.3 shows, North America still has the largest share of the world's "Internet population" – 33.3 percent. This proportion will naturally drop as connectivity to the Internet increases elsewhere (*South China Morning Post*, January 13, 2001). Europe and the Asia Pacific (includes Asia, Oceania, India, and the Pacific Ocean Islands)

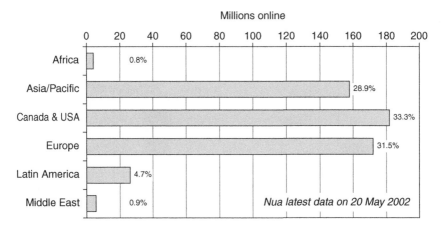

Figure 2.3 Global distribution of Internet users, 2002

Source: compiled from figures available at http://www.nua.com/surveys/howmanyonline/index.html

have just under one-third each, leaving the rest of the world – Africa, the Middle East, and Latin America – with about 5.4 percent between them in a stark manifestation of the "digital divide."

Figure 2.4 shows the change in the regional share of the world Internet population from 1997 to 2002. The North American share has dropped dramatically, as might be expected, and that of Europe and the Asia Pacific have grown in tandem, although growth has been somewhat slower in Europe. The Latin American share has also increased. The Middle East has shown a slight rise, from 0.8 percent to 0.9 percent, while Africa has registered a decline from 1.0 percent to 0.8 percent. It seems likely that aspects of this pattern will continue into the foreseeable future. The North American share will decline as the market becomes saturated, and there will be modest growth in Latin America and relative stagnation or decline in the Middle East and Africa. European growth will slow down because many of those markets are mature (see Figure 2.6). However, percentage uptake in much of Asia is still very low and growth in China, and also in India, will push up the Asia Pacific share in the future. Certainly predictions about Internet growth (and concomitant hardware demand) in the region tend to be optimistic (see e.g. Nua Ltd, December 19, 2000; *Bangkok Post*, January 3, 2001). Gartner Group reports that China is currently the fastest growing ICT market in the world (Hui, 2001).

Behind the Asian region's 28.9 percent share of the global Internet population lie both large numbers of people, and great disparities between countries. Figure 2.5 shows the position of Asian countries in the league table of Internet countries by number online. The top twelve countries

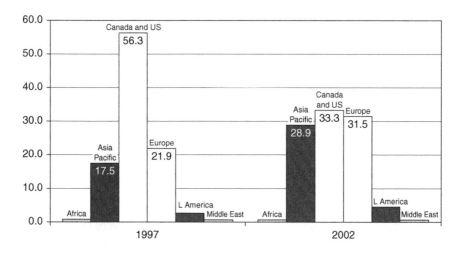

Figure 2.4 Change in regional share of global Internet, 1997 to 2002

Source: compiled from figures available at http://www.nua.com/surveys/howmanyonline/index.html

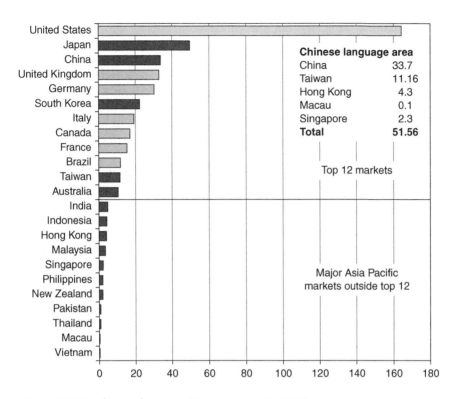

Figure 2.5 Numbers online – top Internet countries 2002

Source: compiled from figures available at http://www.nua.com/surveys/howmanyonline/ index.html

worldwide are given in order, followed by the major Asia Pacific countries outside that ranking. Japan has, not surprisingly, the second largest number of people online in the world, after the United States, and leads Asia with 49.7 million. However, if we consider the Chinese language area – China, Hong Kong, Macau, Taiwan, with Singapore added as a proxy for the Chinese Diaspora in Southeast Asia – then Japan is pushed into third place. Even by these figures, which probably understate the number online in China (see Nua Ltd, April 22, 2002) the Chinese language area has 51.6 million users.

Market forces increasingly ignore national boundaries, and nowhere is this more evident than in cyberspace. Language is an important compo- nent of international Internet use, but is seldom considered in analysis of the digital divide. It seems likely that one of the reasons for the strong showing of the Scandinavian countries and the Netherlands in taking up the Internet in comparison to equally prosperous countries such as France is their higher competency in English, which has been the major language used on the Web. Within Asia, India has the disadvantage of not having a single national language but the concomitant advantage that English is used relatively widely. The Chinese language area, on the other hand, has a basically common written language (ignoring the differences between simplified and traditional characters) and, partly as a result of this, the level of English is quite low (with Singapore and Hong Kong as exceptions). The huge critical mass of Chinese speakers has probably already made Chinese the second language of the Internet and, sometime soon, it will become the major one, supplanting English. Countries such as Thailand and Vietnam, even though they have substantial populations, will have the disadvantage of belonging to small language groups.

While China is currently an important Internet country in terms of numbers online (and growth), its proportion online is very low (Figure 2.2) and so it does not appear among the major Internet countries by that measure. As Figure 2.6 shows, Asia comes out well, with Hong Kong, Taiwan, and Singapore in the top twelve and South Korea (15) and Japan (19) not far behind. All of them are ahead of Germany (20) and France

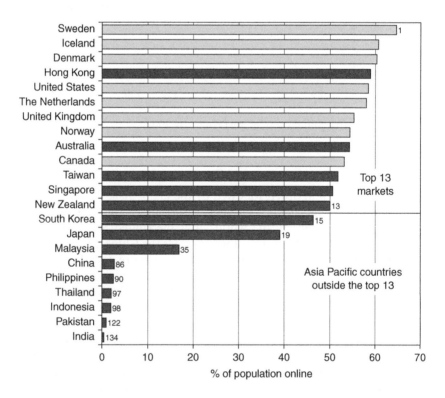

Figure 2.6 Top Internet countries, 2001, by percentage of population online

Source: compiled from figures available at http://www.nua.com/surveys/howmanyonline/index.html

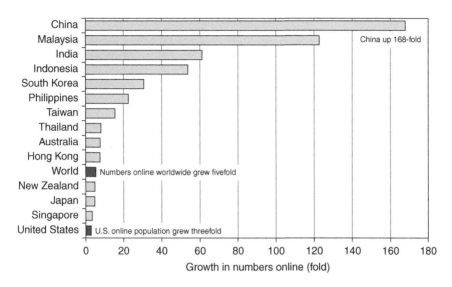

Figure 2.7 Growth in numbers online 1997 to 2002 in major Asian markets

Source: compiled from figures available at http://www.nua.com/surveys/howmanyonline/index.html

(30) and may be considered at the leading edge of Internet use. Japan's relatively low position is interesting, given its wealth and technological level. However, these figures ignore the widespread use of Internet phones, so a change of definition would give another impression, though the relevance of that general economic activity would be marginal. Moreover, there is an explosive growth of broadband in Japan so the situation may be different in a year's time (Creed, 2002).

Growth is, of course, the third key measure, and Figure 2.7 plots the increase in numbers online between 1997 and 2002 for the major Internet markets in Asia. This measure tends to favor countries with large populations and so China is by far and away the star performer. However, sheer population size is not the only determinant, and for this reason Malaysia, with a population of 22 million, appears better poised than both India (1030 million) and Indonesia (228 million).

ASIAN INTERNET: CATCHING UP

Figures 2.2 through 2.7 bring together some basic statistics on Internet use in Asia. This is supplemented by Table 2.1 which gives data on a range of information technology indicators for Asian countries and leading countries worldwide. The picture of the ICT environment painted by these

Table 2.1 ICT Indicators, 1999, top Internet countries and Asia

Country	Internet hosts	Internet users	Estimated PCs	Main telephone lines	Mobile cellular subscriber	Digital cellular subscriber	Television receivers	Cable TV subscribers
Iceland	10.7	53.9	35.9	67.8	39.2	–	52.1	–
Norway	9.9	45	45	70.8	61.7	–	–	–
Sweden	5.9	41.4	45.1	66.5	57.8	–	–	–
United States	19.3	39.8	–	60.7	31.2	–	–	–
Bermuda	4.4	39	–	73.7	–	–	–	–
Canada	5.5	36.1	–	60.5	23	–	–	–
Finland	8.9	32.3	36	55.3	66.7	–	–	–
Australia	5.8	31.7	47.1	52.1	34.4	29.8	–	–
Singapore	4.6	29.5	52.7	57.7	47.5	–	–	–
Denmark	6.4	28.2	41.4	68.3	49.9	–	62.1	25.4
Hong Kong, China	1.7	25.2	29.1	55.8	54.9	–	–	6.6
Switzerland	3.8	24.6	46.2	69.9	42	–	–	–
United Kingdom	3	21.3	30.6	50.2	40.8	–	–	–
Taiwan, China	2.7	20.5	18.1	54.4	52.1	–	–	–
Korea, Republic of	0.6	14.7	18.3	45.7	50.4	–	–	15.2
Japan	2.1	14.5	28.7	49.4	44.9	–	–	–
Malaysia	0.3	6.9	6.9	20.3	5	–	–	–
Thailand	0.1	1.3	2.3	5.9	2.2	–	–	–
China	0	0.7	1.2	8.6	3.4	–	–	–
Philippines	0	0.7	1.7	2.1	0.7	–	–	–
India	0	0.2	0.3	1.3	0	–	–	–
Indonesia	0	0.2	0.9	2.9	1.1	–	–	–
Nepal	0	0.1	0.3	0.4	0	–	–	–
Pakistan	0	0.1	–	2.2	0.2	–	–	–
Vietnam	0	0.1	0.9	1.1	0	–	–	–
Myanmar	0	0	0.1	0.6	0	–	0.7	–

Source: International Labor Organization (2001); World Employment Report (2001), Life at work in the information economy, Geneva.

Note:
Data in italics for "Main telephone lines" and "mobile cellular subscriber" are for 1995.

statistics and assessments is confusing and contradictory in detail but several observations relevant to Asia may be made:

1   Japan, though the most developed Asian economy, has lagged in uti-
    lization of the Internet, and, although broadband is growing fast,
    it seems likely that this trend will continue.

2   Singapore and Hong Kong will continue to be the most advanced Internet economies in Asia. However, other Asian cities should not be overlooked. In particular, country data on China tend to give a misleading impression of the development of the Internet in major Chinese cities, and there are reports of very high Internet access in cities such as Beijing, Shanghai, and Guangzhou (*China Electronics News*, December 28, 2000). Perhaps the same is happening in Bangalore, Hyderabad, and Karachi.

3   Beyond cities and city-states, South Korea and Taiwan will jostle for leadership in Asia (Nielson NetRatings, 2001).

4   China, with its rapidly growing economy and its large language area, will soon be the major Internet market in Asia. Given the network effect, whereby the value of a network to its users grows exponentially with the size of the network, this has huge implications.

As might be expected, as the development of the Internet in a country matures, growth of the network slows. Growth in the United States is slowing down, and while it is not clear what the maximum proportion will ultimately be – there will always be a segment of the population which for reasons of youth, age, poverty, and inclination will never be connected – it is likely that will be approached soon. A recent Pew Research report found that 57 percent of non-Internet users in the United States (i.e. about a quarter of the population) say they have no interest in using the Web (Pew Research Center, 2000). A proportion of Americans with a PC at home are not connected to the Internet (Nua Ltd, January 10, 2002). Even more significant is a report that a substantial number of people are turning away from the Internet:

> 28m people in the United States, and perhaps 2m in Britain, now fall into the category of "former Internet users." Even worse, it is teenagers – the very age group on whom the medium's future supposedly depends – who are disconnecting in the greatest numbers.
>
> (Burkeman, 2000)

This is unlikely to be happening in Asia yet, and the U.S. and British figures may well be inflated, but it does suggest a note of caution. The Internet user base will not continue to grow for ever; more important, after the novelty has worn off, real use of the Internet in terms of effective e-commerce will not grow automatically.

FOLLOWER COUNTRIES AND THE INTERNET

Given the current and likely future state of Internet development, how should Asian nations be approaching the Internet? What can they learn from its short history? Much of what is written on the Internet is based on the American experience, and it is often assumed that "follower countries" will replicate the American model. There are three reasons why this assumption is unwarranted.

1 Leap-frogging with emerging technologies and business models

The Internet has traditionally been based on a landline communications infrastructure – from copper cables in telephone wiring systems to fiber-optic cable. In developing countries where this infrastructure is inadequate, such as China and India (Nua Ltd, January 8, 2001), consumers are leap-frogging into Web mobile phones. It seems likely that the Internet in such countries, which hold not merely a large proportion of the world's population but also a large number of the new middle class, will utilize mobile communications to a large extent (Nua Ltd, November 29, 2000). This will also happen in developed countries, where we "have only begun to see the impact of wireless technologies on business' full potential" (Biggs, 2000), but the effect will be much greater in countries where there is a substantial proportion of the population with spending power but without access to traditional telecommunication networks. A recent article in the American journal *The Futurist* put "portable information devices" as the first of the top ten emerging technologies of the coming decade (Halal, 2000). The ILO suggests that "Leapfrogging has first of all a technological foundation: through wireless applications, developing countries can bypass more costly and time-consuming investments in fixed-wire telecom infrastructures" (International Labor Organization, 2001).

Cheaper computers and communication devices will bring the Internet rapidly within the purchasing power of large segments of fast developing countries such as China and India if they are adapted to local conditions (Nua Ltd, January 12, 2001) and use the technology appropriately (Nua Ltd, January 5, 2001).

2 Adoption truncation

The process of adopting Internet use will be truncated in follower economies. In developed economies fifteen years ago academics were virtually the only users of email; usage has now spread to about half of the population. The spread of knowledge about a new technology, and the acceptance of it as a desirable acquisition, is a key factor in its adoption, especially when, as in the case of the Internet, costs are falling rapidly. The "natural" adoption pattern seen in the United States and similar economies will be truncated elsewhere because of widespread knowledge and desire. As it becomes accessible it will be taken up rapidly, and not necessarily following the American pattern of adoption. For instance, there was a definite movement from male to female in the United States.

However, there are indications elsewhere that growth is being driven by women, for instance, in Italy (Between ICT Brokers, 2000) and South Korea (*ZD Net Asia News*, October 4, 2000). In Taiwan it is claimed that women are as likely to be Internet users as men (Nua Ltd, November 17, 2000).

3 Local variation

Growth of the Internet will also be very much affected by local physical infrastructure, political, social, and cultural constraints. Taking the case of e-commerce, for instance, very few Chinese currently have credit cards, and those who do are not confident of using them online, so that payment tends to be on delivery. Physical delivery is also a problem, from the postal service through to inadequate transportation networks. The penetration of computers is low, and although the percentage of the population owning a telephone doubled between 1995 and 1998, it still only amounts to 10.53 percent (*China Statistical Yearbook 1999*, 2000). In Latin America it is said that only 15 percent of the population can be targeted for e-commerce because of social inequalities (Elkin, 2000). In this context, it is appropriate to note East Asia's relatively egalitarian wealth distribution.

Cyber cafés and kiosks (Misra, 2001) are particularly popular in India, which, like China, has an inadequate telecommunications infrastructure (NetSenseTM, 2000). In Japan it is predicted that much e-commerce will be mediated through the ubiquitous network of convenience stores (Gunji, 2000). Examples of local variation could be continued but the point has been made. The growth of Internet usage and adoption of e-commerce will be affected by a wide range of local factors, including state promotional attempts. While the Internet is a global medium, successful practitioners will be those who are aware of local differences and conditions and adjust their operations, where justified, for best fit. Of particular relevance is the use of the vernacular. English has traditionally been the main language of the Internet and will continue to be necessary for companies, including SMEs, with markets that cross linguistic boundaries. However, what is needed in many places, including Asia, is a more vernacular Internet. One important way to stimulate Internet use in Asia, and to close the digital divide, is to provide website and email in the customer's language, rather than in a foreign one.

With much of the glamor going out of dotcoms, IT firms and investors alike will be looking more closely at applying Internet technology to existing "bricks-and-mortar" companies (*South China Morning Post*, January 17, 2001). Indeed, as the International Labor Organization argues, "While much attention has surrounded the volatile new world of the 'dot.coms,' this is a distraction: the true portent of ICT is how it will transform the 'old economy'" (International Labor Organization, 2001). Asian companies must, in general, embrace the Internet but they must do it wisely if they are to realize the potential of the technologies. They must understand their customers and the business environment in which they are operating.

They must attempt to work out how the Internet fits into this, what changes it will make, and what are the opportunities and dangers. Overseas experience, especially from the United States, will be an uncertain guide, but should be kept in mind and should be applied imaginatively and creatively to their specific situation. They should be wary of "technology fetishism" and should ensure that the Internet is used as a servant to their business, not the master. As elsewhere in the world there will be a constant need to reassess their business and markets, and to cope with the challenges and opportunities of technological change.

The role of government

Virtually all governments have an interest in promoting ICT and have a great, perhaps vital, responsibility to foster and promote effective and efficient ICT use (see Beal, 2001). For example, the ILO notes that "For macroeconomic gains to occur requires a range of commercial, trade, investment, telecommunications and other infrastructure policies to be brought to bear on the development potential of ICT. China's strategy is particularly promising in this regard. It has combined previously separate ministries into the Ministry of Information Industries, and established economic zones particularly devoted to the growth of start-up ICT ventures" (International Labor Organization, 2001). In the Republic of Korea the Ministry of Commerce, Industry and Energy (MOCIE) has just unveiled a plan to promote ICT among 30,000 SMEs (*Korea Herald*, August 4, 2001; UNCTAD, 2001).

There are many ways in which governments can promote ICT use for commercial and individual development. These include:

1 Infrastructure
2 Tax policies
3 Financial support
4 Education
5 R&D
6 Standards
7 Advice and information
8 Portals to promote SME exports
9 B2B promotion
10 E-government
11 E-procurement.

E-government (and e-procurement) are particularly interesting ways in which governments can facilitate ICT take-up. Lunati *et al.* note:

> Another effective government initiative affecting both the development of electronic commerce and SME familiarity with and uptake of it is

the progressive online transfer of government activities. Business-related activities can be grouped into four major types: i) transactions such as business registration, taxation and social security-related transactions; ii) information provision (business and corporate legislation, local government information, building zoning) and information collection (statistics); iii) government purchasing (procurement); and iv) government consultation activities (calls for inputs into new planning or zoning initiatives).

(Lunati *et al.*, 2000)

Governments can set a good example by using ICT effectively, and demonstrating cost-saving and efficiency gains. They can also use a combination of carrot and stick to encourage companies and individuals to use ICT in their inevitable, but expandable, dealings with government. For instance, governments are moving to e-procurement which, while saving costs, enables them to set up a system which is less biased towards large companies than physical procurement (Lunati *et al.*, 2000). By encouraging smaller companies to register and participate in e-procurement it is able to assist them against competition from large foreign companies without infringing WTO regulations. Finally, by phasing out physical procurement it is providing corporations who are involved in supplying government with a powerful incentive to go digital. It is estimated that procurement by public authorities accounts for 11 percent of the European Union's GDP (OECD, 2001). While it is likely that government procurement will be a smaller proportion in at least the developing Asian economies, it still represents a major market for companies. Asian governments are among the leaders in e-government. A recent survey of 195 countries around the world conducted by London-based World Markets Research Centre and Brown University in Boston claimed that Taiwan was second and Singapore eighth in "e-government ranking" (World Markets Research Centre, 2001).

CONCLUSION

In under a decade the Internet, and ICT more generally, has grown enormously and has become one of the defining characteristics of our times. The "digital divide," within countries and between countries, is seen as one of the most pressing economic, social, and political issues of the contemporary world. People, and countries, excluded from the digital revolution are likely to fall further behind with their socio-economic problems compounded and exacerbated. ICT is not a panacea either for economies or for businesses, and must be used wisely and well. However, ICT and its effective utilization is increasingly becoming a prerequisite for a wide range of human activities, economic, political, and social.

A few years ago emails, and websites, were virtually exclusively in English. Now they are increasingly in Chinese, German, or Spanish. Nowhere is the rate of change more bewildering and exhilarating than in Asia. Internet growth in much of Asia, Latin America, and Africa is linked more strongly to economic growth than it is in North America or Europe, where the new technology grew in an already developed economic space. Where economic growth is languishing, as it is in much of Africa, then Internet growth also lags. Where economic development is vigorous, as in much of Asia, then the Internet becomes a significant manifestation of growth, and in turn a major driver of it.

BIBLIOGRAPHY

Bangkok Post (2001) "Asia Pacific net subscriptions to top 72 million in 2001 – study," January 3. Online. Available HTTP: http://www.newsbytes.com/news/01/160014.html (accessed August, 2001).

Beal, T. (2000) "SMEs and the World Wide Web: opportunities and prospects," in M.A. Abdullah (ed.) *Small And Medium Enterprises In Asia Pacific. Vol. III: Development Prospects*, Commack, NY: Nova Science Publishers.

—— (2001) "SMEs and Government Policies on ICT," the Sixth International Conference on Global Business and Economic Development, States and Markets: Forging Partnerships for Sustainable Development, Bratislava, Slovakia, November 7–10.

—— (2002) "Information and communications technologies in the two Koreas: contrasts, commonalities, challenges," *Global Economic Review* (Seoul).

Between ICT Brokers (2000) "Women driving Italian Internet boom." Online. Available HTTP: http://www.nua.ie/surveys/?f=VS&art_id=905356139&rel=true (available as of January 30, 2003).

Biggs, M. (2000) "On the radar: which emerging technologies will succeed, and when should you adopt them," *InfoWorld*, September 18.

Burkeman, O. (2000) "Is it the end of the digital dream?" *Guardian Weekly*, December 21–27.

China Electronics News (2000) "20/100 of families in Beijing, Shanghai and Guangzhou to log on," December 28.

China Statistical Yearbook 1999 (2000) Beijing: China Statistics Press.

Chua, J. (2001) " 'Bricks-and-clicks' card will bridge offline-online worlds," *South China Morning Post*. Online. Available HTTP: http://technology.scmp.com/ecommerce/WEEKLY/20010108181043297.asp (accessed August, 2001).

Creed, A. (2002) "Japan DSL count skyrockets in 2001," *Newsbytes Asia*. Online. Available HTTP: http://www.newsbytes.com/news/02/173724.html (accessed August, 2001).

Elkin, N. (2000) "Profiling the Latin American net user e-marketeer." Online. Available HTTP: http://www.emarketer.com/etopics/articles/20001102_latam.html?ref=dn (accessed August, 2001).

Foley, K. (2001) "A billion customers, anyone?" Online. Available HTTP: http://www.nua.ie/surveys/analysis/weekly_editorial/archives/issue1no164.html (available as of January 30, 2003).

Gunji, T. (2000) "Entwicklungstrends von Informations- und Kommunikationsdienstlesitungen in Japan" ("Trends in information and communications services in Japan"), X Betriebwirstschaftliche Tage zu Schwerin '00 (Tenth Annual Schwerin Business Symposium, 2000), Innovation and Competition in the Service Society – Start into the New Millennium, October 26–27, Schwerin, Mecklenburg-Vorpommern, Germany.

Halal, W.E. (2000) "The top 10 emerging technologies," *The Futurist* (Washington), July/August.

Hui, M.I. (2001) "Small firms account for 40% of exports in 2001," *Korea Herald*. Online. Available HTTP: http://www.koreaherald.co.kr/SITE/data/html_dir/ 2002/01/14/200201140029.asp (accessed August, 2001).

International Labor Organization (ILO) (2001) *World Employment Report 2001: Life at Work in the Information Economy.* Online. Available HTTP: http://www.ilo.org/public/english/support/publ/wer/index2.htm (only overview and statistical annex available online) (available as of January 30, 2003).

International Telecommunications Union (2000) *Internet Indicators 2000.* Online. Available HTTP: http://www.itu.int/ITU-D/ict/statistics/(available as of January 30, 2003).

Korea Herald (2001) "Ministry to aid IT projects of small firms." Online. Available HTTP: http://www.koreaherald.co.kr/SITE/data/html_dir/ 2001/08/04/ 200108040008.asp (accessed August, 2001).

Krammer, M. and Rozwell, C. (2000) "SMBs: embrace the organizational disruption of E-business," Gartner Group. Online. Available HTTP: http://www. gartnergroup.com/public/static/hotc/00094687.html (accessed August, 2001).

Lunati, M., Faverie, M. and Vickery, G. (2000) "Realising the potential of electronic commerce for SMEs in the global economy," background report for workshop at the Bologna Conference (OECD), June. Online. Available HTTP: http://www.conferenzabologna.ipi.it/Eng/dopo_la_conferenza/documenti/WK3_ eng.pdf (available as of January 30, 2003).

McConnell International (2001) "Ready? Net.Go!" Online. Available HTTP: http://www.mcconnellinternational.com/ereadiness/default.cfm (available as of January 30, 2003).

Ma, J. (1997) "China's economic reform in the 1990s." Online. Available HTTP: http://members.aol.com/junmanew/cover.htm (accessed August, 2001).

Misra, N. (2001) "Technology transforms rural India," *South China Morning Post.* Online. Available HTTP: http://biz.scmp.com/ZZZ44UIVPGC.html (accessed August, 2001).

Nairne, D. (2001) "China Net figures inflated, study finds," *South China Morning Post.* Online. Available HTTP: http://technology.scmp.com/internet/daily/ 20010111164531321.asp (accessed August, 2001).

NetSenseTM (2000) "An exhaustive study of the usage and attitudes of the Indian Internet user," September 19.

Nielsen NetRatings Press Release (2001) "South Korea and Taiwan dominate Asian internet usage." Online. Available HTTP: http://209.249.142.22/ press_releases/ PDF/pr_010308.pdf (accessed August, 2001).

Nua Ltd (2000) "eMarketer: gloomy outlook for Hong Kong B2C," October 20. Online. Available HTTP: http://www.nua.ie/surveys/?f=VS&art_id= 905356119&rel=true (available as of January 30, 2001).

Nua Ltd (2000) "Taylor Nelson Sofres: B2C takes off in Taiwan," 17 November.

Online. Available HTTP: http://www.nua.ie/surveys/?f=VS&art_id= 905356178&rel=true (available as of January 30, 2003).

—— (2000) "Xinhua: Wireless Web set to boom in China," 29 November. Online. Available HTTP: http://www.nua.ie/surveys/?f=VS&art_id=905356204&rel =true (available as of January 30, 2003).

—— (2000) "Associated Press: Singapore is role model for e-government," December 12. Online. Available HTTP: http://www.nua.ie/surveys/?f=VS&art_id= 905356237&rel=true (available as of January 30, 2003).

—— (2000) "CNET: Asia: 188 million Internet users by 2004," December 19.

—— (2001) "Newsbytes: B2B market matures in Asia Pacific," January 2. Online. Available HTTP: http://www.nua.ie/surveys/?f=VS&art_id=905356296&rel= true (available as of January 30, 2003).

—— (2001) "BBC Online Network: WAP advocates rebut criticism," January 5. Online. Available HTTP: http://www.nua.ie/surveys/?f=VS&art_id= 905356312&rel=true (available as of January 30, 2003).

—— (2001) "eMarketer: the Net in India: a luxury few can afford," January 8. Online. Available HTTP: http://www.nua.ie/surveys/?f=VS&art_id= 905356319&rel=true (available as of January 30, 2003).

—— (2001) "Context-based research: is the wireless industry missing the point?" January 12. Online. Available HTTP: http://www.nua.ie/surveys/?f= VS&art_id=905356337&rel=true (available as of January 30, 2003).

—— (2001) "Multilingual sites imperative for large firms," May 18. Online Available HTTP: http://www.nua.com/surveys/index.cgi?f=VS&art_id=905356776 &rel=true (available as of January 30, 2003).

—— (2002) "Not everyone wants Net at home," January 10. Online. Available HTTP: http://www.nua.com/surveys/?f=VS&art_id=905357539&rel=true (available as of January 30, 2003).

—— (2002) "Reuters: China number two in home net usage," April 22. Online. Available HTTP: http://www.nua.ie/surveys/index.cgi?f=VS&art_id= 905357873&rel=true (available as of January 30, 2003).

Organization for Economic Cooperation and Development (OECD) (2001) *The Bologna Process: Proposals to Implement the Bologna Charter on SME Policies, Paris.* Online. Available HTTP: http://www.conferenzabologna.ipi.it/Eng/english _2001(9).PDF (available as of January 30, 2003).

Pew Research Center (2000) "Internet naysayers." Online. Available HTTP: http://www.pewinternet.org/reports/reports.asp?Report=21&Section=Report Level2&Field=Level2ID&ID=55 (available as of January 30, 2003).

South China Morning Post (2001) "Asia-Pacific to outpace US Web usage within five years," January 13.

—— (2001) "Dell to double Asia-Pacific capacity," January 15.

—— (2001) "India eyes bricks and mortar firms as dotcoms go under," January 17.

Taylor, N. (2000) "Global surfers prefer to shop locally," *South China Morning Post*, December 21.

UNCTAD (2001) "China's ICT strategy and E-Commerce," in *E-Commerce and Development Report 2001*, section 10.

United Nations Development Programme (UNDP) (2001) "Annual report 2001, partnerships to fight poverty." Online. Available HTTP: http://www.undp.org/ dpa/annualreport2001/ (available as of January 30, 2003).

World Markets Research Centre (2001) "Global e-government survey 2001: London and Boston." Online. Available HTTP: http://www.worldmarketsanalysis.com/pdf/e-govreport.pdf (available as of January 30, 2003).

ZD Net Asia News (2000) "Forty-two percent of Korean Net users are women," October 4. Online. Available HTTP: http://www.zdnetasia.com/news/dailynews/story/0,2000010021,20075519-1,00.htm (accessed August, 2001).

APPENDIX: METHODOLOGICAL NOTE ON STATISTICAL SOURCES

1 NUA Internet surveys

Source: http://www.nua.ie/surveys/how_many_online/index.html (available as of February 10, 2003).
The surveys vary in date. At the time of writing, the latest survey is in February, 2002 and available data from this site is in May, 2002.
NUA methodology note:
Where possible, "How Many Online" figures represent both adults and children who have accessed the Internet at least once during the three months prior to being surveyed. Where these figures are not available, we use figures for users who have gone online in the past six months, past year, or ever. An Internet user represents a person with access to the Internet and is not specific to Internet account holders. When the figure for Internet account holders is the only information available, this figure is multiplied by a factor of three to give the number of Internet users. The figure for "Asia Pacific" includes Australia and New Zealand. When more than one survey is available on a country's demographics, Nua will take the mean of the two surveys or, in the case where Nua feels one study may be more comprehensive/reliable than the other, Nua will quote this figure over the other.
Source: http://www.nua.ie/surveys/how_many_online/methodology.html (available as of February 10, 2003).

2 International Labor Organization (ILO)

World Employment Report 2001, Statistical Annex
Source: http://www.ilo.org/public/english/support/publ/wer/tables/tabl_toc.htm (available as of February 10, 2003).
This site contains four tables, only the first of which – ICT indicators – is used here to compile Table 2.1. The ICT indicators table has 220 countries, but 1999 Internet data are given for only seventy.

3 Catching up and falling behind

Inequality, IT, and the Asian diaspora[1]

Anthony P. D'Costa

INTRODUCTION

The revolution in IT (including the Internet) presents new opportunities for economic development and social mobility. Yet for many belonging to disadvantaged groups, accessibility to new technologies and economic well-being is highly constrained. This tension manifests itself in increasing inequality, set in motion by the rapidity of innovations, itself let loose by global economic integration and unequal access to new technologies. This chapter examines this tension by identifying the economic and social processes behind inequality in some Asian economies and how that inequality is reproduced in the larger world economy.

Inequality is a relative notion. It precludes neither income growth nor a reduction in poverty, although improvements in both are likely to reduce inequality. Inequality is argued to be a composite product of global integration involving pre-existing social structures and processes of inequality. Consequently, they lead to highly uneven economic and social outcomes in Asia (see United Nations Development Program, 2001). Economic interconnectedness among nations allows some to integrate themselves favorably into the world economy due to specific advantages, such as a well-educated workforce and high-quality physical and technological infrastructures. Others might witness a process of immiserization due either to adverse movements in the terms of trade or to a lack of competitiveness in general and the IT industry in particular. Even in the case of those countries that manage to integrate well, well-placed social classes tend to benefit the most. This uneven development on a global scale is characteristic of capitalism, a system that is necessarily expansive but in which greater gains are secured by dominant classes, social groups, and nations (see Shari, 2000).

There are two levels of inequality that result from differential access to higher, especially technical and professional education. The first is the persistent inequality in developing countries due to pre-existing social inequality. Higher education is also in itself a key marker of such inequality. Inegalitarian social structures compound the problem. Second is the mobility of technical, professional talent in an IT-driven, integrating world economy, which contributes to inequality in affluent societies as well. The inability of developing economies to absorb such talent leads to underutilization of local talent at home and encourages emigration. As a result, many Asian countries are contributing to a global talent pool, standing out professionally as a visible community in affluent countries, such as the US. The economic and educational gaps between them and other ethnic minorities in the U.S. are significant, but the gulf between these workers and their developing country counterparts in non-technical, non-integrating sectors is worse.

In analyzing the relationship between Asia and Asians in the global IT industry, we can postulate a self-reinforcing, cumulative process (James, 2001) whereby pre-existing inequality is reproduced both at the national and global levels (see Figure 3.1). For a variety of institutional reasons, unequal access to tertiary education leads to a few joining the ranks of a transnational technical pool. Consequently, an Asian diaspora in the IT area emerges, involving Japan, Singapore, Malaysia, South Korea, Taiwan, China, Philippines, and India. These countries have been major exporters of IT products and services and recipients of transnational investments (see D'Costa, 2003a). These are also the economies that have either succeeded in educating the masses or have created good-quality tertiary education systems, emphasizing technical and professional programs. The HPEAEs (high performing East Asian economies) have had the added advantage of

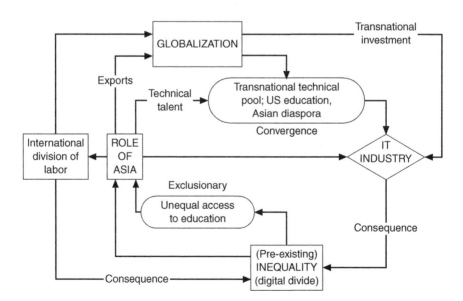

Figure 3.1 The self-reinforcing process of globalization, IT, and inequality

Source: author's compilation

ensuring greater equity accompanying high economic growth, through the spread of universal education, labor-absorbing export activities, land reforms, and public goods. South and Southeast Asia have been less successful in promoting economic growth with distribution. Consequently, their participation in the IT loop has been peripheral. However, countries such as India, with slower growth than East Asia and poor income distribution, are tackling pre-existing inequality by gradually widening educational and social opportunities, increasing access to IT, and exporting.

The global development of the IT industry and Asia's role in it has ambiguous outcomes for development. For example, as skilled IT workers move from core markets back to the home (developing) markets and found new start-ups, they induce local development and reduce core market hegemony. This is typically true in countries that have either emphasized mass education with attention to distributive justice or have fostered the development of a large pool of technical and professional workers. On the other hand, pre-existing inequality in Asian countries could be exacerbated as global opportunities arising from the IT industry are captured only by those Asians who have the requisite education, skills, and social connections. Consequently, the IT industry and Asia's participation in it remains double-edged, with dual tendencies – an equalizing trend for the upwardly mobile and an inegalitarian one for the already impoverished. What is evident in this era of globalization is that there are select Asians and Asian countries that benefit from global integration but clearly there are others that do not.

This chapter illustrates these themes in three main sections. The first section lays out the relationship between the processes of globalization and world inequality as it pertains to the IT sector. It suggests that unequal access to technical education within countries produces global inequality. The second section examines Asia's role in the global IT industry, particularly its role in technical education and employment in core markets, such as the US.[2] The third section discusses the interrelationships between inequality, education, and social mobility at three levels: the domestic economy, foreign markets, and Asian social networks in the global IT industry. By embedding the analysis at different levels, the connections within the global IT industry, as well as the networks between IT professionals and entrepreneurs, are illustrated. Furthermore, by extending this analysis to the issues of access to education and the international division of labor, I hope to produce a more nuanced account of IT-based globalization and the opportunities this provides for countries and individuals.

GLOBALIZATION AND IT

The IT industry is a good illustration of the self-reinforcing processes of inequality. As the growth of world demand for IT workers is met increasingly by development-aspiring states, more and more IT professionals become part of a transnational workforce. Based on this development it could be anticipated that there would be some convergence in the incomes of professionals in the global IT industry. This assumes that the rate of increase in compensation for developing country IT workforces is faster than their industrialized country counterparts. The reduction in poverty in most of Asia suggests that inequality is less severe (Pangestu, 2001). But intuitively, IT growth also suggests that income inequality could rise within countries that generate such talent for two reasons: (1) if the incomes of the IT industry are rising faster than other sectors; and (2) if the IT sector does not have strong linkages with other sectors, thereby limiting the trickle down effect (Morley, 2001). The IT workers are urban-based, better educated, English-speaking professionals. They are relatively few in number compared to the vast numbers of undereducated, impoverished, unskilled workers in Asia. The IT sector's links to other sectors may or may not be strong. Much would depend on what is produced, how, where it is sold, and government policy. For example, in the electronics industry, a locally based design, hardware manufacturing, including semi-conductors and chips, and final assembly are likely to have a greater economic impact on incomes as a whole. On the other hand, a heavily export-dependent sector for software services could result in a skill premium for the professionals but worsen inequality due to unbalanced growth (D'Costa, 2003b). To stem the polarizing trend, the supply of skills will have to be increased and greater linkages established with other sectors of the economy.

The IT-based global economy offers ample opportunity to those who are technically qualified and able to exercise their human capabilities in a wider global, networked system. In the post-dot.com bubble in the US this may appear unconvincing, given the massive number of failures in the Internet-based businesses leading up to the most recent recession. However, it should be pointed out the IT industry is more than new start-ups in e-commerce. There is hardware manufacturing, demand for which seems unceasing, and software services, whose applications border on the fantastic. Virtually every industry, including the service sector, is subject to and rejuvenated by IT applications. As prices of IT products fall and the speed of innovations intensifies, the wider diffusion of IT for affluent economies and high income groups is only a matter of time. In poor economies, the high income groups are typically the first to benefit from IT diffusion, though some governments facilitate greater access to the less privileged. The point is that the production and consumption of IT-related products and services has a class bias – the poor, the illiterate, the impoverished, and socially underprivileged remain at the periphery of this very dynamic IT sector. On the other hand, those with high levels of education, social connections, and greater receptivity to new technologies are able to insert themselves favorably into the global IT loop. The large identifiable swathes of Asians (from India, China, Hong Kong, Singapore, South Korea, Taiwan, the Philippines, Japan, among others) catering to the global IT industry indicate the region-specific involvement with globalization. Asian diasporas circumscribed by professional requirements are contributing to the technological, organizational, and financial dimensions of the IT industry. At the same time, the exclusion of the vast majority, in many impoverished Asian countries, along with the poor in affluent societies, from the benefits of IT suggests a more sober view of such technologies in networked economies.

Globalization is a multifaceted process driven by capitalist logic that transcends national boundaries and national actors. Investment by transnational firms, economic reforms by national governments, and external pressures from supranational agencies such as the World Bank, the IMF, and WTO contribute to economic interconnectedness. The IT industry is a quintessentially global one. Broadly speaking, the IT sector comprises several interrelated industries, high and low technology, hardware and software, manufacturing and services. The Internet is a composite subset of this sector, connecting people in global spaces and transforming economies in novel ways. Most states are eyeing some facet of the IT industry, both as an immediate response to the changing global competitive conditions and as a long-term strategy for national development.

Recent discussions on inequality have reinforced the importance of understanding the functioning of the capitalist global economy (Streeten, 1998; Stewart and Berry, 1999). As the complexities of innovations for world competitiveness increase, firms are compelled to form global alliances. This alliance capitalism (Phillips, 2000) is a harbinger of inter-industry networks, imperative to the systemic nature of contemporary knowledge-based innovation. Networks are also intra-firm, as in the internalization of market transactions, between the parent firm and its subsidiaries abroad (Dunning, 2000). The strategy of networking for corporate profitability has been catalyzed by the proliferation of digital information and communications technologies (ICT) (Castells, 2000). These strategies are designed to sustain a firm's core competence, leaving many of its other functions to be outsourced. Firms that are networked are typically from the advanced capitalist economies, exploiting their firm-specific advantages cultivated in supportive home environments in geographically dispersed locations.

In this networked global system, the distribution of gains is dependent on who controls and operates what part of the value chain (see Kaplinsky, 2000). As advanced capitalist firms specialize in the more knowledge-intensive core competency, such as design, their developing country suppliers work hard to master routine technology-based production. This is not to suggest that it is impossible to break out of structural dependency, as clearly many East Asian economies and a few large, industrialized countries such as Brazil and India have done. Rather it is to indicate that an innovation-based high road to capital accumulation is challenging, given the rapidity of technological change, the structural conditions that constrain the reproduction of new technologies easily, and the social conditions in poor economies that limit diffusion of recent innovations (D'Costa, 2003a). Inequality is inherent in this international division of labor for two reasons: (1) core competency also includes other high value-added segments, such as marketing, undertaken by advanced country firms in advanced country markets; and (2) because of the dynamic process of cumulative causation, the first-comer advantages of advanced capitalist economies lead to "self-reinforcing advantages" over time (James, 2001).

Technological spill-overs accrue to core markets, generating new industrial and knowledge clusters, while developing countries typically must contend with backwash effects. This uneven development at the global level is reproduced regionally within countries, especially those that have been able to break the monopoly of the core economies. Singapore, Hsinchu in Taiwan, and Seoul in South Korea are prime examples of new global regional agglomerations based on technological upgrading and knowledge-based learning. Continuous industrial upgrading has meant the shift in IT industries from Taiwan to Shanghai and from Hong Kong to mainland China, while many of the higher-order design activities remain centered in Hong Kong and Hsinchu. The government of Taiwan is planning to recruit 20,000 Indian software professionals for its Kaohsiung software zone (Bhuyan, 2002). Bangalore and Mumbai in India fit the bill as well, but they are also part of an impoverished national economy. Interestingly, mimicking the Taiwanese and Hong Kong experience, Indian software entrepreneurs from Bangalore are currently eyeing China both as a market and a center of production (Trivedi, 2002). China's dynamic IT industry (Smith, 2001, 2002) and its relatively lower costs make it attractive even for Indian IT firms. In all this reshuffling over economic space, uneven development is both smoothed out somewhat and accentuated elsewhere. Thus, as Bangalore caters to core markets and it begins to reproduce core market features in alliance with Chinese firms, the inequality between Bangalore and its immediate surroundings becomes stark. In the absence of countervailing forces, class-based polarization based on income, education, and social connections is inevitable. Two simultaneous forces are present in this process of globalization: divergence between Bangalore and the rest of the country, and convergence between core markets in advanced capitalist centers and Bangalore.

The intersection of class and space is readily apparent, though not in any simple way. On the spatial front we have the interlinking of economies through trade, investment, and increasingly, through flows of talent. Thus we have uneven development at the global level with countries and regions witnessing different rates of economic change. However, with spatial integration dominant classes from different national economies are likely to have some shared class identity at the global level, which Leslie Sklair

(2001) calls the "transnational capitalist class." However, because this class is nationally based, subject to the exegesis of local class politics, state policies, local institutions, and culture, the global class overlap is likely to be narrow and fluid (Hoogvelt, 2001). Class differentiation at the local level parallels the spatial inequality at the global level but the one-to-one correspondence between class and space is not completely established. The bourgeoisie in Bangalore is distinct from the toiling masses in India precisely because it joins the ranks of the transnational capitalist class. But it remains very much a local bourgeoisie competing with other dominant classes located elsewhere in the global economy. Contemporary globalization accentuates the uneven development process and class differentiation.

GLOBALIZATION, IT, AND ASIA

Notwithstanding the problem of defining Asia and whether such continental categories are intellectually useful, Asia as defined here denotes a group of countries in the region actively participating in an emerging global IT industry. Japan is excluded from this analysis (see n. 2). The involvement of Asia in the IT industry is significant, as producers of export products and services from home countries and by working directly in foreign markets. Asia is also a major importer of foreign hardware and software, from Microsoft and others. In electronics and other related hardware manufacturing, onshore production at home has been important, and so a wide range of consumer durables is produced and exported from East and Southeast Asia. With the exception of South Korea and to some extent Taiwan, most of these exports have been TNC-led, albeit with considerable state and local participation. Similarly, software services, such as maintenance, debugging, porting, and conversions, began with on-site provision, but contract workers had to be physically present in foreign locations. Now, offshore production of software is becoming more important. With the growing maturity of the Indian software sector and continued attractiveness of low wages, outsourcing of software services by foreign clients is increasingly becoming the norm in India and elsewhere.

Asia's participation in the global IT industry may be viewed in terms of economic integration. This could mean intra- and or inter-regional links. For the purposes of this chapter, intra-regional interactions, though complementary to the process of globalization, are not examined. Cost considerations and development aspirations led TNCs to seek and host governments to promote stable, low-cost supplies of labor. The promotion of low-wage-based electronics manufacturing, followed by gradual industrial upgrading in East and Southeast Asia to maintain international competitiveness, contributed to a new and changing international division of labor. Today, as IT-related technologies converge, firms and governments in Asia are concerned increasingly with competing in the globally expanding sector.

Taking the Asian region as a whole, the net results of capitalist development in widely varying institutional contexts have been very uneven. For some, global participation resulted in rising incomes and better income distribution initially as export growth was labor-absorbing. In addition, redistributive policies by governments, including widespread tertiary education, countered the tendencies towards increasing inequality associated with deepening, capital-intensive industrialization. Overall, however, the Asian experience has been highly variable. The high performing East Asian economies have experienced high growth rates, considerable industrial upgrading, and maintained relative equality, while South Asia has remained poor and highly unequal. Southeast Asia lies somewhere in between, though Indonesia may fare worse than India. However, as production becomes more knowledge- and skill-based, we can argue intuitively that heightened participation by many Asian countries in the global IT industry is likely to lead to inequality. The unequal access to higher education at home and subsequent inclusion of those who benefit from education in global social networks contribute to persistent inequality, and by extension, to the digital divide.

The ambiguity of benefits of global participation and structural dependence is captured nicely by India's IT sector. Of India's US$6.2 billion software exports in 2000 to 2001 (with domestic market size of US$2.06 billion), about 60 percent was to the US, with only six OECD countries (the US, Japan, UK, Germany, France, and Italy) accounting for nearly 80 percent of exports. The international division of labor for software development is quite clear-cut: India is a major center for outsourcing for the industrialized world and this trend is expected to grow. Recent projections place India's export level at US$9.5 billion by 2001 to 2002. India's National IT Task Force has set a target of US$50 billion of annual software and services exports by 2008; domestically, the goal has been set at US$35 billion. Both the actual and projected export figures are impressive by any standard. However, the sector continues to provide a large absolute volume of low-level services (see D'Costa, 2002a, 2002b, 2002c).

At the lowest level, this is a temporary transfer of Indian technical talent by a recruiting agency to the overseas client's site for a flat fee (man-month basis), pejoratively known as "body shopping." The agency's profit is based on the fees minus the costs of the transfer, such as airfare and living costs, including an agreed-upon salary for the worker. On-site services include a range of activities, such as programming, conversions, testing, debugging, porting, installing, and maintaining systems (see Heeks, 1996). Most of this work is tedious, uncreative, and requires lower-level skills, since the bulk of the instructions and specifications come from the client. The strength of the Indian software industry is in programming, and not in systems design and project management (Bacani, 2001). At the other end, turnkey projects, which entail design and systems integration, demand greater skills. Turnkey projects accounted for a significant

37 percent of software exports. However, even this activity includes low-value work, such as coding, conversions, debugging, and testing, carried out mostly offshore (in India) for cost reasons.

The transfer of software development to India is a welcome change as the local economy begins to capture more of the gains of higher value-added services. This is reflected in the rise in local salaries by job classification (Table 3.1). However, the inherent inequality associated with this development cannot be ignored. On the one hand, the global salary differential persists between Indian and US salaries (fifth column, Table 3.1), and, on the other, the rapid growth of IT-related salaries relative to other services – industrial and agricultural – means inequality across sectors (D'Costa, 2003b). IT professionals in India and elsewhere represent a new, globally mobile upper class in the country.

Inequality is produced within the software industry. As large firms have greater resources they also tend to secure better prices for their services. For example, revenues per employee were the lowest for firms with ten employees or fewer (US$11,528) and highest for those with 500 employees or more (US$36,373). The revenue income also takes into account the revenues earned by 100 percent-owned foreign subsidiaries. It is evident that large firms have higher revenues per employee due to increasing returns resulting from more employees and possibly more capital equipment. The size of firms is also correlated with export competitiveness, with larger firms being more competitive.

INEQUALITY, EDUCATION, AND SOCIAL MOBILITY

The home front

One significant institutional barrier to digital opportunities is unequal access to education. While most high performing East Asian economies have excelled in providing extensive educational opportunities to broad segments of their people, several Asian countries, especially those in South Asia, have failed on this score. The inherent class bias in South Asia's tertiary education is reflected by the growing prominence of India's higher educational institutions, especially in engineering and the sciences, and the woeful conditions of its primary and middle school systems (Drèze and Sen, 1998). The middle class has a vested interest in maintaining access to and expanding opportunities in higher education as it provides considerable social and economic premium over those without such training and credentials. Consequently, economic and social inequality is inherent in the unequal spread of education. Those with a solid technical education are rewarded well by the market. Those who make it to the IT sector experience considerable economic and social mobility, and pull many others (family members, friends, and college alumni) along with them.

Table 3.1 Comparative costs and revenues

Size of firm	Revenue/employee (1998)		Type of worker	Salary per annum (1997)		Indian salaries as a % of US salaries (1997)*
	INR	USD		INR	USD	
0–10	484,166	11,528	Programmer	105,000	2500	6.8–7.4
10–50	686,704	16,350	System analyst	392,500	9345	17.8–18.6
50–100	617,832	14,700	Programmer analyst	257,500	6131	13.8–14.0
100–200	681,197	16,219	Network administrator	725,000	17,262	43.6–34.9
200–500	689,418	16,415	Database administrator	725,000	17,262	29.1–28.4
500–	1,527,652	36,373	Help-desk support technician	392,500	9345	21.6–19.7
			Software developer	725,000	17,262	32.0–28.4

Source: INFAC (1998) and Okazaki (1999), Arora *et al.* (2001, Table 12, p. 1278).

Notes:
INR = Indian Rupees, USD = US Dollars, exchange rate used is 1USD = 42INR, *The "Indian salaries" column was derived from Arora *et al.* (2001) and % share based on lower and upper values of Indian salaries corresponding to US salaries.

However, it is clear that the vast majority is unable to access higher educa-tion for various structural and institutional reasons. In India, the clamor for reserved admissions in universities by *dalits* and "other backward castes" testifies to the structural oppression of such groups. In addition, it reflects the importance these groups place on education for social mobility. Pre-existing inequality limits access to education, thereby shutting out opportunities the expansive IT sector might offer. Table 3.2 presents data on income, literacy and education, income distribution, and new economy characteristics for selected Asian economies.

This demonstrates that there is considerable divergence among Asian countries in terms of level of economic development, the diffusion of mass education, and the development of high skills. Income gaps appear to widen, even as all of them have experienced rising per capita income and economic development in general. Income polarization is persistent. With respect to the new economy, divergence is the norm among these countries (see Table 3.2). South Korea and Malaysia are far ahead relative to others in terms of PCs and Internet hosts. There were 157 PCs for every 1000 people and sixty Internet hosts for every 10,000 people in South Korea compared to India's three PCs for every 1000 people and 0.23 Internet hosts for every 10,000 people. Both Myanmar and Vietnam lag well behind India's new economy indicators (UNDP, 2001). East and Southeast Asian economies relying on manufactured exports have experienced greater IT development. East Asia has a better record than others in distributing the benefits of IT as well. India, on the other hand, has only more recently begun to gain from the integration of its competitive sectors with the world economy. Export of high technology (broadly defined), as a share of total manufactured exports, is on the rise for most Asian economies, including India. What is troublesome is that the gains from IT growth in economies with a high degree of income maldistribution accrue narrowly to those with professional and technical qualifications. In Asian countries where entrenched structural poverty is rampant, such as India or the Philippines, the unequal access to technical education exacerbates existing inequality, especially when IT such as the "Internet is grafted on to existing forms of inequality" (Abbott, 2001). Just as many Asians join the ranks of a transnational bourgeoisie, vastly more are systematically excluded due to lack of IT literacy, especially women, the poor, rural residents, and minorities.

Unequal access to education in heavily populated India and China with large economies, sizable industrial and knowledge-driven sectors, suggests that even a small percentage entering the technical ranks contribute to a large technical talent pool. It has been estimated that India is generating about 200,000 bachelor degree holders in the sciences and 240,000 science degree holders at all levels annually (World Bank, 2000). In the context of globalization, developing countries with technical talent liberalizing their economies witness increased demands for skilled professionals at home

Table 3.2 Pre-existing inequality and new economy indicators

	GNP/capita 1981, 1982, 1999	Adult illiteracy (% of people 15 and above, 1998) Male	Female	No. enrolled in higher ed. (% of 20–24)	Income distribution Lowest 20%	Highest 20%	Year of estimate	# of PCs/1000 (1998)	Internet hosts/10,000	High tech exports
Bangladesh	140	49	71	14	6.9	42.2	1973–74	–	0.00	0
	220			17	9.5	38.6	1988–89			
	370			27	8.7	42.8	1995–96			
India	260	33	57	26	7.0	49.4	1975–76	2.7	0.23	5
	310			27	8.8	41.3	1989–90			
	450			25	8.1	46.1	1997			
Philippines	790	5	5	37	5.2	54.0	1970–71	15.1	1.58	71
	770			33	6.5	47.8	1988			
	1020			31	5.4	52.3	1997			
S. Korea	1700	1	4	39	5.7	45.3	1976	156.8	60.30	27
	6790			45	7.4	42.2	1988			
	8490			44	7.5	39.3	1993			
Malaysia	1840	9	18	36	3.5	56.1	1973	58.6	25.43	54
	2790			–	4.5	53.8	1989			
	3400			44	4.6	53.7	1995			
Indonesia	530	9	20	42	6.6	49.4	1976	8.2	1.00	10
	670			40	8.7	42.3	1990			
	580			45	8.0	44.9	1996			
Thailand	770	3	7	28	5.6	49.8	1975–76	21.6	6.46	31
	1840			39	6.1	50.7				
	1960			40	6.4	48.4	1998			
China	300	9	25	46	–	–	–	8.9	0.57	15
	470			34	6.4	41.8	1990			
	780			50	5.9	46.6	1998			

Source: World Bank, *World Development Report*, various issues.

and abroad. TNCs are tapping increasingly into local talent markets for their global operations. In 1998, nearly 34,000 Indian students and 30,000 professionals went to the US alone (Department of Education, India, 1999, in World Bank, 2000). The consequence of this demand is heightened income and wage differentials in national economies (Stewart and Berry, 1999). The dominance of English in IT invariably adds another layer to the inequality equation, favoring certain classes, urban locales, and cultures. Here too, some Asian countries, such as India, are better positioned than others to take advantage of the opportunities in the global IT industry.

Recently the US raised the number of B1 visas that permit foreign workers to work in the US software industry, most of which are expected to be issued to Indians. In unprecedented moves, Germany and Japan are introducing Indian professionals as guest workers. Last year the German Chancellor Gerhard Schroeder, against political opposition, proposed a US-style "green card" program to allow software engineers to enter Germany from India and other developing countries (Drozdiak, 2000). German businesses estimated that there was a shortage of 300,000 specialists in modern technologies in Germany. More recently, both Germany and Japan are eyeing Indian talent, complaining about the difficulties in competing for such talent with the US (Ignatius, 2001). Many countries are increasingly relaxing immigration rules for IT professionals. Already in Japan more than forty Indian software companies have opened offices to offer outsourcing services (Bacani, 2001).

The unequal access to technical and professional education has its self-reinforcing tendencies. With rising global demand for IT workers, a premium is paid for these workers. Structurally, core economies such as the US capture more of the gains, as they can offer higher wages and better professional opportunities (D'Costa, 2002a). They also initiate outsourcing of many of the IT activities to low-cost sites – reaping the benefits of global talent and integrated production operations (D'Costa, 2002b). Over time, a network of professional technical talent is formed at the global level. As many of the technical professionals transform themselves into entrepreneurs, they too begin to transnationalize their operations (Saxenian, 1999). As outsourcing becomes routine in the world economy, local wages and salaries in these internationalized skill-based sectors increase substantially. In addition, many non-residents of developing countries living in core economies become expatriate workers in their countries of origin. The convergence of income among certain professional groups within an internationalized sector is not inconsistent with income polarization found in national economies. These professionals continue to experience rising incomes at a faster rate than do workers in other sectors.

The foreign frontier

Economic integration produces some income convergence at the global level and considerable dispersion within national economies. At the same time, the rigid core–periphery hierarchy and associated class structures also come under strain. For example, core citizens as a whole are economically better off than those in the periphery. Income distribution, even if unequal, is better in the core. However, with globalization, the introduction of new technologies has a negative impact on equality in the core. This is accentuated as IT workers from Asia become a visible force in the core economies. For example, as core economies, especially the US, continue to dominate the IT industry in terms of technological trajectories, markets, infrastructures, and talent – home-grown and immigrant – it is not surprising to find a flow of technical talent to these countries.

The US offers considerable higher education opportunities, allowing a large number of non-residents to pursue science and engineering education in US universities (National Science Foundation, 2001). What is noteworthy is that the proportion of non-residents rises significantly with higher level degrees, suggesting a process of inequality between foreigners and residents in the US. Thus, in 1998, 3.6 percent of Bachelor's degrees in science and engineering were earned by non-residents, while for Master's and Ph.D.s the figures were 24.6 percent and 33.1 percent respectively. It is evident that foreigners were disproportionately represented in higher levels of education, thereby introducing income dispersion on ethnic lines in core economies. The prominence of Asians within the non-resident group, especially at the Ph.D. level (see Figure 3.2), should be noted. Furthermore, Americans of Asian origin as well as recent non-citizen residents from Asia studying in the US prefer science and engineering fields. For example, of the total bachelor's degrees pursued by resident Asians, nearly 50 percent in 1998 were in science and engineering. The proportion of computer science degrees for the Asian residents was higher (9.1 percent) than for all students (6.6 percent).[3] The result of technical education among Asians is that they are much better situated to be socially and economically mobile than other groups, both at home if they return, and abroad if they do not.

Inequality in Asian countries is reproduced in core countries as well. As Asians pursue higher education and employment in core countries, they distance themselves from other ethnic groups. Not only are their average incomes higher than other minority populations, such as African Americans and Latinos in the US, but they are also higher than the average Caucasian.

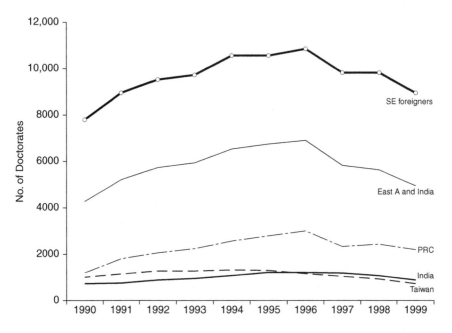

Figure 3.2 Science and engineering doctorates awarded in the US
Source: National Science Foundation (2001)

The diasporic dimension: inter-firm and interpersonal linkages

Technically trained at home, with education and employment abroad, a new Asia-born class of transnational entrepreneurs is in the making (see Sklair, 2001). As the skills of this growing but exclusive group rise, Asia-based firms are also beginning to develop high-end competency in serving core markets.[4] Consequently, firms from developing countries, such as India, are increasingly establishing overseas offices to expand their clientele directly but also to enhance learning opportunities by being close to buyers. This also enables Indian firms to cultivate domain expertise from a large user base, which is not available in a structurally poor economy. Thus far a few premier Indian companies, such as Wipro (ranked number one by sales of software in India), NIIT (ranked number six), and BFL Software have located their CEOs in the US. Many medium-sized firms have opened up marketing and liaison offices in their major export markets. Mindtree has recently transferred one of its top executives to New Jersey to take advantage of being close to the market. The increasing physical presence of Indian firms in the export markets suggests not only the shortcomings of an earlier arms-length export model but also the formation of a transnationally linked technical professional pool that differentiates itself fundamentally from other segments of the home societies.

To access markets and tap into knowledge bases, acquisition of foreign firms by Indian companies seems a logical route. Several acquisitions of foreign firms by Indian firms are setting new precedents. In the software business, DSQ, an Indian firm based in Chennai, recently purchased San Vision Technologies in the US for US$30 million. Silverline Technologies of Mumbai recently acquired e-business consulting firm SeraNova of the US for US$99 million. Insignificant as these may be, as India becomes a significant offshore site for the world market, it begins to attain a headquarter status for select firms. For example, Pune, India, is now the world headquarters of SAS Global Services, a subsidiary of SAS Inc., the world's largest privately held software company. System Logic of the US was converted to a subsidiary of System Logic, India. BFL Software was considering the purchase of MphasiS in the US and making it a subsidiary.

As software firms across countries consolidate to access knowledge, international integration encompasses the financial sphere as well. Riding on the bullish wave of high technology firms, successful Indian firms are attempting to leverage their acquisitions by raising capital abroad. Dollar-denominated prices for foreign firms mean that Indian firms must secure capital from international markets, such as American Depository Receipts and Global Depository Receipts. Most recently, Wipro, among others, raised several hundred million dollars from the New York Stock Exchange. Other firms are beginning to follow this practice. Infosys Technology, one of India's leading software firms, was the first Indian company to be listed on the American NASDAQ Stock Exchange. An Internet service provider, Satyam Infoway, became the second.

Foreign capital is also facilitating domestic acquisitions. Satyam Infoway is in the process of purchasing IndiaWorld Communication for nearly US$100 million. The Indian government is actively assisting the sector not only through infrastructure development but also in setting up venture capital funds, especially to tap into intellectual capital abroad. The Small Industries Development Bank of India and the newly formed Ministry of Information Technology have set up a US$50 million fund to finance new entrepreneurs in Silicon Valley. Even private firms in India are joining foreign firms to set up venture capital funds to promote start-ups, just as successful non-resident Indian entrepreneurs in the US are also actively scouting out Indian firms for incubation.

The presence of a visible expatriate Indian professional community in the US and their interaction with Americans of Indian origin is contributing to new social networks of knowledge (Saxenian, 1999). Several US-based companies, small and large, have established Indian operations with Indian personnel. Many Indian-owned companies in the US, themselves spin-offs from larger American companies, have now become suppliers to their former US employers using Indian employees. For example, Aditi, established by a former Microsoft employee, does its work for Microsoft in Bangalore. Hence the CEO of the Seattle-based Aditi must spend a large portion of the year in India.

This movement of skilled professionals in a reverse direction – from user markets to producer markets – along with increasing physical presence of Indian companies in export markets, is consolidating a globally based technical community.[5] The regional concentration of Indian professionals in Silicon Valley, the Pacific Northwest, and New Jersey in the US, in the UK, and Singapore is linking Indian firms with foreign ones. Whether the talent-flow is significantly two-directional depend on opportunities in home countries. As demonstrated by Saxenian (1999), few Indians, unlike their Taiwanese counterparts, return to India. If they do, as more are doing today, it is rarely on a permanent basis. There are various reasons for Indians not returning, even if family and cultural ties remain strong. The US is still perceived to offer better professional opportunities and economic rewards. In addition, unlike the aggressive steps taken by the Taiwanese government to attract its US-trained students back home, the relationship between Indian policy makers and Silicon Valley-based Indian entrepreneurs has not been strong. Saxenian, in a recent survey report, suggests that 18 percent of the 40 percent immigrant professionals surveyed have invested in their home countries and 40 percent of the foreign-born respondents indicated that they would consider returning home (PTI, Silicon Valley, 2002). No doubt the nature of the economic development process would be different with the intensification of global links, possibly raising growth rates. However, in the absence of major redistributive policies most of this growth will accrue narrowly to the well-trained, technical professionals. Income polarization is unlikely to be altered under the possible scenario.

To summarize the main points of this section, Asians may be seen as part of internationally organized social networks, who in turn contribute to the globalization of IT as employees and as entrepreneurs, in the process separating themselves structurally from other social groups in their adopted countries as well as forming strong links to their originating countries and regions:

1   At the home front, the class bias in educational opportunities means that the middle classes are in a better position to take advantage of opportunities in the global IT industry.
2   As Asians pursue higher education and employment abroad, they distance themselves from other ethnic groups. Not only are their average incomes higher than other minority populations, such as African Americans and Latinos in the US, but they are also higher than the average Caucasian.

3   Some Asians become techno-entrepreneurs in high tech industry. In her survey of Silicon Valley's new immigrant entrepreneurs, Saxenian (1999) suggests that one-third of the Valley's scientific and engineering workforce are immigrants and that Chinese and Indians run 25 percent of the high technology firms. In 1990, 55 percent of Indians, 40 percent of Chinese, and 18 percent of whites in Silicon Valley had an MS or Ph.D. degree (US Census 1990, in Saxenian, 1999). Since these are "new" immigrant entrepreneurs they are all Asia born.

4   The concentration of such successful Asian professionals and entrepreneurs in California has led to the creation of numerous ethnic-based professional associations, including networks of Korean, Singaporean, and Filipino engineers. For example, two India-based organizations were set up: the Silicon Valley Indian Professionals Association (SIPA) in 1991 and The Indus Entrepreneur (TiE) in 1992. There were eleven such organizations for the Chinese Americans, in manufacturing and software (Saxenian, 1999).

5   The presence of a large number of professionals from similar ethnic backgrounds is conducive to forming social networks that span both their home country and region, say, Taiwan and China, and their adopted one, the US. Whether the flow is significant in either direction depends on relative opportunities in home and adopted countries. These networks are also exclusive in that only those with the high technical skills, solid educational background, and professional socialization are able to join these networks. They are best positioned to take advantage of the opportunities offered by globalization. The others, in lacking the requisite skills and education, are largely unable to do so.

CONCLUSION

This chapter has delineated a complex, self-reinforcing process by which Asia and Asians in the IT sector are intricately linked to processes of globalization and inequality. It is also a nuanced presentation of a case where globalization offers new opportunities, generates multi-directional flows of technical personnel, and creates options by which core and peripheral economies are being bridged in contingent ways. While the empirical materials have been drawn from the Indian experience, it made a case that globalization is inherently selective, benefitting only those who are best placed to capitalize on the opportunities that open up. Specifically, in the IT sector, technically trained professionals are well positioned to capture the benefits of economic integration. The unequal access to tertiary education, significantly influenced by class politics, provides the proverbial stepping-stone for this minority to join the ranks of a global talent pool. The social–educational divide is reinforced by further technical education and employment abroad. Transnational networks also introduce subtle forms of inequality in advanced capitalist countries. For example, the concentration of technically trained Asians, mainly Chinese, Taiwanese, and Indians in Silicon Valley, both as employees and entrepreneurs, also implies considerable social and economic differentiation from other ethnic minorities. Inequality or the digital divide associated with the IT industry is not just a national, developing country problem but one that occurs, even if in subdued form, in core markets.

The relationship between globalization and the IT industry shows the formation of transnational networks, of Chinese and Indian origin. In the first instance this translates into disparity between non-residents and their fellow citizens at home, but it also suggests considerable economic mobility among Asians. Just as Asians contribute to inequality, they also induce egalitarian tendencies. For example, the rise of East Asia over the last generation has narrowed the income gaps between the advanced capitalist and late industrializing countries. At the same time there is a widening and narrowing of inequality within Asia as we examine spatial and class dimensions in a variety of venues. However, the continued expansion of meritocracy and education is likely to erode the power of older elites and contribute to a social penchant for education, energizing peripheral economies in new ways. There is plenty of evidence of a percolating effect on rural residents in India who send their children to the towns and cities for modern education. The rise of the Indian middle class is a testimony to the process of embourgeoisment, a process in which the IT sector is playing a transformative role. There are many Indian software entrepreneurs with humble, rural backgrounds who, simply with their educational attainments, have broken down the social barriers to wealth generation. The real question is whether their success will be reproduced on the wider social front and the wealth shared, or if it will remain the preserve of those who have the right mix of education, class position, and social background.

With reference to national policy, India's software export performance and the large numbers of Indians involved in the global IT industry suggests that global integration is indubitably the best course for economic policy. This is certainly the case with industries, such as computers and other related IT sectors, that are subject to rapid technological change (Kraemer and Dedrik, 2001). Policy has to move on several fronts. There must be an explicit government policy and industry strategy to move up the value chain. There are signs that Indian firms are already moving towards higher value services or retaining a greater portion of the revenues by moving away from on-site projects to offshore development in India. This is being facilitated by Indian government investment in data communication links so that companies can maintain direct satellite links to various foreign clients as well as a number of improvements by India-based companies such as timely deliveries and cost competitiveness. It is also apparent that without increased educational opportunities for the masses and a policy environment for nurturing domestically driven entre-preneurs, export-led development could remain exclusionary. As it is, poor countries such as India are essentially demand-constrained because of the inegalitarian social structure, allowing only a minority (and perhaps because of it) to move into more rewarding employment.

The socially grounded analysis of IT-based globalization used here sug-gests that the nature of the digital divide in the global economy and between Asian countries is an extension of both persistent internal inequal-ity and selective Asian mobility within diasporic networks. Even though the movement of such talent is initiated in the advanced capitalist coun-tries, the mobility of technical talent spills over in developing countries as well. What this means is that, in the absence of countervailing policies, income growth due to global integration could result in income dispersion. The selective yet growing participation by Asians is reflected in the recent projections of Internet use. It has been estimated that Internet users in India are expected to reach 37.5 million by 2005 compared to 4.47 million in 2000 (*Economic Times*, 2001). This is a ninefold increase in five years. Yet the number of projected users will remain under 4 percent of India's population. These numbers are a cause for both optimism and concern. While more people are moving up the digital ladder, huge swathes of the population remain outside the orbit of the new economy (Main, 2001). Kattuman and Iyer (2001) wonder at the relevance of an otherwise suc-cessful IT enclave for India's half and one-third billion people who are illit-erate and poor respectively. The one certainty we have is the recognition that concerted national efforts will be critical to addressing inequality in Asia.

NOTES

1 I thank the organizers of the 2001 Internet Political Economy Forum Confer-ence in Singapore and the International Studies program at the University of Washington for facilitating my participation, K.C. Ho for his enthusiastic support, K. Lal, A.K. Bagchi, Routledge's anonymous reviewer for detailed comments, and Janette Rawlings for her meticulous substantive and editorial suggestions. All errors and omissions are my sole responsibility.
2 Japan is excluded from the analysis because for all practical purposes its eco-nomic structure and level of development is qualitatively different from the rest of Asia, and therefore its relationship with the world economy is also qualita-tively different. Relatedly, Japanese are less mobile globally than others, emi-grating less than other Asians, preferring their own (Ph.D.) education system over foreign ones, and those who do study abroad tend to return to Japan (per-sonal communication with Marie Anchordoguy). The implication of this is that there is lesser likelihood of a Japanese diaspora in the same way as there might be one for the Chinese or Indians.
3 Asians in the US who arrived as refugees such as Vietnamese, Cambodians, and Laotians have had less success due to the severity of their dislocation. Their

particular class position in their homeland will also have a bearing on their economic position in their adopted land.

4 A number of Indian firms have begun the process of skill deepening. In addition to solid systems integration skills, several companies are engaged in imaging and scientific programming, such as GIS and CAD/CAM, and real time programming, such as telecom, multimedia, and e-commerce (D'Costa, 2002c).

5 These networks are different from those resulting from international migration. While it is true that semi-skilled migrant labor through their foreign exchange remittances contributes more in monetary terms to the national balance of payments than more skilled professionals (Patnaik and Chandrasekhar, 1998), skilled labor mobility fosters technological synergy that can lead to increased international competitiveness.

BIBLIOGRAPHY

Abbott, J.P. (2001) "Democracy@internet.asia? The challenges to the emancipatory potential of the Net: lessons from China and Malaysia," *Third World Quarterly*, 22, 1: 99–114.

Arora, A., Arunachalam, V.S., Asundi, J., and Fernandes, R. (2001) "The Indian software services industry," *Research Policy*, 30, 8: 1267–87.

Bacani, C. (2001) "I.T. crunchtime," *Asiaweek*, 27, 19.

Bhuyan, R. (2002) "Taiwan to recruit 20,000 Indian software professionals," *Cyber News Service*, April 25.

Castells, M. (2000) "Materials for an exploratory theory of the network society," *British Journal of Sociology*, 51, 1: 5–24.

D'Costa, A.P. (2002a) "Software outsourcing and policy implications: an Indian perspective," *International Journal of Technology Management*, 24, 7/8: 705–23.

—— (2002b) "Technological leapfrogging: the software challenge in India," in P. Conceição *et al.* (eds) *Knowledge for Inclusive Development*, New York: Quorum Books.

—— (2002c) "Export growth and path-dependence: the locking-in of innovations in the software industry," *Science, Technology and Society*, 7, 1: 51–89.

—— (2003a, forthcoming) "The Indian software industry in the global division of labor," in A.P. D'Costa and E. Sridharan (eds) *India in the Global Software Industry: Innovation, Firm Strategies and Development*, London: Palgrave.

—— (2003b) "Uneven and combined development: understanding India's software exports," *World Development*, 13, 1: 211–26.

Drèze, J. and Sen, A. (1998) *India: Economic Development and Social Opportunity*, Oxford: Clarendon Press.

Drozdiak, W. (2000) "Call for foreign tech workers raises hackles in Germany," *Seattle Times*, 11 April.

Dunning, J.H. (2000) "Regions, globalization, and the knowledge economy: the issues stated," in J.H. Dunning (ed.) *Regions, Globalization, and the Knowledge-Based Economy*, Oxford: Oxford University Press.

Economic Times (2001) "India's net base to touch 3.75 cr," July 4.

Heeks, R. (1996) *India's Software Industry: State Policy, Liberalisation and Industrial Development*, New Delhi: Sage Publications.

Hoogvelt, A. (2001) *Globalization and the Postcolonial World: The New Political Economy of Development*, Baltimore, MD: The Johns Hopkins University Press.

Ignatius, D. (2001) "If Germany competes for immigrants, it can't stay the same," *International Herald Tribune*, June 25.

(Information Products and Research Services (I) Pvt. Ltd.) INFAC (1998) *Software Industry: Market Status*, Mumbai: INFAC.

James, J. (2001) "Information technology, cumulative causation and patterns of globalization in the third world," *Review of International Political Economy*, 8, 1: 147–62.

Kaplinsky, R. (2000) "Globalization and unequalization: what can be learned from value chain analysis?" *Journal of Development Studies*, 37, 2: 117–46.

Kattuman, P. and Iyer, K. (2001) "Human capital in the move up the value chain: the case of the Indian software and services industry," in M. Kagami and M. Tsuji (eds) *The 'IT' Revolution and Developing Countries: Late-Comer Advantage?*, Tokyo: Institute of Developing Economies, Japan External Trade Organization.

Kraemer, K.L. and Dedrick, J. (2001) "Liberalization and the computer industry: a comparison of four developing countries," *The Information Society*, 17: 83–90.

Main, L. (2001) "The global information infrastructure: empowerment or imperialism," *Third World Quarterly*, 22, 1: 83–97.

Morley, S.A. (2001) "Distribution and growth in Latin America in an era of structural reform: the impact of globalization," technical papers no. 184, December, Paris: OECD Development Centre.

National Science Foundation (2001) "Science and engineering degrees, by race/ethnicity of recipients: 1990–98," June, Washington, DC: NSF.

Okazaki, T. (1999) "The productivity of the Indian software industry" in "New dimensions of Indian industrial development," *Konodai Bulletin of Economic Studies*, 11, 1: 135–48.

Pangestu, M. (2001) "The social impact of globalization in Southeast Asia," technical papers no. 187, December, Paris: OECD Development Centre.

Patnaik, P. and Chandrasekhar, C.P. (1998) "Notes on international migration suggested by the Indian experience," in D. Baker, G. Epstein and R. Pollin (eds) *Globalization and Progressive Economic Policy*, New York: Cambridge University Press.

Phillips, R. (2000) "Approaching the organisation of economic activity in the age of cross-border alliance capitalism," in R. Palan (ed.) *Global Political Economy: Contemporary Theories*, London: Routledge.

PTI, Silicon Valley (2002) "Silicon Valley's Indians building networks back home," HindustanTimes.com. Online. Available HTTP: http://www.hindustantimes.com/ (accessed June 5, 2002).

Saxenian, A. (1999) *Silicon Valley's New Immigrant Entrepreneurs*, San Francisco: Public Policy Institute of California.

Shari, I. (2000) "Globalization and economic disparities in East and Southeast Asia: new dilemmas," *Third World Quarterly*, 21, 6: 963–76.

Sklair, L. (2001) *The Transnational Capitalist Class*, Oxford: Blackwell.

Smith, C.S. (2001) "China's high-tech industry approaches critical mass," *International Herald Tribune*, May 29.

—— (2002) "China catching up to U.S. in chip technology," *International Herald Tribune*, May 6.

Stewart, F. and Berry, A. (1999) "Globalization, liberalization, and inequality: expectations and experience," in A. Hurrell and N. Woods (eds) *Inequality, Globalization, and World Politics*, Oxford: Oxford University Press.

Streeten, P. (1998) "Globalization: threat or salvation?" in A.S. Bhalla (ed.) *Globalization, Growth and Marginalization*, London: Macmillan Press for IDRC, Canada.

Trivedi, A. (2002) "India's software supremacy and the Chinese threat," Siliconindia.com. Online. Available HTTP: http://www.siliconindia.com (accessed September 7, 2002).

United Nations Development Program (UNDP) (2001) *Human Development Report, 2000*, New York: Oxford University Press.

World Bank, *World Development Report*, various issues.

World Bank (2000) "India: scientific and technical manpower development in India," Washington, DC World Bank, Education Sector Unit, South Asia Region, report no. 20416-IN.

4 Cyberspace, surveillance, and social control

The hidden face of the Internet in Asia

David Lyon

Cyberspace is often thought of as a realm of freedom, even of fun. At least until recently, few would have associated surveillance with cyberspace. The "cyber" prefix has been attached to fiction ("cyberpunk"), and to fashion, as well as to entertainment, education, finance, architecture, and city planning. Cyberjaya, within the Malaysian Multimedia SuperCorridor, is one of the world's first cities to include "cyber" in its name. This in itself is paradoxical, because at first cyberspace was popularly associated with the immaterial, the virtual, the displaced, and the disembodied. In William Gibson's novel, *Neuromancer*, cyberspace seems to be apart from the corporeal, institutional world. But in Cyberjaya, the integration of the built environment and the global economy with "cyberspace" is taken for granted. The fiber-optic broadband links that provide the infrastructure for cyberspace are tied tightly to government plans and a changing economy, but not necessarily to surveillance.

In Asian countries, no less than in others outside Asia, cyberspace is a realm of surveillance. Personal data are gathered, sorted, stored, and traded – processed for the purposes of management, influence, and social control. Most innocent, seemingly, would be the efforts of e-commerce online marketers to use customer profiles to create consumer clusters in order to target specific persons and groups for advertising and solicitation. Most sharply, perhaps, would be the use of Internet data-tracking techniques to discover the whereabouts and plans of Al Qaeda members since the devastating "terrorist" attacks of September 11, 2001. In March, 2002, for instance, American Internet intelligence experts detected Al Qaeda email-use patterns in airports, Kinkos, and public libraries in Indonesia, the Philippines, and Malaysia as well as Afghanistan and Pakistan (Risen and Johnson, 2002). At either end of this spectrum, I shall argue, some critical questions are raised about the "hidden face" of the Internet. Although he acknowledges Ho, Baber and Khondker's (2002) argument that civil society may use the Internet to extend freedoms in Singapore, Manuel Castells also points out that the Internet is used in Asian countries as elsewhere for repressive and illiberal surveillance purposes (Castells, 2001).

Whatever freedom and fun may be generated in cyberspace, the reality is that the Internet does not create a "space apart," a realm of technologically enabled liberty. Rather, as the Internet is increasingly integrated with everyday life in Asia as elsewhere, so it provides some new ways of engaging in old practices. It may well be that our relationship to our bodies alters, subtly, as we are able to do more things at a distance. Organizational behaviors and expectations may also develop in new ways as the Internet and its associated intranets become embedded in bureaucratic routines. It may well be that we can discern changes in the very notions of time and space that structure human social activity, but none of this means that fundamental changes in social relationships, and especially in the political economy of power, are occurring. It is easy to forget that even in Gibson's novel, however much utopian cyberpunks may have been parasitic on it.

While not wishing to promote dystopian perspectives on the Internet, it would be irresponsible to ignore what might be thought of as a dark side, a hidden face of cyberspace. This has to do with how we conceive of cyberspace. For a brief period in the 1990s, it seemed to some that cyberspace had only a bright side. Sociologically, however, it is appropriate to use the term "cyberspace" to connote the convergence of what were once thought of as different spheres: information technologies and telecommunications. The Internet tilts things decisively towards communications, and assumes that computing machinery provides the media for flows of information. Cyberspace, then, refers to the social and cultural relations involved in computer-mediated communication. Even if we avoid referring to cyberspace and use the more precise-sounding term "Internet," there is no escaping the social shaping and thus mixed influences on its development.

The Internet is by definition a techno-social, evolving medium. It is in many ways a process rather than a "thing." As Janet Abbate shows, "The turbulent history of the Internet may be a reminder of the very real material considerations that lie behind this technology and of their political and economic consequences" (Abbate, 1999, p. 5). Abbate has in mind in particular the American military concerns built into the Internet at its origin, but also networking philosophies in other countries, and end users everywhere, which help to shape the Internet as a medium of communication, using electronic mail and the World Wide Web. Like other technological innovations, the Internet represents human social activity, and as such manifests all the ambiguities and contradictions that are common to such activity.

The particular "material considerations" discussed here are ones that relate to the coordination and control capacities of the Internet. Just as it is a mistake to focus on the supposedly virtual aspects of the Internet, as if these were separate from bodily life in geographical places, so it is wrong to think of cyberspace as a new domain of human activity. Rather, the

Internet is superimposed upon and integrated with already existing forms of communication. In a world where nation-states have simultaneously been trying to shore up their cultural and social defences while ceding much power of regulation to the marketplace, new media of communication such as the Internet have become increasingly significant. The capacities of cyberspace for information processing have a huge impact both on how nation-states govern their populations and how corporations marshal the behavior of consumers. These are the processes that I refer to as "surveillance" (Lyon, 1994).

Surveillance is personal data processing for particular purposes. Put another way, surveillance is focused attention on behaviors and trends of persons and of populations with a view to managing, controlling, protecting, or influencing them. Coordination and control are thus built into this understanding of surveillance. In the last quarter of the twentieth century, computers became the vital medium of surveillance, allowing collected data to be stored, matched, retrieved, processed, marketed, and circulated (Lyon, 2001). Above all, searchable databases became the key to surveillance practices, permitting new levels of classifying, categorizing, and cataloguing of personal data. This is generated by systems of the kind that permit citizens to gain online access to government departments (which I will be able to do in Ontario from 2002; see Blumler and Coleman, 2001; Ghafour, 2001) or that seek niche markets in specific neighborhoods of people with similar socio-economic characteristics (see Gandy, 1993). Similarly, these systems have an impact on organizational practices of human resources management and of policing. It is worth stressing that activities such as these may be construed positively. They permit greater efficiency and speed, and may well result in increased benefits for citizens and consumers, who experience them as enhancing their comfort, convenience, and safety.

Without suggesting that surveillance is intrinsically sinister, however, it must be admitted that all forms of human categorizing and classifying carry risks. Surveillance using searchable databases is no exception. During the same quarter century as computers became established in administration, questions were raised, protests mounted, and regulation emerged, mainly in an effort to protect personal data and to try to safeguard privacy, which was where the primary perceived risks lay. Laudable results of this include the development of Fair Information Practices, the European Data Protection Directive, and the OECD Guidelines for handling personal data. Several Asian countries, including Japan and Korea, base their management of computer-based personal information held by government departments on the OECD Guidelines, while others such as Malaysia and Hong Kong refer positively to those Guidelines.

But by the 1990s, the emergence of the Internet as a medium for commercial, management, policing, and government activities including military intelligence and war-making spelled the birth of cyberspace surveillance, which almost immediately accelerated the pace of personal data-processing operations. Today, surveillance is the norm. So, far from personal data being processed only in unusual situations, where there is a suspicion of inappropriate behavior, or a special rationale for focused attention, surveillance is universal, ubiquitous, continuous, routine, multi-faceted, and networked. Although many life-spheres are touched by numerous agencies and new surveillance technologies, including biometric, video, DNA, and general dataveillance, the Internet offers both new opportunities to bring these together, and a number of fresh directions for surveillance within the emerging medium itself. These in turn point up the need for considering both national differences in cyberspace surveillance, and certain kinds of risks that have hitherto been underplayed.

EVERYDAY SURVEILLANCE AND ASIAN SITUATIONS

Everyday surveillance has become the normal routine in informational societies. At all times and in all places, citizens, employees, travellers, and consumers are subject to systems that check, trace, track, monitor, and record transactions, communications, and movements. Numerous different agencies and organizations are responsible for this personal data process-ing, which occurs using a broadening panoply of new technologies, from basic dataveillance through biometrics, video, DNA, and GPS. The key technique relates to searchable databases that are used to classify, categor-ize, and catalog data on populations and persons. Increasingly, the Internet is implicated in surveillance. These social sorting devices are not innocent "cyber" associations that have no impact in the real world. Rather, they interact intimately with ongoing practices of daily life in the real world to influence people's choices and life-chances.

Few people are unaware of the kinds of surveillance that is carried out in these routine ways, although it may be fair to say that few understand the multiple ways in which everyday surveillance occurs. Although this not necessarily sinister or malevolent, it would be premature to suggest that fears of "Big Brother" are entirely misplaced. If people have concerns about surveillance, these concerns are often couched – at least in the West – within discourses of privacy and data protection which, though not at all irrelevant, are now hardly adequate for the multitude of ways that surveil-lance touches our lives today. These discourses may have some salience in Asian situations as well, but there are also notable moments of divergence or inappropriateness. Moreover, these discourses relate only indirectly to questions of social sorting that are so central to surveillance today.

Much debate about surveillance has occurred in North America and Europe, and it tends either to ignore Asian situations or to imagine or imply that discourses developed elsewhere will be appropriate in Asian countries. If one shifts the focus to Asian societies, however, several things become apparent. One is that, although searchable databases are still significant as the technological means underpinning surveillance practices, the nature of surveillance does differ. Nation-states have different attitudes to the Internet, and companies operate in different ways in monitoring and sorting their actual and potential customers and employees. True, globalization does mean that both techniques and social practices flow more readily from country to country, but they still have to reckon with quite different cultural expectations and political realities. In addition, supposed solutions to problems raised by everyday surveillance may have a poor cultural fit. Privacy itself, for example, has no direct equivalent in the Japanese language, and the very individualism that lies behind (all too) much privacy discourse is also somewhat alien in some Asian situations.

Surveillance is at present theorized inadequately in the social sciences, and policy tends to revolve around some helpful but limited ideas of fair information practices. Both areas are dominated by non-Asian perspectives. Focusing on Asian societies is a useful corrective, first, because it involves breaking out of non-Asian paradigms to understand how surveillance is developing in non-Western contexts, and second, because Asian cultural perspectives also have something to offer. In this underdeveloped field of surveillance studies, much may be gained by a new look at the actual nature of surveillance today, in its various settings and manifestations, and at what Asian situations may offer by way of fresh perspectives that could affect both analysis and policy. My main focus here is on the former.

In what follows, some examples of surveillance are discussed, first, in relation to government, and second, in relation to corporations. State surveillance is of course the *locus classicus* for understanding the power of information, but how this occurs differs from country to country. Asian situations may be different in some respects from North American or European, but they are also different from each other, depending on their particular development origins and trajectories. Corporations have for a long time operated surveillance systems to keep tabs on employees, and this practice only shifted to customers in the first half of the twentieth century. But market research was always a mild and imprecise science – until the advent of database marketing. Harnessing computer power to the analysis of market segments, and now using the Internet as a multimedia tool for interactive consumer solicitation, are the powerful means of corporate cyber-surveillance. Alongside these, of course, are technological developments that sometimes enable surveillance convergence between quite different institutional sectors.

INTERNET SURVEILLANCE BY GOVERNMENT

It is important to recall that modern governments, by definition, engage in systematic surveillance of citizens. Those in power have always taken an interest in populations for the purposes of taxation or conscription, but the bureaucratic methods adopted by modern administrations ensured that this would become routine, universal, and inescapable. Positively, it meant that legal, civil, and political equality and access could be ensured more easily, but at the same time, other inequalities also emerged as personal data became a source of power over citizens.

Computerization of government departments deepened the penetration of surveillance into the everyday lives of the populace in all modern societies and, as networking became increasingly important in the later twentieth century, so that accelerated the process. Many see the administrative uses of the Internet as an advantage, permitting the possibility of online access to government services by citizens, and even versions of digital democracy. But it simultaneously raises questions about who has access to the mushrooming quantities of personal data that circulate, what third-party purposes they are used for, and how far data subjects retain control over them.

Having painted with a broad brush, it is immediately important to qualify what has been said about technology and government. There is no simple causal correlation between levels of technological development and degrees of democracy. Extensive computer networks have been revealed in the now defunct Stasi system of East German secret police services, but it is not clear whether they helped or hindered the process of discovering and rooting out dissidents of that now discredited and dismantled regime. On the other hand, countries that are often associated popularly with high degrees of democratic accountability – such as the USA or the UK – pursue surveillance practices that utilize the most sophisticated systems for draconian purposes. For instance, in April 2001, when anti-globalization protesters were demonstrating in Quebec City against the proposed Free Trade Areas of the Americas, FBI and US Secret Service agents raided the Seattle-based offices of an alternative media website, and used a court order to demand the Internet addresses of everyone who had visited the site during the Quebec protest. The act was defended because Canadian police plans for protecting world leaders had been removed and posted on the site; but numerous innocent protesters were thus caught in a category of suspicion (FT, 2001).

This example provides direct evidence of government surveillance using the Internet, which, according to Andy Oram (for Computer Professionals for Social Responsibility (CPSR)), was the "most pressing policy issue in cyberspace" during 2000 (Oram, 2000). The trends discerned by Oram (and elaborated for Asian situations) are these: The debate over Echelon, the global tracking system based in the USA, UK, Canada, Australia, New Zealand and elsewhere, now in the open, will continue. Numerous governments – including South Korea, Japan, Singapore, and Hong Kong – are requiring Internet service providers (ISPs) to preserve information on users and to help law enforcement agencies track their online activities. Old restrictions on the export of encryption (from the USA) were lifted by the Clinton regime, but, as we shall see, this does not mean they are welcome in some Asian countries such as China. Wiretapping has again become controversial, given the development of digital telephones and so-called third generation mobile cellphones. The Japanese Wiretap Law of 1999 (that came into force in August 2000), which covers emails and faxes as well as voice-calls, is particularly contested. It is opposed by a Committee for the Repeal of the Wiretapping Law which collected 180,000 signatures against it, and even the NTT asked that its employees should not be required to be present when taps are installed (EPIC/PI, 2000).

These are the kinds of trends in Internet surveillance, and what drives them can all be traced to a cluster of concerns, which nevertheless differ in emphasis from country to country. Criminal activity is generally taken to be the main reason to justify Internet surveillance by states, especially in activities such as drug handling, (inter)national terrorism, money laundering, and pornography marketing. In Japan, for instance, the existence of criminal organization such as Yakuza and cult groups like Aum Shinrikyo is used to justify message interception. But in several countries cracking down on dissent is another rationale, more or less explicitly stated. As we have seen, this may occur in any country, not only in ones with notoriously authoritarian regimes. Maintaining social order may, more modestly, be seen as an aim of Internet surveillance. Since the "terrorist" attacks of September 11, 2001, however, reinforced state surveillance of many kinds – including Internet surveillance – has been undertaken by many governments, North American, European, and Asian (see Lyon, 2001b).

In the case of Singapore, for instance, as recently as 1986 Lee Kwan Yew defended his interference in the private lives of citizens by saying that "without the slightest remorse, we wouldn't be here, we wouldn't have made economic progress, if we had not intervened on very personal matters – who your neighbour is, how you live," and so on. This attitude is perpetuated in current legislation, such as the Computer Misuse (Amendment) Act, the National Computer Board (Amendment) Act, and the Electronic Transactions Act which, though protecting the confidentiality of records from peers, give police powers to require disclosure of documents without a warrant. In addition, the Telecommunications Authority of Singapore permits the government to monitor anything considered a "threat to national security" under the Internal Security Act. These matters do not pass unnoticed, however. After 200,000 SingNet ISP users were scanned unknowingly in 1999 new guidelines were produced by the Infocomm Development Authority, stating that consent must be sought before such scanning occurs (EPIC/PI, 2000).

South Korea, which has adopted the OECD Guidelines on Protection of Privacy and Transborder Flows of Personal Data, nonetheless has recently been the site of some lively debates over surveillance. President Kim Dae-Jung, for instance, used his opposition to surveillance – in the form of the proposed Electronic National Identification Card – as a platform in his successful election campaign in 1997. In 1998 Kim Dae-Jung also ordered a probe into illegal wiretapping by police and security services (which no doubt also covers some Internet tracking too). In Korea, the drive towards e-commerce also sparked controversy over surveillance, as we shall see below. The Citizen's Action Network also mounts campaigns that release information about surveillance trends, including those involving the Internet.

The Japanese situation is different from the South Korean, but also from the Chinese. A 1988 Act, in Japan, based on OECD Guidelines, protects personal data in computerized files held by government departments, but some critics – such as the social economist Toshimaru Ogura – worry that the *de facto* situation is one of extensive government surveillance using computer communication networks. The late 1990s wiretap controversy hints at this. The Chinese experience, on the other hand, is one of fairly blatant government control. As in Japan, banned movements such as the Falun Gong religious group ("sect" for purposes of discreditation) spur threats of instant detection if their websites are visited. Major news sites such as the BBC, *New York Times*, and *Washington Post* are blocked by the "Great Firewall" but curiously, given its coverage, including articles from the *New York Times* and *Washington Post*, the *International Herald Tribune* is not (Gittings, 2001). In a departure from the trend towards mainly targeting ISPs, the Chinese returned, in April 2001, to focusing on users, particularly in the Internet cafés that have sprung up, especially in Shanghai. But this move seems to be directed against pornographic sites and network games, as well as "superstitious" sites (which probably means *Falun Gong*).

There is, in other words, a variety of ways in which, and purposes for which, surveillance by the state is used in Asian societies. These vary depending in particular upon the history of citizen–state relationships within the country in question. China has a long history of surveilling its citizens. Since at least the fourth century BC (in Western dating), China has kept accurate population records and limited the movement of her citizens from home. It is hardly surprising that new technological means are sought to update old practices. But in Indonesia, where a colonial past is the context of development, it seems that there is a high degree of mistrust of the state by citizens, so the quest for government transparency – citizens watching the state – is at least as significant as the state watching citizens. Indeed, attempts to digitize records and to use the Internet for surveillance purposes are still augmented, paradoxically, by networks of spies (Simon, 2001).

In all these situations, however, one common factor is that the desire to develop e-commerce has raised the stakes in the debates over surveillance. China, South Korea, and others are keen to open up their markets to electronic consumption, and this liberalizing trend flies in the face of attempts to close up and crack down on ISPs and site users. The arguments for processing personal data seem to have strong economic justification, even if the political rationales for doing similar things sometimes seem dubious. It is important to look at surveillance by corporations as well as by the state, both to understand the intrinsic dynamics of this sector as well as to see how pressures towards one kind of data collection have effects on the other.

INTERNET SURVEILLANCE BY CORPORATIONS

If the use of searchable databases opened new doors to marketers, then the advent of the Internet has encouraged many more to try to rush through them. But this did not happen overnight. In a long process, starting early in the twentieth century, corporations steadily augmented their interest in monitoring processes of production by attempting also to manage processes of consumption. Employees continue to be extensively and increasingly monitored at work, including by use of and in their use of the Internet. This chapter, however, focuses more on the Internet relations of consumption. Taylorist principles of scientific management, in the hands of General Motor's Alfred Sloan, were retooled for use with customers. From the 1920s data were collected on buying habits to create profiles on customers, and this was collated with demographic and socio-economic data. From the 1930s IBM provided data services to computers engaging in these early forms of consumer surveillance (Webster and Robins, 1989). However, market research entered a new phase of development with searchable databases and a further phase with online networking.

Searchable databases made possible systematic and automated social sorting processes, to sift customers according to their purchasing choices and preferences. Oscar Gandy's work (Gandy, 1993) was the first comprehensive scholarly study of such processes in the USA Using data collected from actual purchase transactions or from applications and enquiries, customers are classified as members of particular groups or market segments. "The American Patriot Donors List" is one such, mentioned by Gandy (1995). Contributors to this list support conservative causes such as opposing gays in the military, gay rights issues, pornography, government waste, and tax increases, and such lists (this one is managed by Response Unlimited) are used to enhance current information on customers in the database. The point is to predict who will buy what and to direct marketing efforts accordingly.

The channeling of the Internet towards increasingly commercial ends meant from an early stage that these kinds of practices would be perpetuated and enhanced online. In 1994 Lou Montulli, a young Netscape employee, invented the cookie (Schwartz, 2001). This is the means whereby each website's computer places a small file on each visitor's machine that tracks what the visitor does at the site. At a stroke, relative anonymity on the World Wide Web became a dinosaur. Transactions, movements, and desires from then on were stored, sorted, mined, and sold. Since then, massive profits have been made by companies specializing in online personal data processing. In some celebrated cases, companies have tried to combine online with offline data, to create comprehensive and fine-grained profiles of consumers. Doubleclick is the best known case, which in 1999 bought Abacus (which specializes in geo-demographic marketing data) in order to collate these two very valuable personal data sources into programs of increased predictive power (see also Lyon, 2001a).

Recently, several new devices have appeared which enhance the quality of personal data that can be gleaned from the web. So-called "web-bugs" send information from personal websites to market research and advertising companies. But the presence of these may themselves be discerned by other tools, surveillance "bots" that check on businesses to see what they are up to. Companies such as Cyberalert or Cyveillance offer investigative and tracking services, mainly to other corporate clients, in a form of mutual business surveillance (Profitt, 2001). It is hardly surprising, then, to discover that many companies fail to meet EU/US guidelines for the privacy of consumer information. A recent survey by Andersen Consulting showed that not one of seventy-five American corporate websites achieved a full score. Out of six areas, some met one or two, but only two met five (Reuters, 2001).

The desire to be involved in e-commerce is as strong in many Asian countries as it is in Europe and North America, which means that these practices are not unknown here too. Steps have been taken to limit potential abuse. In China, for instance, while many regulations enable government security to keep track of transactions, the Ministry of Information and Industry in 1999 required Intel to disable its "Processor Serial Number" from Pentium III chips, that make it possible to identify and track Internet users engaging in e-commerce (EPIC/PI, 2000). Following the North American route of distinguishing between public and private data-processing agencies, Japan has sought self-regulation for e-commerce, although a Bill on processing of personal data by businesses will be introduced during 2001. Korea has gone further than this, with its "Basic Act on Electronic Commerce" of 1999, and the creation in 2000 of a Cyber Privacy Center that issues guidelines including the need for consent before collecting information of a sensitive nature (to do with political or sexual orientation, or birthplace). ISPs are also required to display their privacy policies (EPIC/PI, 2000).

While there is little doubt that e-commerce is growing (albeit as erratically as elsewhere) in Asian countries, what is less clear is how it will develop and what limits will eventually be placed on personal data processing for profit. While many in North America and Europe claim (in relevant surveys) that they are concerned about their lack of anonymity online, only a small proportion actually do anything about it. In a Pew Internet and American Life survey, 86 percent of online users were "very concerned" or "somewhat concerned" about others obtaining their personal information, but only 10 percent set their browsers to reject cookies (Associated Press, 2000). It appears to be a trade-off, where one reluctantly loses privacy for the sake of enhanced participation in the marketplace. On a broader scale, there seems to be a certain cynicism among some countries, and perhaps companies too, that see privacy policies as a cost of doing business, rather than as a public good in themselves. For example, it may be argued that what actually prompted the timing of Canada's Bill C-6, which offers some protection for the private sector and came into force in January, 2001, was the requirement to comply with the European Directive on Data Protection, rather than internal political will.

But this also assumes that "privacy" is the real issue. While it may be a strategic way of approaching the issues in North America and Europe, given that modern Western individualistic societies place a fairly high premium on privacy (however defined), it may not be the best perspective there, let alone in Asia. Without falling into egregious generalizations about Asian societies (which are often almost as culturally different from each other as they are from North American and European societies (Robison and Goodman, 1996)) it can at least be said that individualism does not always take the same forms as the West in Asian societies (see e.g. Turner, 1994). Thus while discourses of privacy may offer some limited leverage on the issues raised by commercial Internet surveillance, they do not tell the whole story by any means.

Issues other than privacy are raised by the loss of control over personal information, and these are economic and political ones. Surveillance seen as social sorting suggests that database marketing, both online and offline, is a discriminatory means of distinguishing between different groups of consumers (Lyon, 2002, see also Lyon, 2003). People are assigned to categories of winners and losers; the winners are creamed off for special treatment, and the losers are cut off from opportunities. Already, in North America, aspects of this process are referred to as "weblining" in which certain combinations of geo-demographic data and online consumer profiles produce categories that are, for example, ineligible by definition for certain kinds of health insurance (Stapanek, 2000). Customers, in other words, are classified according to their relative worth to corporations. And in the case of the major U.S. company Acxiom, names are matched against demographic data to include "B" for black, "J" for Jewish, and "N" for Japanese. These are by no means innocent categories!

Over the past decade, much public attention has been paid to the notion of a digital divide. Usually, this is thought of as a way of indicating how access to communication and information technologies, but especially the Internet, is divided along class, gender, and regional lines. Surveillance as social sorting, however, suggests that another, perhaps more significant digital divide is created by information rather than having to do with access to information. If so, then the question of personal data and e-commerce is one, not merely of transgressions of privacy (however defined), but of threats to justice and to equality of opportunity.

THE HIDDEN FACE OF THE INTERNET

Cyberspace does turn out to have some interesting connections with surveillance, and with social control. Cyberspace and the Internet are evolving socio-technical systems in which both designers and users have a part to play, and in which some prominent users are governments and corporations. The Internet is seen frequently as the realm of free communications, but this is clearly nonsense. As Lawrence Lessig observes astutely, cyberspace is already governed, in its very constitution, by "code" (Lessig, 1999). The real question is who codes it for what purposes? In the case of surveillance examined here, it is clear that systems are set up with the express purpose of extending state governance, and of managing consumers. Governments justify what they do in terms of national security or internal order, and corporations justify what they do in terms of lubricating market mechanisms. To maintain strong states, then, and to develop mature markets, surveillance is necessary.

Some will argue that the Internet ought not to be subject to regulation and control, because its genius is to provide channels of communication, the means to participate. Thus the USA is willing to assist Chinese efforts to get around Internet censorship. The CIA, through its Washington-based technology company In-Q-Tel, offers SafeWeb as a means of using the Internet without leaving tracks (Campbell, 2001). Curiously, this occurs at the same time as Chinese left-wing publications have been taken off the Internet for criticizing President Jiang Zemin's desire to see capitalists play a role in the Communist Party (Fong, 2001).

In Malaysia, too, some see the Internet as a means of retaining freedom. The website Malaysiakini.com is a paperless newspaper which publishes information on such controversial matters as the illness of Anwar Ibrahim and the ordeal of Irene Fernandez, who publicized the brutal conditions at the Semenyih immigration detention camp in Selangor (See Chin, Chapter 8, this volume). Without the Internet, this site could not exist, but because the Malaysian government wants the country to be open for business, it cannot simply shut the site down. As Peter Preston sees it, the view is that "Opting out of the world wide web is opting out of your country's future" (Preston, 2001).

While these situations certainly exist, it is hard to use them as a justification for *laissez-faire* approaches to cyberspace, particularly when it comes to surveillance. As far as government and policing surveillance is concerned, there is no substitute for the constant monitoring by bodies such as the Electronic Privacy Information Center, Privacy International, or the Global Internet Policy Initiative (from the Center for Technology and Democracy) – although it would be preferable if these became truly global concerns.[1] State surveillance will continue to be mounted using the Internet, and constant vigilance is called for from all who value political freedom and participation. For those who value social freedom and participation, however, questions are raised by commercial Internet surveillance that do not yet have champions who are taken seriously where it counts. As we have seen, the debate tends to be siphoned off into questions of privacy that largely miss the point of surveillance as social sorting. The "other" digital divide that reinforces difference and creates new informational classes of relative privilege and relative disadvantage requires urgent analytic and policy attention.

Without denying the usefulness of privacy protecting technologies (PETs) and the array of encryption devices now available, approaching surveillance from a more radical angle seems appropriate. Privacy and data protection laws and policies, and PETs of all kinds, simply assume that personal data processing will continue to grow on a massive scale. Another approach, however, would be to ask whether all the data are really needed in the first place. This would place the burden of accountability on those who collect and process personal data, rather than on data subjects who are in any case always at a disadvantage in not knowing all about how their personal data are being used, and with what consequences for their life-chances and choices (Hamelink, 2000, esp. ch. 5). Accountability in this area of surveillance, as in others (I have in mind CCTV in public places, DNA and biometrics, for instance), is woefully inadequate. It is all too often assumed that, just because some worthy end is in view (public order, crime prevention, expanded markets), the means to that end – particularly if they are apparently neutral, technological means – are appropriate. As we have seen, both major means of surveillance today carry with them major risks – to political, personal, and social freedom, and thus also to justice.

The title of this chapter was however, intended as a *double entendre*. The "hidden face" of Internet surveillance has two meanings. It is not merely that few are aware of the extent of surveillance using the Internet, either in government or in corporate contexts. It is also the case that the crucial feature of "surveillance" – watching over – in this context is that no "face" is seen. All digital data are abstracted from the real life flesh-and-blood person who lives and relates to others in particular geographical places. The face is hidden from view within computerized bureaucratic administrative systems whether they are operated by governments, police, employers, intelligence services, or online database marketers.

Cyberspace, as noted above, is never a separate realm from embodied, social, place-bound life. Yet all forms of surveillance nevertheless have an influence on and impacts within the everyday lives of persons and groups in their everyday lives. The implications of this are huge, and much too large to expand on here (but see Lyon, 2001b). Simply and economically put, however, the implications are that persons should be put before profit and systems should be developed as if persons were directly involved – face to face – at every point. This is to seek an appropriate ethics of surveillance rather than assuming that technology or the market will somehow sort things out. It is also an ethics of surveillance that may overcome some limitations of merely Western approaches.

However cyberspace surveillance develops over the next few years, it is clear that its development will be the outcome of neither technological destiny, nor of benign government departments and corporations. Risks abound at every point. Surveillance using Internet technologies is now an established and routine aspect of everyday life in the twenty-first century, in Asian countries as in North America and Europe. The question is: Who is willing to be accountable for the ways in which surveillance is developed? Who is willing to go beyond the North American fixation with privacy or the European assumption that data protection can cover all eventualities? Are there insights from Asian countries that might help overcome this impasse – especially in asking whether personal data processing could be limited in the first place?

NOTE

1 The establishment in 2003 of the Asia-Pacific Privacy Charter Council is a positive move from the point of view of those who believe that appropriate policies for personal data handling have been insufficiently discussed in this region.

BIBLIOGRAPHY

Abbate, J. (1999) *Inventing the Internet*, Cambridge, MA: MIT Press.
Associated Press (2000) "Internet users seek assurances over online use of personal data," *Washington Post*, August 21. Online. Available HTTP: http://www.washingtonpost.com/ac2/wp-dyn?pagename=article&node=&contentld=A60984-2000 Aug20&notFound=true (current as of February 12, 2003).
Blumler, J. and Coleman, S. (2001) *Realising Democracy Online: A Civic Commons in Cyberspace*, London: Institute for Public Policy Research.
Campbell, D. (2001) "CIA funds cyberwar against Beijing censor," *Guardian*, September 4.
Castells, M. (2001) *The Internet Galaxy: Reflections on the Internet, Business, and Society*, Oxford and New York: Oxford University Press.
EPIC/PI (2000) *Privacy and Human Rights 2000*. Online. Available HTTP: http://www.privacyinternational.org/survey/phr2000/countrieshp.html (current as of February 12, 2003).

Fong, T.H. (2001) "Mainland leftist sites taken off Net," *South China Morning Post*, September 3. Online. Available HTTP: http://technology.scmp.com/ZZZRZ60FQQC.html (accessed April 11, 2002).

FT (2001) "Dark side of cybercrime fight," *FT.com Financial Times*, May 10.

Gandy, O. (1993) *The Panoptic Sort: A Political Economy of Personal Information*, Boulder, CO: Westview Press.

—— (1995) "It's discrimination, stupid!" in J. Brook and I.A. Boal (eds) *Resisting the Virtual Life*, New York: City Lights.

Ghafour, H. (2001) "Next year, licences can be renewed on Internet," *The Toronto Star*, September 5.

Gittings, J. (2001) "Great leap forward," *Guardian*, July 12. Online. Available HTTP: http://www.guardian.co.uk/online/story/0,3605,520016,00.html (current as of February 12, 2003).

Hamelink, C. (2000) *The Ethics of Cyberspace*, London and Thousand Oaks: Sage.

Ho, K.C., Baber, Z. and Khondker, H. (2002) "'Sites' of resistance: alternative web sites and state–society relations," *British Journal of Sociology*, 53, 1: 127–48.

Lessig, L. (1999) *Code and Other Laws of Cyberspace*, New York: Basic Books.

Lyon, D. (ed.) (1994) *The Electronic Eye: The Rise of Surveillance Society*, Cambridge: Polity Press/New York: Blackwell.

—— (2001a) *Surveillance Society: Monitoring Everyday Life*, Buckingham: Open University Press.

—— (2001b) "Facing the future: seeking ethics for everyday surveillance," *Information Technology and Ethics*, 3, 3: 171–81.

—— (2001c) "Surveillance after September 11," *Sociological Research Online*. Online. Available HTTP: http://www.socresonline.org.uk/6/3/lyon (accessed on April 11, 2002).

—— (2002) *Surveillance as Social Sorting: Privacy, Risk, and Digital Discrimination*, London and New York: Routledge.

—— (2003) *Surveillance after September 11*, Cambridge: Polity Press, New York: Blackwell.

Ogura, T. (2000) "Towards global communication rights: movements against wiretapping and monitoring in Japan," Paper at Jimbo Net, October 18, and ASEM People's Forum, Korea, October 19. Online. Available HTTP: http://marux.org/~ogura/global_communication_rights.html (accessed April 11, 2002).

Oram, A. (2000) "Year-end world-wide round-up on Internet surveillance," Computer Professionals for Social Responsibility. Online. Available HTTP: http://www.praxagora.com/andyo/ar/roundup_surveillance.html (current as of February 12, 2003).

Preston, P. (2001) "The Internet is a friend of freedom," *Guardian*, January 30. Online. Available HTTP: http://www.guardian.co.uk/Archive/Article/0,4273,4126873,00.html (current as of February 12, 2003).

Profitt, B. (2001) "Surveillance bots scope out competition." Online. Available HTTP: http://www.botspot.com/news/feature010501.html (current as of February 12, 2003).

Reuters (2001) "Web sites fail global privacy standards." Online. Available HTTP: http://news.excite.com/news/r/010816/11/net-tech-privacy-dc (accessed April 11, 2002).

Risen, J. and Johnson, D. (2002) "Intercepted Al Qaeda email is said to hint at regrouping," *New York Times*, March 6. Online. Available HTTP: http://www.nytimes.com/2002/03/06/international/asia/06INQU.html (current as of February 12, 2003, access to members only).

Robison, R. and Goodman, D.S.G. (eds) (1996) *The New Rich in Asia: Mobile Phones, McDonald's and Middle Class Revolution*, London and New York: Routledge.

Schwartz, J. (2001) "Giving the web a memory costs its users privacy," *New York Times*, September 4. Online. Available HTTP: http://www.nytimes.com/2001/09/04/ technology/04COOK.html (current as of February 12, 2003, access to members only).

Simon, B. (2001) "Theorizing dissimulation: superpanopticism and unruly subjects in surveillance societies," Paper given at a research workshop of The Surveillance Project, May.

Stapanek, M. (2000) "Weblining," *Business Week*, April 3. Online. Available HTTP: http://www.businessweek.com/2000/00_14/b3675027.htm (current as of February 12, 2003).

Turner, B. (1994) *Orientalism, Postmodernism, and Globalism*, London and New York: Routledge.

Webster, F. and Robins, K. (1989) "Plan and control: towards a cultural history of the information society," *Theory and Society*, 18: 323–51.

5 Global technology meets local environment

State attempts to control Internet content[1]

Carolyn Penfold

INTRODUCTION

The regulation of Internet content has been topical for some time, but no consensus has arisen as to whether or not there should be any such regulation, the extent to which there should be regulation, nor as to the means by which regulation might be achieved. However, in recent years a number of attempts have been made by individual nations to regulate content, or access to content, on the Internet. One such attempt, the Australian Broadcasting Services Amendment (Online Services) Act 1999 (Commonwealth), which was introduced specifically to regulate Internet content, serves as an excellent case study in examining the purposes and mechanisms of regulation. In this chapter I will discuss this attempt in detail, and briefly contrast the Australian example with similar attempts to regulate Internet content in Singapore and China. The very different methods applied in each country, and the differing degrees of regulation, reflect to a great extent each nation's historical, social, legal, and political environment. This environment may, in fact, be a most important indicator of the level of content control achieved, due to the technological difficulties encountered in attempting to control Internet content.

THE INTERNET AS A NEW MEDIUM

As the Internet grew ever more user-friendly, and became more accessible to people around the world, it was hailed in many quarters as the harbinger of democracy and freedom throughout the globe. The speed of Internet communications, the possibilities for interactivity, the anarchic and non-hierarchical structure, the promise that anyone could be author, publisher, and recipient of an infinite quantity of content, and the ability for communications to route around interruptions, all led to a belief that the Internet would change the world. Many believed that those living under repressive regimes, starved of news and information, and kept out of contact with free, liberal, democratic nations, would be able through the Internet to access enlightening information, to organize, and to spread their own information. There was consensus, for example, "among politicians and pundits in the United States that the Internet poses an insurmountable threat to authoritarian regimes" (Kalathil and Boas, 2001). Beliefs in the Internet's capabilities for spreading freedom and undermining censorship and control of information had a number of bases, both technical and non-technical.

It had been widely assumed, and explicitly argued, that censoring the Internet was technically impossible. Developed initially for defence purposes, the Internet was designed specifically to overcome interruptions, and to circumvent broken links. The claim that when one route was blocked a message would re-route and re-route, indefinitely, until the message reached its intended destination, was used repeatedly to argue that intervention in Internet communications is impossible. Further, the ability to disguise, to hide, to encrypt, and to tunnel data meant that there were further technological means of circumventing proxy filters, thus increasing the democratizing potential of the Internet (Coroneos, 2000). Advice to the Australian government prior to the enactment of the Broadcasting Services Amendment (Online Services) Act 1999 (Commonwealth) concluded that "content blocking implemented purely by technical means will be ineffective" (McRea *et al.*, 1998).

However, technology was also developing that could assist in content control. For example, restricted access systems requiring passwords or keys to enter, and software to block and filter content, have developed considerably. Developments such as the Platform for Internet Content Selection (PICS) allowed labeling of Internet content, and thus for the selection or rejection of content based on the labels it carried.[2]

Devices to detect a user's geographical location have also been developed, and the efficacy of such devices was examined by the French Superior Court in the case of LICRA et UEJF vs. Yahoo! Inc. and Yahoo France 2000. In that case, action was brought against Yahoo France and Yahoo Inc. (USA) for allowing anti-Semitic and pro-Nazi material to be accessed from within France, in contravention of French law. Yahoo Inc. argued, among other things, that the nature of the Internet as a global medium made it impossible to stop French users accessing its material, short of removing the material from the Internet. Having found the contravention proven, but mindful of Yahoo Inc.'s assertions, the court appointed a panel of international experts to look into the possibility of preventing French Internet users from accessing such material from overseas servers (Yahoo France carried but did not host the material in question, which was located on a server in the USA). Based on evidence from these experts, the French Superior Court held that geographical location devices may be as much as 90 percent effective in determining a user's location when combined with other methods, and thus such devices may allow content hosts and providers to restrict access to content based on a user's location. In summary, it was found that users' geographical locations could in fact be sufficiently differentiated to restrict access substantially to users in particular areas.

Such developments contradicted claims of the technological impossibility of controlling Internet content, but did raise normative issues. One issue which arose was that the development of technological methods which would improve the ability of states to censor could be argued also to encourage them to do so. Of PICS, one critic argued that the:

> technology which empowers parents to control the access of their children, equally empowers governments to control the access of their adult citizens.... Many of the original PICS advocates have become alarmed by the extent to which PICS makes the Web censor friendly. Increasingly, PICS is said to be the devil.
>
> (Graham, 1999; see also Bohorquez, 1999)

The French decision likewise led to fears of increased censorship. *The Economist*, for example, said that the result of that case could be to hand to "authoritarian governments the tools they need to censor the Internet" (*The Economist*, 2000). Such censorship was contrary to the notions of freedom of speech embraced and promoted by early Internet users as one of the basic "values" of the Internet. In the words of Gibbons, "although "the First Amendment is a local ordinance" in cyberspace, Cyberians throughout the world often invoke its talismanic force against those attempting to hinder free and robust speech" (Gibbons, 1997: 475). "Information wants to be free," a phrase attributed generally to Stewart Brand, a board member of Electronic Freedom Foundation, was another catch-phrase of early Internet users. To counter accusations of cultural imperialism, proponents argued that the adherence to free speech principles was not derived from US law, but rather from the architecture and development of the Internet itself.

Further, users rejected not only the right of governments to curtail freedom of speech on the Internet, but also the rights of national governments to legislate for the Internet at all. John Perry Barlow's (1996) *Declaration of Independence in Cyberspace* is oft quoted, and was echoed by noted scholars who also argued that nation-states had neither sovereignty nor jurisdiction in cyberspace. Johnson and Post (1996), for example, argued that "real world" sovereignty, or the acceptance of one state governing for a particular area, is based on four main precepts: power, effect, legitimacy, and notice. First, in real space government has the physical "power," within a particular space, to enforce its laws. Second, actions in real space cause "effects" in real space, and thus can be governed by the laws in force where those effects occur. Third, "legitimacy" is given to laws which are made by the people, or by the government of the people, within the space to be governed. And fourth, the need to cross physical borders when moving between jurisdictions in real space means that those crossing them have "notice" that they are moving from one territory, and therefore one legal system, to another.

Cyberspace makes a mockery of these notions from which "real space sovereignty" is derived. There is no sovereign existing which has sufficient physical connection with "the territory" of cyberspace to physically enforce rules there; there is no sovereign state within which all effects of actions in cyberspace will necessarily be more heavily felt than another; there is no sovereign state whose rule over cyberspace could be seen as legitimate, given that cyber-citizens come from all sovereign states; and in "seamless" cyberspace no notice is given of movement from one legal sphere to another; it is rare in cyberspace for users to be aware of the physical locations of materials they access or indeed distribute. "The Net thus radically subverts the system of rule making based on borders between physical spaces" (Johnson and Post, 1996), leading many to argue that individual states should step out of cyberspace regulation, and allow cyberspace itself to develop appropriate methods of dealing with problems and disputes. Johnson and Post (1996) claim an analogy with such areas as the laws of clubs and associations, or of religious bodies, where communities of interest are allowed and in fact encouraged to develop appropriate rules to govern themselves, without posing any threat to the existing legal system. This delegation of rule-making authority gives responsibility to those who "best understand a complex phenomenon and have an interest in assuring the growth and health of their shared enterprise."

The belief that censoring or regulating Internet content was impossible, that individual states had no legitimacy in cyberspace, and that free communications were somehow a basic tenet of the Internet, fails to recognize the varied social and political perspectives and systems which exist around the world. While US legislative attempts to censor or control Internet content have so far been unsuccessful on constitutional grounds, in much of the world Internet content or access to it *is* censored or regulated, individual nations *do* legislate for and assert control over Internet content within their borders, and many free speech notions have been ignored by nations intent on controlling Internet content as they would control the same material in any other medium. While individual nations may not control "cyberspace," they do have an interest in controlling real world participants, real world infrastructure, and real world effects within their jurisdictions (Goldsmith, 1998). An examination of Internet content regulation in Australia and Asia shows that nations have found and employed a variety of methods in attempting to regulate Internet content, and that, to overcome technological difficulties, technical restrictions are often combined with legal, social, and political pressure to regulate Internet content more effectively.

ATTEMPTS AT CONTROLLING INTERNET CONTENT

The ultimate method of censoring Internet content is prohibition; namely prohibiting or limiting access to computers, or at least to Internet connections. Where the state has been heavily involved in the licensing and development of press and other media, and of communications methods and technologies, prohibition is an option, but Internet development and proliferation has promised such economic potential that many nations are caught in a dilemma: how to ensure the economic rewards offered by embracing the technology, without surrendering the society's values and expectations.

Most nations, not only those branded "authoritarian," do try to protect their own values by regulating speech and communications to some degree. It is likely, though, that different types of content will be controlled or censored depending on the concerns of individual nations, which tend to reflect to a great extent the history, religion, society, and day-to-day political situation of the nation or area in question. As Lessig and Resnick (1999) note, "What constitutes 'political speech' in the United States (Nazi speech) is banned in Germany, what constitutes 'obscene speech' in Tennessee is permitted in Holland. . . . What is harmful to minors in Bavaria is Disney in New York." Each society will maintain what it believes are legitimate views on the topic.

Further, attempts to regulate Internet content reflect not only the "content" concerns of individual governments and societies, but vary also according to the existing legal or regulatory structures of that society. While the Internet does introduce special technological challenges to those wishing to regulate its content, it will be seen from the examples below that in many countries technological constraints on content may be less important than the other constraints available within individual societies.

AUSTRALIA'S ATTEMPT TO REGULATE INTERNET CONTENT

Many criticisms were made of the enactment of the Broadcasting Services Amendment (Online Services) Act 1999 (Commonwealth).[3] It was said that by enacting the legislation the government showed a lack of understanding of Internet technology, a disregard for the Internet industry, and a contempt for freedom of speech rights in Australia. In Australia however there is no specific constitutional protection for freedom of speech. It is necessary to look instead to the common law, to rights "implied" in the Constitution, or to international provisions.

First, the common law in Australia has never recognized a right to free speech. It has recognized a general freedom to do anything not restricted by law, and thus the right to freedom of speech exists only where there is nothing to prevent its exercise (*Australian Capital Television*, 1992).

Second, the Constitution of Australia does not explicitly give any guarantee of freedom of speech, although the High Court has held that a right to freedom of political communication must be implied (*Lange*, 1997). If the government were to try to restrict political communications within Australia, it would be subject to restrictions, but the OSA does not seek to restrict such content.

A third possible source of freedom of speech protection is the International Covenant on Civil and Political Rights (ICCPR), which has been signed and ratified by Australia. The ICCPR has not however been enacted under domestic law, as would be needed if the Australian government were to be required to uphold it domestically. However, the protections for freedom of speech found in the ICCPR (Art. 19), and so often used to support arguments against governments' curtailing freedom of speech, allow freedom of speech to be restricted if necessary for the protection of national security, public health, or morals (Art. 19(3)(b)). It is likely then that even if the ICCPR were enacted into domestic Australian law, there would be no conflict with the enactment of the OSA.

The provisions of the Broadcasting Services Amendment (Online Services) Act 1999 (Charter)

The Broadcasting Services Amendment (Online Services) Act (the OSA) operates through a system of co-regulation, whereby the Australian Broadcasting Authority (ABA) investigates and makes decisions about Internet content, and industry bodies develop codes or standards which specify the technical aspects of how those decisions are to be applied.

The ABA is given the power to investigate complaints made (s26) about prohibited or potentially prohibited content accessible via the Internet (s22), and may also investigate material of its own volition (s27).[4] "Prohibited content" includes Australian hosted R-rated material which is not subject to a restricted access scheme, and all material rated X or RC wherever hosted (s10).

Internet content is classified in the same way as film. Under the Australian scheme for the classification of films an R rating means "unsuitable for a minor to see"; an X rating means "unsuitable for a minor to see, and explicitly depicts sexual activity without violence, non-consent or coercion, and likely to cause offence to a reasonable adult." RC means the film is or would be refused a classification (Dickie, 1998). The main focus for restriction of content in Australia is hard-core pornography, graphic violence, and instruction in matters of crime. The ABA may issue take-down notices to Australian sites hosting what is believed to be X or RC material. For overseas hosted material ISPs are notified of prohibited content and must then provide an approved filter or filtered service to subscribers. The ABA also refers overseas hosted material to makers of content filters for inclusion in their block lists.

The ABA is also empowered to register and monitor compliance with industry codes, and further functions include advising and assisting parents and adults in relation to supervision and control of children's Internet access, conducting and co-ordinating community education programs, conducting and commissioning research into related issues, liaising with regulatory and other bodies involved in the Internet industry, and gathering information on technological developments and service trends in the industry (s94).

Effects of the Australian legislation

The Australian legislation, read in conjunction with the Internet Industry Codes of Practice, does not, in fact, restrict or control access to Internet content. While the legislation aimed initially to "restrict access to certain Internet content that is likely to cause offence to a reasonable adult, and to protect children from exposure to Internet content that is unsuitable for children," (s3(1)(l) & (m)), this has not been achieved. The legislation does prohibit the hosting of X and RC material in Australia, but does nothing to stop access to the same material hosted overseas. While the legislation itself required ISPs to "take all reasonable steps to prevent end-users from accessing that content" (s40(1)(c)), this requirement has been greatly undermined by the Internet Industry Codes of Practice which allow ISPs to fulfill their responsibilities simply by offering subscribers access to a content filter or filtered service (IIA Content Code 2.6.2). There is no requirement that the filters be actually used!

While the legislation could have placed much heavier burdens on industry, or the Industry Code could have been refused registration as not allowing for sufficient content control, the government was very concerned about stymieing growth in the Internet industry. The government felt that the legislation it enacted "steered a middle course between heavy handed prohibitions *that could hinder industry development* and a laissez-faire 'do nothing' approach" (Alston, 2000, p. 4; italics added). The government wished to be seen to be doing something to regulate Internet content, although its desire not to place too great a burden on industry meant that the law it enacted did not in fact restrict access to any material. However, the regulations, in conjunction with the Industry Codes of Practice, do raise awareness of the dangers of some Internet content, prevent minors from gaining Internet access accounts without adult approval, provide an avenue for complaints about Internet content and for the removal of restricted content hosted in Australia, and provide some funds for research and development of better filtering and labeling technologies. In this way, Australia's Internet content regulation regime well fits the legal and political environment; Internet content is classified in accordance with a preexisting and familiar classification scheme, and the industry regulates itself with oversight from government, as occurs in most similar industries. The usual process of government-initiated censorship and classification has been recognized as too difficult to apply fully to the Internet, and so responsibility for content control has been placed on users, with some assistance regarding the provision of filters, pursuit of a labeling scheme, and community education campaigns. The Australian regulations seem to have achieved the government's aim that Internet regulations "enable public interest considerations to be addressed in a way that does not impose unnecessary financial and administrative burdens on the Internet industry" (Broadcasting Services Amendment [Online Services] Act 1999 [Commonwealth]).

OTHER ATTEMPTS TO REGULATE INTERNET CONTENT

Other governments have also tried to regulate Internet content without forgoing their economic interest in an emerging Internet industry. However, while in Australia pornography is the main focus of censorship, in many nations governments seek to control or censor broader categories of content, including, for example, content critical of government or of political structures, or content likely to cause unrest or dissent within a community. Control of such material may be expected to require stronger methods than used in Australia, and in fact this appears to be the case in a number of Asian countries. I will discuss content regulation in Singapore and China to illustrate some of the different methods of control being employed. These two nations are not put forward as "representative" of Asian nations, but as examples of the variety of methods used, the type of content controlled, and the methods available within these societies.

Internet content regulation in Singapore

Singapore is not a signatory to the ICCPR, but its Constitution gives every citizen of Singapore the right to free speech and expression (14(1)(a)). That right may be curtailed where "necessary or expedient in the interests of the security of Singapore.... Friendly relations with other countries, public order or morality and.... To protect the privileges of Parliament" (14(2)(a)). In fact, Singapore has a reputation for censorship (Ang, 1997), and speech is tightly controlled in every medium in order to enhance social harmony, to avoid ethnic tensions, to uphold morality, and to ensure a suitable environment for continued economic growth. In denying calls for greater freedom in public speaking, for example, a Director in the Ministry of Home Affairs replied, "In multi-racial and multi-religious Singapore, we cannot put at risk the racial harmony and sense of public order, peace and safety built up over the years" (Rozario, 1999).

Equally, Singapore has a reputation for embracing new technology, and consequently the government has encouraged the take-up of Internet services, while continuing to control the content of communications. Singapore's Internet content regulation scheme is overseen by the Singapore Broadcasting Authority (SBA), and the scheme relates only to content of concern to Singapore. For example, "In the case of racial and religious material, [SBA's] purview covers only materials which may incite racial or religious hatred among the races in Singapore" (SBA, 2002b); it is not concerned with hate speech generally.

A class license scheme requires registration of many participants in the Internet industry, including ISPs and ICHs (Internet Content Hosts), political parties providing content on the Internet, and anyone else propagating, promoting, or discussing political or religious issues relating to Singapore (SBA, 2002c). Under the Internet Code of Practice "licensees" must use their best efforts to ensure that "prohibited material" is not broadcast via the Internet to users in Singapore (SBA, 2002a). ISPs are not required actively to monitor material they carry (Anil, 2001), nor are hosts required to monitor material they host over which they do not have editorial control (SBA, 2002b), but must block or remove prohibited material of which they become aware, or of which they are notified by the SBA (SBA, 2002b).

Prohibited material is "material that is objectionable on the grounds of public interest, public morality, public order, public security, national harmony, or is otherwise prohibited" (SBA, 2002b; Anil, 2001), and the Internet Industry Guidelines list factors to be taken into account in assessing such content. These offer some clarification, but uncertainty remains, and it is likely that industry will err on the side of caution as the SBA may modify licenses, impose additional conditions on license holders (Anil, 2001), or even remove licenses if an Internet business does not act in accordance with the regulations or the Internet Code of Practice. This threat may discourage those in the industry from challenging decisions or notifications of the SBA.

Internet Industry Guidelines note that the registration of content providers is not intended to censor content, but rather "to emphasise the need for the content providers to be responsible in what they say ... given the multi-racial, multi-religious nature of our society" (SBA, 2002b). In such a situation self-censorship may flourish even where specific restrictions look less stringent. The recent closure of Singapore's Sintercom site is just one example of this. After being pressured to register as required of sites "engaging in propagation, promotion, or discussion of political issues" (Ellis, 2001), Sintercom's convener closed down the site, denying it was a political site but claiming he was "too tired" to continue running it (Ellis, 2002).

However, this reflects Singapore's history and social and political situation. Interestingly, although free speech advocates decry the Singapore Internet Code of Practice as violating "free speech guarantees enshrined in democratic institutions and international law" (Anil, 2001), Singaporeans overwhelmingly support their government's censorship policies. A recent poll showed 85 percent of Singaporeans believed that censorship was necessary, and 82 percent were satisfied with the level of censorship in Singapore (Anil, 2001).

Internet content regulation in China

Unlike Singapore, China is a signatory to the ICCPR, although it has not ratified the covenant. Like Singapore, the Constitution of China provides protection for freedom of speech (Art. 35 and 41), but also has provision for this to be read subject to other rights; for example, the exercise of these "freedoms and rights may not infringe upon the interests of the state, of society and of the collective, or upon the lawful freedoms and rights of other citizens" (Art. 51). Like Singapore and Australia, China has been keen to embrace information technology and to reap its economic rewards, but has remained keen also to maintain control over the information available through the medium. In China, "state strategies toward media and ICTs have historically addressed the balance between economic modernization and political control" and thus "although the Internet may differ radically from past forms of media, we can also place it against a wider history of state control of media and ICTs" (Kalathil and Boas, 2001). Therefore, contrary to assumptions that broad Internet penetration meant the beginning of the end for authoritarian governments, the government has encouraged uptake of the Internet, while controlling its development, and has introduced restrictions to avoid potential political challenges.

In October, 2000, the Chinese government released a document entitled "Measures for Managing Internet Information Services," which lists information which may not be produced, reproduced, released, or disseminated (Xinhuashe, 2000: Art. 15), including information contrary to the Constitution or which endangers national security, is detrimental to the honor of the state, instigates ethnic hatred or discrimination, undermines national unity, disturbs social order, or spreads pornography or other salacious material.

A variety of technological and other types of controls have been employed, including official scrutiny of websites prior to publication (Miles, 2000), access being routed through state-sanctioned providers, and requirements that content accessed, and user identities, be recorded (Liang, 2001). Other controls include "blocking specific websites, monitoring chatrooms and on-line content, selective arrests and crackdowns, and promoting self-censorship" (Kalathil and Boas, 2001). Thus, in addition to restrictions on specific content, generalized monitoring, or even the possibility of it, is likely to ensure that Internet users are careful about what material they access, and service and content providers are careful about material to which they provide access. Occasional well-publicized events, such as the government's closure of numerous Internet cafés, the closure of

Falun Gong websites, and the arrest and conviction of a man alleged to have provided email addresses to a pro-democracy journal, demonstrate further to both users and the industry that their activities may always be under surveillance, and under threat. Thus while it may be difficult to effectively censor the Internet technically, there are in China many additional factors which serve to restrict Chinese Internet users from accessing and distributing information to which the government objects.

CONTENT REGULATION IN CONTEXT

Australia, Singapore, and China have each embraced new information technologies for economic gain and continue to increase their modernization and technological advances. Each has attempted to control Internet content in ways very much in keeping with their traditions, and their legal, political, and social structures. Consequently, a variation both in the methods used and the degree of control exerted can be clearly seen, with a progression in the number and levels of restriction; Australia restricts content at the level of content hosts only, Singapore, at the levels of content providers, hosts, and service providers, China, at the levels of content providers and hosts, service providers, and users. Moreover, the philosophies and histories of government involvement in media and communications in each of these nations are apparent both in the methods they employ and in the content they seek to regulate.

It is important to emphasize that most nations wishing to exert control over Internet content are both restrained and compelled by their legal, social, and political structures. Malaysia appears to be an exception, in that to promote its multimedia super corridor to outsiders it has promised no Internet censorship, although it is anticipated that existing legislation controlling speech and communications will continue to apply to Malaysians using this medium (Davidson, 1998; see also Chin, Chapter 8, this volume). At the other extreme are nations such as Myanmar, which has opted to regulate the Internet through restricting access to both computers and Internet connections (Barron, 2000).

Most Asian nations though, wishing to benefit from broad Internet penetration, have allowed access but introduced specific regulations to try to curtail access to and distribution of "inappropriate" material, using combinations of technological and other methods, generally to control content already restricted in other media. Such restrictions are not confined to Asia, as nations all over the world are attempting to regulate Internet content in ways that meet the expectations of their communities, confirm their values and beliefs, and protect their political systems or actors.[5]

It is true that no nation has legitimacy to govern the Internet as a whole, but it is also true that each nation has a legitimate interest in governing the Internet in which its residents or citizens participate. It appears that most nations do have at their disposal a number of methods by which to do this; technology is only one factor in exerting such control. It should not be forgotten, however, that censorship of other media has not been achieved by technological or physical means alone. While some access is prevented in this way, social disapproval, a dislike of acting illegally, the danger of being caught, the fear of punishment and so on all combine to discourage attempts to access censored or restricted information, even when it can be accessed. The same will be true of the Internet; while a user may be able physically to access prohibited or restricted content, restrictions may still be effective.

CONCLUSION

At the same time that many commentators were proclaiming that the Internet assured certain freedoms, many nations were carefully planning and implementing policies and regulations to ensure that they could harness the Internet's economic promise without compromising local social and political structures, beliefs, and values. While Cyberians may cringe at the restrictions placed on Internet freedom, and human rights activists wring their hands at an opportunity lost, individual nations, for the most part, have found ways to incorporate Internet communications into existing frameworks which protect and promote their own values and expectations, and their historical, religious, social, legal, and political structures. While greater protection for freedom of communication may be desired by many both within and beyond a particular society, present indications are that despite initial promises of the Internet as a haven for free speech and communication, in the foreseeable future Internet content is likely to remain regulated in most nations in a manner and to a degree similar to other media.

NOTES

1   An earlier version of this chapter was published in Sin, K.F. (ed.) (2003) *Legal Explorations: Essays in Honour of Professor Michael Chesterman*, Sydney: Lawbook Co.
2   For further information see W3C at http://www.w3.org/PICS/ (accessed July 1, 2002).
3   Now incorporated to become Schedule 5 of the Broadcasting Services Act 1992 Commonwealth.
4   Section numbers used hereafter refer to the section in Schedule 5 of the Broadcasting Services Act (1992) Commonwealth.
5   For further discussion and references regarding Internet regulation, see Penfold, 2001.

BIBLIOGRAPHY

Alston, R. (2000) "The government's regulatory framework for Internet content," *University of New South Wales Law Journal Forum, Internet Content Control*, 6, 1.

Ang, P.H. (1997) "How countries are regulating Internet content." Online. Available HTTP: http://cad.ntu-kpi.kiev.ua/events/inet97/B1/B1_3.HTM (current as of January 21, 2003).

Anil, S. (2001) "Re-visiting the Singapore Internet code of practice," *Journal of Information, Law and Technology*, 2.

Australian Broadcasting Authority (ABA) (1996) "Investigation into the content of on-line services," Report to the Minister for Communications and the Arts, Sydney: ABA.

Australian Capital Television Pty Limited v The Commonwealth (1992) 177 CLR 106 at 182, per Dawson J.

Barlow, J.P. (1996) *Declaration of Independence in Cyberspace*. Online. Available HTTP: http://www.eff.org/Publications/John_Perry_Barlow/barlow_0296.declaration (current as of January 21, 2003).

Barron, S. (2000) "Myanmar works hard to keep the Internet out," *New York Times*, July 14.

Bohorquez, F.A. (1999) "The price of PICS: the privatization of Internet censorship," *New York Law School Law Review*, 43: 523.

Coroneos, P. (2000) "Internet content control in Australia: attempting the impossible?" *UNSWLJ Forum, Internet Content Control*, 6, 1.

Davidson, A.D. (1998) "I want my censored MTV," *Vanderbilt Journal of Transnational Law*, 31: 97.

Dickie, J. (1998) "Classification and community attitudes," Research Paper no. 5, Centre for Media, Communications and Information Technology Law, Law School, University of Melbourne.

Ellis, E. (2001) "Hot potato: the Singapore government should leave Sintercom alone," *Time Singapore*, July 17. Online. Available HTTP: http://www.singapore-window.org/sw01/010717ti.htm (current as of January 21, 2003).

—— (2002) "Tech talk: Sintercom no more," *Time Asia*, July 24. Online. Available HTTP: http://www.time.com/time/asia/digital/column/0,9754,171971,00.html (current as of January 21, 2003).

Gibbons, L.J. (1997) "No regulation, government regulation, or self-regulation: social enforcement or social contracting for governance in Cyberspace," *Cornell Journal of Law and Public Policy*, 6: 475.

Goldsmith, J.L. (1998) "Against cyberanarchy," *University of Chicago Law Review*, 65: 1199.

Graham, I. (1999) *The Net Labelling Delusion: Saviour or Devil?* Online. Available HTTP: http://libertus.net/liberty/label.html#Sindex (current as of January 21, 2003).

Internet Industry Association (IIA) (1999) *Internet Industry Codes of Practice*. Online. Available HTTP: http://www.iia.net.au/codes.html (current as of January 21, 2003).

Johnson, D. and Post, D. (1996) "Law and borders – the rise of law in Cyberspace," *Stanford Law Review*, 48: 1367.

Kalathil, S. and Boas, T. (2001) "The Internet and state control in authoritarian regimes: China, Cuba and the counterrevolution," Carnegie Endowment for International Peace, Global Policy Program, no. 21.

Lange v Australian Broadcasting Corporation (1997) 189 CLR 520.

Lessig, L. and Resnick, P. (1999) "Zoning speech on the Internet: a legal and technical model." Online. Available HTTP: http://cyberlaw.stanford.edu/lessig/content/articles/(current as of January 21, 2003).

Liang, C. (2001) "Red light, green light: has China achieved its goals through the 2000 Internet regulations?" *Vanderbilt Journal of Transnational Law*, 34: 1417.

LICRA et UEJF vs. Yahoo! Inc and Yahoo France (2000) Tribunal de Grande Instance de Paris (Superior Court of Paris), November 20. Online. Available HTTP: http://www.gigalaw.com/library/france-yahoo-2000-11-20-lapres.html (current as of January 21, 2003).

McRea, P., Smart, B. and Andrews, M. (1998) *Blocking Content on the Internet: A Technical Perspective*, CSIRO.

Miles, J. (2000) "Can governments control the Internet?" *BBC News*. Online. Available HTTP: http://news.bbc.co.uk/1/hi/world/asia-pacific/623339.stm (current as of January 21, 2003).

Penfold, C. (2001) "Australia's Internet content regulation in the international context," *Computers and Law*, 45.

Reno vs. ACLU 117 S Ct 2329 (1997) (USA).

Rozario, C. (1999) Director, Public Affairs Division, Singapore Ministry of Home Affairs, quoted in *Straits Times*, January 28.

Singapore Broadcasting Authority (SBA) (2002a) *Internet Code of Practice*. Online. Available HTTP: http://www.sba.gov.sg/sba/i_codenpractice.jsp (current as of January 21, 2003).

—— (2002b) *Internet Industry Guidelines*. Online. Available HTTP: http://www.sba.gov.sg/sba/i_guidelines.jsp (current as of January 21, 2003).

—— (2002c) *Registration of Internet Class Licences*. Online. Available HTTP: http://www.sba.gov.sg/sba/i_register.jsp (current as of January 21, 2003).

The Economist (2000) "Vive la liberte!," November 25.

W3C (World Wide Web Consortium) (n.d.) "Platform for Internet content selection." Online. Available HTTP: http://www.w3.org/PICS/ (accessed July 1, 2002).

Xinhuashe (Xinhua News Agency) (2000) "Measures for managing Internet information services." Online. Available HTTP: http://www.chinaepulse.com/html/regulation.html (current as of Jaunary 21, 2003).

6 Piracy, open source, and international intellectual property law

Debora Halbert

As Asia faces the global economy of the future, it is necessary to take stock of the once arcane issue of intellectual property. The ability to manufacture cheaply computer software, music, movies, and textbooks that are of the same quality as the original has resulted in a threat posed by intellectual property consumers to intellectual property owners (Negroponte, 1995). While the philosophically oriented may see the digital age as an opportunity to rethink authorship, creativity, and private property, others view it as an era of massive theft (Grabosky *et al.*, 2001). When the ease of reproduction is combined with the networked world of the Internet, the laws of copyright created in the eighteenth century seem ready to topple. In response, expansive new laws are passed in an effort to maintain control of information even as that control becomes impossible.

Industries that rely upon intellectual property law perceive piracy as a threat and the Internet as a tool for wrongdoing rather than as a more efficient mode of communication. Copyright violations around the globe have led to a huge multi-pronged anti-piracy effort with intellectual property interests successfully lobbying governments to change laws to enhance protection, and to shut down troublesome Internet sites. These industries have developed educational campaigns to define piracy as a moral issue and they have established hotlines for people to report piracy by employers or neighbors (Gutterman and Anderson, 1997).

The development of the Internet, along with other information and communication technologies in Asia, has tremendous significance for several reasons. First, as "information" has become the key ingredient to participation in the information society, governments have invested heavily in these technologies in order to bring about economic development and participate more fully in the new global economy (see Ho, Kluver, and Yang, Chapter 1, this volume). Second, the availability of information on the Internet means that unlike traditional property, information is not exclusive and can exist in multiple forms and locations, without diminishing the ability of the original owner to use it. Finally, the Internet enables rapid and inexpensive duplication of information, allowing an enlarged sphere of participation in economic, political, and cultural life. However, the negative side of the transformation to an information society is the easy availability of copyrighted works that can be defined as piracy.

As Asian economies face the future of information technology and the networked world made possible by the Internet, it is important to assess critically the meaning of piracy, intellectual property, and exchange of information in the context of centralized information ownership. First, this chapter will examine the politics of piracy in the global context. I will argue that piracy is the inevitable consequence of a property model which outlaws the exchange of information and that the language of piracy has political and economic ramifications. Second, I will attempt to demonstrate how information technology can regain its developmental role, by using the open source movement as an example.

One preface is necessary. It is impossible to generalize about "Asia" as a common cultural system. It is also difficult to generalize about a common economic approach to development in Asia. When the region under discussion includes such disparate development models as Japan's advanced industrial economy and North Korea's communist economy in crisis, not to mention China's new hybrid economic model, generalizable claims are difficult to make. Each country within the region is taking its own path to development (Clark, 1999). In addition, international intellectual property relationships are complex and multifaceted. While it is true that there are individuals, organizations, and governments that benefit from these property regimes throughout the globe, it is also important to evaluate the ways in which powerful actors such as the US and the EU have constructed the playing field for claims regarding copyrights and patents. I hope that given the difficulties of the task, I can capture adequately the problems faced by Asian countries as they adopt and deal with intellectual property law.

INTERNATIONAL INTELLECTUAL PROPERTY REGIMES WITHIN THE ASIAN CONTEXT

The idea of copyright originates in English law during the eighteenth century (Rose, 1993) and finds its modern-day advocate in the United States. At the international level, the US has been the primary actor in lobbying for intellectual property protection through the trade negotiations leading up to the creation of the WTO and the Trade Related Aspects of Intellectual Property Rights Agreement (TRIPs) (Ryan, 1998; Sell, 1998). As negotiations surrounding the passage of TRIPs indicate, the debate breaks down into a contest between developed, intellectual property-producing nations and developing, intellectual property-consuming nations. Those with strong intellectual property industries to protect favor much stronger laws at the international level than do those with weaker intellectual property industries. It is of course also important to recognize that piracy remains rampant in the US and many developing nations have growing intellectual property-related industries seeking stronger protection. These complexities make the "problem" of piracy even more difficult to address because the issue seems to be a political one. By political, I am suggesting that property rights and piracy are political boundaries placed upon the debate over property protection. By evaluating the context within which claims of piracy are made, we are better able to understand how to address the issue.

While critical voices abound (Alford, 1995; Litman, 2001; Martin, 1998; Vaidhyanathan, 2001), the "problem" of international piracy exists in part because it has been assumed that there is a universally applicable model for intellectual property development. However, it may be helpful to investigate the economic relationship between these so-called "pirates" and those who claim to be the victim of piracy, mainly the developed world. The following analysis focuses primarily on the actions of the US government because US industries have been the most interested in ensuring protection of intellectual property at the international level (Sell, 1998). The focus on the US should not be interpreted to mean that they are the only actors interested in strong intellectual property protection. However, the US was an early advocate of strong protection and we will never know how protective systems might have developed in Asia without the strong lobbying effort of these early actors.

Despite the fact that Asian scholars point to political, economic, and cultural factors that play an important role in how intellectual property is defined throughout the region (Yu, 2001), virtually all countries in Asia have now placed laws on the books that protect copyrights and patents. These laws were enacted primarily in response to trade threats by the United States and later by pressure put upon countries that wanted to participate in the WTO. Thus, it is important to evaluate the legal and economic factors contributing to claims of piracy and how Asia should address this "problem."

The "problem" of piracy emerged during a period of declining US economic competitiveness and a shift in the US economy. The United States offset the loss of its manufacturing base to Asia by emphasizing intellectual property-based goods. Carlos M. Correa (2000) best summarizes the economic transformation that led the United States to the focus on intellectual property piracy:

> [D]uring the 1980s, US supremacy in manufacturing and technology had been eroded by catching-up processes in Japan, first, and in Asian newly industrializing countries (NICs) later. These countries emerged as aggressive competitors in consumer electronics, microelectronics, robotics, computers and peripherals, as well as in various services (e.g. engineering and construction). The erosion of the technological leadership of US firms in certain high-tech areas, coupled with the high US trade deficit, was partially attributed to a too-open technological and

scientific system which allowed foreign countries to imitate and profit from US innovations. Thus, a major source of declining American competitiveness was conceived to be the losses from overseas piracy and counterfeiting activities.

(Correa, 2000, p. 4)

As the United States economy shifted to one reliant on knowledge-based innovation, rather than manufacturing and industrial strength, piracy became a major concern. The shift to an intellectual property-based economy occurred at the same time as the US was experiencing record trade deficits, a condition that remains in place today (Crutsinger, 2000; Egan, 2000; Somerville, 2000). These changes in the global economy threatened US economic stability (Gilpin, 2000).

Since 1945, intellectual property-related US exports more than doubled, with current profits from licensing reaching over US$8 billion (Nerona, 2000). Within the rapidly developing new information-based economy, openness of ideas was replaced with private property rights. All aspects of the system, from code to content, were subject to privatization and control (Bollier, 2002; Lessig, 2001). Thus, strong international intellectual property protection became necessary to stave off the threat posed by the developing economies, most of which had no intellectual property protection on the books (Rosser, 1999).

As the global economy developed and focus shifted to the East, technology-based firms, software, record, and movie companies began to publicize more vocally the "problem" of piracy in Asia. Despite rampant piracy throughout the United States and Europe (Software and Information Industry Association, 2000), it was Asia that became the focus of anti-piracy campaigns. China, for example, became the target of early anti-piracy activism (Alford, 1995; Halbert, 1997). The reasons countries in Asia have been targeted as pirate nations are complex, but they seem to be based upon the combination of an early lack of intellectual property laws and enforcement, combined with rapid economic development that threatened countries producing and exporting intellectual property goods.

Once the problem of piracy was defined, the United States used both unilateral and multilateral methods to enforce their intellectual property laws abroad. For example, in the mid-1980s, Indonesia came under fire for producing pirated cassette tapes. Despite the fact that Indonesia had no intellectual property laws and was not party to any international agreement on copyright, they were condemned by Western recording interests for pirating recordings (Rosser, 1999). The conflict escalated when Indonesian businessman Anthony Darmawan Setiono was arrested for importing illegally produced cassettes into the United States (Rosser, 1999). The Indonesian government responded by drafting new intellectual property laws that resulted in refinements to the existing legal regime that would protect music along Western lines (Rosser, 1999).

With the passage of the Trade Related Aspects of Intellectual Property Agreement (TRIPs), the rather esoteric topic of intellectual property became a crucial part of the World Trade Organization (WTO). Prior to TRIPs, the primary international body dealing with intellectual property was the World Intellectual Property Organization (WIPO). However, as early as the late 1970s, many businesspeople felt that WIPO was too weak to protect their intellectual property in the developing world, especially as it related to patent protection (Ryan, 1998). Because many developing countries were members of WIPO, the US could not use the organization to protect their interests without being vetoed by developing countries. Thus, the United States turned to unilateral trade sanctions and the General Agreement on Tariffs and Trade (GATT) to protect intellectual property (Sell, 1998).

Prior to TRIPs, the United States used the Trade Act of 1974, Special 301, as a weapon to curb piracy and impose stronger intellectual property laws (Nerona, 2000; Ryan, 1998). The US Trade Representative's (USTR) office established watch lists and priority watch lists for countries with known piracy records and used Special 301 to force countries to change their behavior. If a country did nothing to improve its piracy rates, it could face trade retaliation by the United States (Nerona, 2000). Threat of sanctions was used against countries to force them to the bargaining table during the Uruguay round of the GATT (Ryan, 1998).

The TRIPs agreement replaced WIPO as the dominant force in the intellectual property world (Sell, 1998). While WIPO remains important as an educational body and as a patent clearing-house, it lacks the enforcement mechanisms built into the WTO. Any WTO member country that wishes to trade internationally must adhere to the laws built into the TRIPs agreement. Under TRIPs, domestic intellectual property laws of member countries must conform to the global standard. TRIPs established a schedule for harmonization, with lesser-developed countries (LDCs) allowed the most time to meet the legal requirements (Nerona, 2000). The WTO is a powerful tool because a violation of international intellectual property law can result in trade sanctions, a device not available to WIPO.

Changes in international law have made intellectual property one of the most significant topics debated in the international arena over the past twenty years. However, the fact that the law has reached new international heights does not mean all countries are ready to adopt the same intellectual property standards as the United States and Europe. In addition, while specific states may officially endorse TRIPs in order to retain trade status within the WTO, individuals operating within the state may have different ideas of how to proceed.

While most governments now see, if reluctantly, that intellectual property protection is necessary for industrial development, it does not follow that all citizens will immediately see the benefit of strong copyright and patent protection. Again, the realities of the situation are complex, with numerous resistances to strong intellectual property springing up around the globe. Certainly, there is an active resistance to the further expansion of copyright in the United States (Berkeley Center). There is no reason to believe that other countries may not also benefit from a more relaxed intellectual property atmosphere as well. Despite the complexities of the issue, intellectual property law appeared on the agenda of developing Asian countries because it was considered a high priority by the US, not Asian leaders. Early debates indicate that intellectual property concerns appeared because of a US dominated global information-based business environment.

There is economic evidence to suggest that it is not in the best interests of developing countries or newly industrialized countries (NICs) to provide strong intellectual property protection. La Croix (1992) argued prior to the adoption of TRIPs and the WTO that uniform standards of international protection will not yield immediate benefits for many countries. Only as developing countries "accumulate capital, develop new manufacturing industries, reduce the proportion of the Gross National Product derived from agriculture, and improve the efficiency of institutions governing law enforcement and dispute adjudication" will intellectual property rights make economic sense (La Croix, 1992, p. 94). He argues, "A country reaching intermediate stages of development (such as South Korea) may experience welfare gains when it adopts stricter IPRs, while a country in the early stages of development (such as Indonesia) may experience welfare losses when it strengthens its IPRs." La Croix affirmed these results in 1995 (La Croix, 1995). Thus, the war on piracy may make economic sense for advanced industrial nations, and explains Singapore's transformation into a center for intellectual property in Asia, but it does not make economic sense for many developing countries.

Maskus (2000) agrees that a "one size fits all" patent system makes little sense. Instead, countries at different stages of development require different levels of domestic protection. Since international intellectual property protection is based upon viable domestic laws in all countries, making the system stronger is pushed at the international level. However, as Maskus (2000) points out, a universal international approach to intellectual property does not reflect the specific needs of countries at different levels of development. Only when a country reaches an advanced stage of development does it make economic sense to have strong IPRs. Maskus (2000) does suggest that strong IPRs may help in areas of foreign direct investment and imports. He ultimately sees both costs and benefits for developing nations using stronger IPRs. In addition, there is evidence that the returns from both legal and illegal piracy (copying product designs without violating patents or copyrights as well as the more popular illegal copying) to NICs can be high (Evenson, 1992).

Political factors may also feed rates of piracy. A country in the process of development may not place intellectual property rights high on the agenda for political change until forced to do so. Without an adequate system of enforcement, which can be costly to implement, these intellectual property laws will do little good. A general lack of enforcement should have been an obvious outcome of coercive anti-piracy tactics. A more effective approach would have been to develop the economic and legal systems as a whole. The current dual system, where public and state acknowledgment of intellectual property protection sits alongside informal noncompliance, does little to promote the end of piracy.

The cultural factors leading to piracy may be the most difficult to assess. Given different conceptualizations of community and individual rights, a system of intellectual property based upon individual rights, as is explicit in the West, may not be immediately obvious to many people. From the standpoint of the government, it often makes greater sense to support activities beneficial to society as a whole. Strong protection of patents or copyrights which require high licensing fees that transfer money away from the local economy may not be the most beneficial to society. In addition, because very few people can actually afford the expense of most Western products, providing pirated versions may be seen as a larger good. Access to something such as engineering textbooks that will help the country further its development will take precedence over the publisher's copyright.

Ultimately, it is probably a combination of political, economic, and cultural factors that lead to what American corporations call piracy in Asia. However, it is important to note that piracy exists everywhere because it is the inevitable result of a private property system. As strong international laws come into existence and as Asia continues to develop, piracy may decline. However, strong copyright and patent protection tends to halt innovation as protection of property replaces exchange of information. Thus, piracy will always be with us regardless of nationality because the act of being human means exchanging information, ideas, art, and music. It would make better sense for our "intellectual property laws" to reflect our systems of exchange (Litman, 2001). In the next section of this chapter, I would like to develop the argument that the open source revolution is a far better model for development than the proprietary system and one which countries in Asia should consider.

SHIFTING PARADIGMS: THE OPEN SOURCE REVOLUTION, AND POSSIBLE FUTURES

The growing power of Asian economies has transformed international trade. Countries such as Singapore, Hong Kong, Taiwan, and Korea specifically targeted information technology as the way in which they would become part of the world economy (Corbett and Wong, 1999; Hanna *et al.*, 1996). By focusing upon technological development, many Asian economies have been successful in creating a technologically sophisticated workforce and a networked economy. The successful strategic planning and futures thinking of many governments in Asia helped contribute to the economic success of the region (Hanna *et al.*, 1996).

One possible future for Asian economies, especially those NICs that are at the heart of information and technology development, is that they will become the intellectual property powerhouses of the future, much like Singapore has claimed they will be. Certainly, the shift to Asian-dominated technology markets continues as American companies outsource work to countries such as China, Singapore, Taiwan, and Indonesia to take advantage of cheaper labor markets. For example, American firms can hire Indian or Chinese computer programmers using the Internet to cross the geographical divide instantaneously. Not only can a company gain a twenty-four-hour workforce, but it can make use of a much cheaper labor force to do so (Linden, 1998). Given the shift of manufacturing to Asia, it is not too large a leap to assume that intellectual property industries, facilitated by the Internet, will also shift to Asia. After all, the global communications network that makes piracy a problem also creates enormous opportunities for business networks as well.

While Asia will be a dominant force in information technology industries, the critical transformation that must happen for countries such as China, Singapore, and South Korea to take advantage of the intellectual property system is to become technology innovators as well as technology producers. Technology development in Asia has relied on technology transfer, the purchase of proprietary systems from the United States, and piracy. None of these strategies will provide an adequate framework for Asian independence and/or economic domination without addressing a crucial development layer. If countries in Asia can become lead innovators in the area of communication technology development, then they will be able to take advantage of the current intellectual property system and dominate world markets. If, however, the critical step towards innovation and away from licensing already existing technology cannot be taken, the future will look less optimistic for Asian economic growth.

At the level of business development, there are very serious decisions that must be made. Technology is both an industry and a platform upon which business of all kinds is based. Who develops and owns this technology is important for the future viability of the economy. Thus, a second possible future scenario should be discussed. This future assumes that countries in Asia would like to see their business opportunities grow without the worry of claims of piracy and without the expensive licensing fees necessary to remain in the current intellectual property paradigm.

The open source movement may provide Asia with a viable alternative model for innovation that avoids many of the traps of proprietary systems. While the open source model applies specifically to software development, it serves as a valuable example of technological innovation that can be employed in an Internet-enabled world. It is important to note that while open source may have advantages, I use it here only as an example of an alternative to already existing intellectual property models. This alternative may be worth examining because of the fundamentally different approach it takes to the idea of ownership of information. Certainly, open source should not be seen as the solution to all the world's problems. However, it is a distinctly different paradigm of development that does not emphasize strong ownership and can allow us to think differently about intellectual property.

Asia Computer Weekly first publicized open source technology in Asian markets in 1999. Despite the fact that Linux was still in its infancy, the first Linux-based conference in Asia was held in 1999 and the open source revolution began to gain ground (Ramos, 1999). Many argued that Linux would provide a means for Asia to gain ground in the economic battlefield of high technology and that the open source movement would make Asia the next Silicon Valley (Keong, 2000). Robert Hart, an executive at Red Hat Asia-Pacific, noted that "Open source levels the playing field by breaking down the entry barriers put up by proprietary software companies" (Keong, 2000). For example, China developed an indigenous version, suited to its own needs, called Red Flag Linux (*AsiaPulse*, 2000). U-Jin Kim, chief executive of LinuxOne in Seoul, argued, "Most people think Linux is just an operating system. In Asia, it's an IT trend" (Rabano, 2000). The growth rate for Linux use in China, for example, is forecast at 50 percent each year for the next five years (Rabano, 2000).

There are significant commercial, practical, and philosophical advantages to the open source movement that should be considered by any country thinking strategically about the future. First, and crucial to developing countries, open source software is cheaper than proprietary software. Although the basic operating system is available for free over the Internet, technical support is available for about one-fifth of the cost of an original version of Windows 98 (Rabano, 2000; *TurboLinux News*, 2000). TurboLinux wants the Chinese to "pirate" their software and has handed out thousands of copies in order to create a critical mass (Speedie, 2000). Given the strategic advantage of cheaper software, it makes economic sense to move to open source, both as a means of developing an indigenous software industry and as a means of having access to the best software and the best prices.

In 1999, several Chinese domestic computer companies began shipping Linux as the operating system for their computers, as it is significantly cheaper than Windows and can be purchased more easily by the average Chinese family (McMahon, 1999). In 2001, IBM announced that it would spend US$200 million on Linux-based development in the Asia Pacific region in order to provide an alternative to proprietary operating systems, with the hope that it would improve its own business opportunities in the Asia Pacific region. According to IBM Asia Pacific President Kakutaro Kitashiro, Linux is gaining popularity in Japan, China, Korea, and India (*Computerworld*, 2001).

Moreover, licensing is easier, as open source technology does not come with monopolistic licenses. Open source, with its less restrictive licenses and its collaborative framework, establishes an ideal setting for growth in software development in the Asia Pacific region. As the Chief Operating Officer of MIMOS, a Malaysian computer company, said, "In the Malaysian context, this translates into the enablement and propagation of creative and innovative software development activities in a collaborative manner over the Internet" (Keong, 2000). In other words, Asian companies, and nations, have a greater chance of developing new technology models without becoming indebted to Western firms.

A second advantage of open source is the ability of local software companies to tailor code to specific needs. The specific software needs of Malaysia, Singapore, or China may be addressed more directly with an open source system. The building blocks are free, and each contribution furthers the greater good. Placing the good of the society ahead of the good of the individual, while still respecting and rewarding the work of the individual, is an important attribute of open source technology. Japanese and Chinese programmers are already creating their own open source programs engineered for the needs of Asian clients.

Third, open source gives Asian companies and institutions more control over their own operating systems. At least 75 percent of computer programming is done in-house as software engineers and systems operators do "vertical maintenance," or attempt to make various proprietary systems work in harmony, according to open source advocates (*Open Source Initiative Online*, 2001). Open source provides all programmers with access to a vast toolbox when writing software that can make a business more efficient. The company also has access to the "guts" of their programs. Businesses with proprietary software packages lose control over their business process because they cannot refine the programs, and this can cost more money (Raymond, 1999). In addition, unlike some proprietary packages which have "back doors" that allow the software vendor to deactivate the program if they feel it violates the licensing agreement, open source software is the property of the company (Minasi, 2000).

Finally, there are strong philosophical reasons for the growth of the open source movement. Open source begins from different assumptions than proprietary software about what motivates people to create the best possible program (Raymond, 1999; Torvalds and Diamond, 2001; Young and Rohn, 1999). Perhaps the most interesting advantage of the open source philosophy is the shift in meaning of piracy. It is only possible to "steal" information under open source by removing it from circulation, so it cannot be used by anybody, or using open source code without contributing back to the general community. Contrast this understanding of piracy with the more traditional definition – which defines any unauthorized use as an act of theft; unauthorized in this sense meaning that the original writer has not been given monetary compensation. By redefining the rules of the game, the "problem" of piracy is eliminated.

Open source recognizes that while programming is creative, it is also more efficient to copy or improve upon already existing code than to write a new program. Copyright, as it is traditionally conceived, prohibits this functional approach by walling off source code behind proprietary walls. Open source encourages sharing – even if sharing will disrupt proprietary boundaries.

The open source movement is an important alternative model to the global standards established by TRIPs and the WTO. Virtually all international agreements and organizations are devoted to stamping out a type of piracy that does not exist in the open source model. The open source model will eliminate piracy without the huge buildup in police power necessary for the current anti-piracy effort.

While open source technology may not be a panacea, it does help overcome some of the privatizing tendencies that may impact the future of information technology development in Asia. It is one possible alternative to proprietary systems that will allow for many Asian economies to continue to develop their information infrastructures without the overwhelming presence of intellectual property owners dictating their every move. In addition, open source allows for money to stay within the local economy instead of leaving for multinational headquarters in the form of licensing fees. Thus, not only will it be possible to develop resources that fit the needs of each economy more specifically, but it will also perhaps be possible to make the next logical leap towards competitiveness in information technology.

CONCLUSION

It may be argued that adopting some sort of open source paradigm might actually hinder the ability of Asia to compete globally by keeping countries that adopt open source models out of the economic loop. However, while it is certainly true that major multinationals which produce proprietary software see a threat from open source technology, it must be recognized that the Internet was created and remains primarily an open source model (Lessig, 2001). Much of the underlying software responsible for the day-to-day functions of the World Wide Web is open source. In fact, while this chapter argues that the open source model is appropriate as a computer software business model, open source software has long been the background of Internet communications. Thus, the viability of the open source model is the ease with which it can provide communication. Open source serves as an example of a larger idea. It is not an operating system so much as an attitude towards exchange and development in the information society. Open source stands in contrast to a development model that creates pirates by creating property. The two models may not be mutually exclusive, but they can provide interested parties with some development options, options that do not exist under the current intellectual property system.

While the open source battle is focused currently on the source code and computer programming levels of Internet development, it is clear the tension between open and closed systems should also be examined at other levels of information exchange made possible by the Internet. It is not entirely clear that a proprietary system of ownership is the best way to facilitate exchange in the information age. The Internet was based initially upon the premise of free exchange at all levels. The struggle to keep the source code level of the Internet free from privatization should provide an example for the areas of cultural communication.

The open source philosophy is enthralling because it provides a new set of rules that structurally eliminate piracy as a problem. If the core of what one sells is open, then the businessperson must focus on providing the best services in a market environment. This model has applications in many different areas of innovation. It is my contention that the law of intellectual property has moved too far in the direction of private property. Asia now has the opportunity to shift the debate back towards the public good.

BIBLIOGRAPHY

Alford, W. (1995) *To Steal a Book is an Elegant Offense: Intellectual Property Law in Chinese Civilization*, Stanford, CA: Stanford University Press.

Asia Pulse (2000) "Edgematrix partners Linux Group to deploy M commerce in HK," October 20 [Lexis-Nexis].

Bollier, D. (2002) *Silent Theft: The Private Plunder of our Common Wealth*, New York and London: Routledge.

Clark, D. (1999) "The many meanings of the rule of law," in K. Jayasuriya (ed.) *Law, Capitalism and Power in Asia: The Rule of Law and Legal Institutions*, London and New York: Routledge.

Computerworld (Philippines) (2001) "Philippines: IBM to spend $200m on Linux dev't in Asia," February 12.

Corbett, P.S. and Wong, Y. (1999) "Seeding the clouds of change: the planned evolution of Singapore into an intelligent island," in F.B. Tan, P.S. Corbett, and Y. Wong (eds) *Information Technology Diffusion in the Asia Pacific: Perspectives on Policy, Electronic Commerce and Education*, Hershey and London: Idea Group Publishing.

Correa, C.M. (2000) *Intellectual Property Rights, the WTO and Developing Countries: The TRIPs Agreement and Policy Options*, Penang: The Third World Network.

Crutsinger, M. (2000) "IMF: America's trade deficits and inflation pose risk to world markets," *The Associated Press*, September 11 [Lexis-Nexis].

Egan, M. (2000) "US imports swell to record level," *National Post*, September 14.

Evenson, R.E. (1992) "Intellectual property rights for appropriate invention," in

J.A. Roumasset and S. Barr (eds) *The Economics of Cooperation: East Asian Development and the Case for Pro-Market Intervention*, Boulder, CO: Westview Press.

Gilpin, R. (2000) *The Challenge of Global Capitalism: The World Economy in the 21st Century*, Princeton, NJ: Princeton University Press.

Grabosky, P., Smith, R.G., and Dempsey, G. (2001) *Electronic Theft: Unlawful Acquisition in Cyberspace*, Cambridge: Cambridge University Press.

Gutterman, A.S. and Anderson, B.J. (1997) *Intellectual Property in Global Markets: A Guide for Foreign Lawyers and Managers*, London, The Hague, Boston: Kluwer Law International.

Halbert, D. (1997) "Intellectual property piracy: the narrative construction of deviance," *International Journal for the Semiotics of Law*, 10, 28: 55–78.

Hanna, N., Boyson, S., and Gunaratne, S. (1996) "The East Asian miracle and information technology: strategic management of technological learning," World Bank Discussion Papers No. 326, Washington, DC.

Keong, L.M. (2000) "Showfloor: LinuxWorld Malaysia shows OS potential," *Asia Computer Weekly*, November 27 [Lexis-Nexis].

La Croix, S.J. (1992) "The political economy of intellectual property rights in developing countries," in J.A. Roumasset and S. Barr (eds) *The Economics of Cooperation: East Asian Development and the Case for Pro-Market Intervention*, Boulder, CO: Westview Press.

—— (1995) *The Rise of Global Intellectual Property Rights and Their Impact on Asia*, Honolulu, Hawaii: East-West Center.

Lessig, L. (2001) *The Future of Ideas: The Fate of the Commons in a Connected World*, New York: Random House.

Linden, E. (1998) *The Future in Plain Sight: The Rise of the "True Believers" and Other Clues to the Coming Instability*, New York: Plume Books.

Litman, J. (2001) *Digital Copyright*, Amherst: Prometheus Books.

McMahon, W.J. (1999) "TurboLinux strikes three bundling deals, extends China reach," *ChinaOnline*, December 8 [Lexis-Nexis].

Martin, B. (1998) *Information Liberation*, London: Freedom Press.

Maskus, K.E. (2000) "Intellectual property rights and economic development," *Case Western Reserve Journal of International Law*, 32: 471–506.

Minasi, M. (2000) *The Software Conspiracy: Why Software Companies Put Out Faulty Products, How they can Hurt You, and what You Can Do About It*, New York: McGraw Hill.

Negroponte, N. (1995) *Being Digital*, New York: Vintage Books.

Nerona, G.P. (2000) "The battle against software piracy: software copyright protection in the Philippines," *Pacific Rim Law & Policy*, 9: 651–80.

Open Source Initiative Online (2001) "Jobs for hackers: Yes, you can eat open source." Available HTTP: http://www.opensource.org/advocacy/jobs.html (accessed June 19, 2001).

Rabano, B. (2000) "The penguin takes flight," *Asiaweek*, 64, September 8.

Ramos, G.P. (1999) "Linux invasion seen starting next year," *Computerworld* (Philippines), July 15.

Raymond, E. (1999) *The Cathedral & the Bazaar: Musings on Linux and Open Source by an Accidental Revolutionary*, Beijing and Cambridge: O'Reilly.

Rose, M. (1993) *Authors and Owners: The Invention of Copyright*, London: Harvard University Press.

Rosser, A. (1999) "The political economy of institutional reform in Indonesia: the case of intellectual property law," in K. Jayasuriya (ed.) *Law, Capitalism and Power in Asia: The Rule of Law and Legal Institutions*, London and New York: Routledge.

Ryan, M.P. (1998) *Knowledge Diplomacy: Global Competition and the Politics of Intellectual Property*, Washington, DC: Brookings Institute Press.

Sell, S.K. (1998) *Power and Ideas: North-South Politics of Intellectual Property and Antitrust*, Albany: State University of New York Press.

Software and Information Industry Association (SIIA) (2000) *SIIA's Report on Global Software Piracy 2000*, Washington, DC.

Somerville, G. (2000) "US trade deficit reaches record high in June: 'no signs of going away'," *National Post*, August 19.

Speedie, A. (2000) "TurboLinux CEO follows Amazon's lead," *WideOpen News*, April 13. Online. Available HTTP: http://linuxtoday.com/news_story.php3?ltsn =2000-04-14-004-06-PS (accessed June 19, 2001).

Torvolds, L. and Diamond, D. (2001) *Just for Fun: The Story of an Accidental Revolutionary*, New York: HarperCollins.

TurboLinux News (2000) "TurboLinux outsells Windows in China," January 10. Online. Available HTTP: http://www.turbolinux.com/news/pr/federal.html (accessed June 19, 2001, hard copy on file with author).

Vaidhyanathan, S. (2001) *Copyrights and Copywrongs: The Rise of Intellectual Property and How it Threatens Creativity*, New York and London: New York University Press.

Young, R. and Rohm, W.G. (1999) *Under the Radar: How Red Hat Changed the Software Business – and Took Microsoft by Surprise*, Scottsdale, AZ: The Coriolis Group.

Yu, P.K. (2001) "Piracy, prejudice, and perspectives: an attempt to use Shakespeare to reconfigure the US-China intellectual property debate," *Boston University International Law Journal*, 19: 1–86.

Part II

Issues and impacts

Case studies

7 From real to virtual (and back again)

Civil society, public sphere, and the Internet in Indonesia

Merlyna Lim

The ability of the Internet to facilitate communication and distribution of information has caused many to identify it as the "new technology of democracy" – as the principal means to enable the expansion of a newly emerging public sphere of political discourse and decision-making actively involving civil society. Yet despite the utopian perspectives on the impact of the Internet upon global society, the Internet, as a technology originating in the U.S. but now existing all over the world, is always localized. Its democratic potential is thus indeterminate and must be worked out in the context of local constellations of power. As elsewhere, the Internet that has been developing in Indonesia has its own character and configuration as it is transformed in important ways by localized power structures.

Technological transformations are imbedded in these power relations, and localities – nations, cities, communities, including cyber-communities – are sites of the nexus struggles over the choice, use, and transformation of technologies such as the Internet. No one source of power is predetermined to "win" in these contests. Rather, dynamic tensions continue in a process of historical change, which, as an open-ended trajectory, allows human agency, when collectively empowered, to make a difference. Indonesia during and after the overthrow of the Suharto regime shows how such moments of the interplay of technology and society allows for the possibility of its people to make history.

In the relations among the state, corporate economy, and civil society, a focal point of contests of power is over the creation and assertion of identity. These contests over identity are driving forces that are interpreting and transforming technological processes of the Internet in Indonesia. More than merely creating a self-image that stands in relation to larger social, economic, and political forces, emerging identities is part of a struggle for power. In its extreme, such identities work against hegemonic systems of belief, loyalty, and action. This has been the case with the so-called "developmental state," which has used various controls and manipulation of media to cast a rigid identity congruent with political regimes that, in not a few cases, have remained in power for decades.

With the collapse of these regimes one by one, the new source of hegemony comes from globalization and takes the form of commodification of social relations that, through the accompanying neo-liberal policies dismantling state regulation over the economy, attempts to shift socio-political identities to those of citizen as consumer. At the same time, the rise of civil society as a potent political force interacts with state and capitalist identity formation, sometimes legitimizing them, other times resisting, and occasionally leading to mass mobilization to create alternative social projects centering on alternative identities. The Internet is intricately involved in these relationships, both as a means of communicating and forming identities, and as a technology that is transformed through shifting power relations that revolve, in part, around identity formation.

CIVIL SOCIETY, PUBLIC SPHERE, AND IDENTITY

Three concepts underlie the exploration of the Internet as a technology received and technology transformed in the context of the localized processes of social change. The first, *civil society*, refers to the organized face of society outside of direct state or capitalist control. This concepts draws from de Tocqueville's (1969) idea of voluntary association and Gramsci's (1971) separation of civil society from both the state and market in the public realm as being integral to processes of democratization and political participation by the masses.

The second term, *public sphere*, is given attention as a means to clarify a central point; namely that "public" does not simply indicate what the government oversees. Rather, it should be understood as a realm in which civil society and corporate interests form political communities and become engaged in relations of power along with the state. As such, the public sphere is conceptualized as a shifting forum situated between the private sphere and the sphere of public authorities (Habermas, 1989). This interplay between civil society and corporate interest directs action in the public sphere in both time and space.

In the triangle of relationships among civil society, the state, and the market, there are at least three widely observed configurations of power: (1) The authoritarian "developmental state" marked by the dominance of the state, though possibly in alliance with corporate interests as it suppresses civil society; (2) the now ascendant neo-liberal corporate economy model with its diminished state and transformation of society into individualized brand name consumers, and (3) the ideal of the active society marked by a public sphere mediated through civil society and its many organizational faces and forms. Which of these models will prevail is a question not only of whose voice will be empowered but is also equally one of a struggle over identity, which is itself both a source and expression of power.

Both state and market make use of the public sphere to create and assert their identities. The state, in its quest for legitimization, seeks to use media of all types to create images and symbols to make citizens identify with it as a positive force caring for society. Corporations seek to transform people into consumers who are loyal to and identify with certain brand names and, at a more general level, are aligned with the wonderful benefits of a supposed "free" market, despite the monopolistic tendencies of contemporary capitalism. At the same time, civil society struggles to create its own identities without the domination of those imposed by the state and market.

As noted above, the Internet is eminently suited to creating and disseminating visual symbols and stylized information that various actors call upon to create shared identities and accompanying social power when these coalesce. As such, the Internet is intricately part of the rise of civil society and the reformation of the public sphere in Indonesia. As a fundamental facet of human social existence (Castells, 1997), creating shared identity is one source of motivation in the use of the Internet technology. This tendency imbeds the Internet in a potentially larger societal process of political transformation revolving around identity struggles. While identity is multi-layered, and often contradictory, it provides "symbolic identification" which links a person to collective alliances that coalesce as resistance to globalization and the rise of network societies. Castells (1997) articulates three types of identity:

1   Legitimizing identity introduced by dominant institutions to extend and rationalize their domination.
2   Resistance identity generated by those who are devaluated or stigmatized by the logic of domination.
3   Project identity, or collective actions of people to build a new identity that redefines their position in society and, by so doing, seeks the transformation of the overall social-political structure.

Identities that start as resistance can induce projects and, in the course of history, may become dominant, but history is not linear and the values or identities must be viewed in the context of historical moments when they emerge or prevail. In the case of Indonesia, the world space of flows – the Internet society – descended on to the country at a juncture of traumatic socio-political transformation. The following sections look at how the Internet in Indonesia has developed in relation to the state–corporate–civil society struggles over identity in the public domain.

THE PRE-INTERNET ERA IN INDONESIA

With its history of Dutch colonization and independence, nation-building in Indonesia became a conscious political, cultural, and economic project of the state. Consequently, the control of communication and information flows also became important as a strategic tool for national integration. Media and telecommunications were seen as the most powerful tools to forge national unity. The Government of the Republic of Indonesia saw telecommunications and media as tools for "development," which was promoted as a central means of legitimizing the regime in power, notably the New Order regime of President Suharto, which lasted for thirty-two years from 1966 to 1998.

Television of the Republic of Indonesia (TVRI), established in 1962, functioned mainly in a development role that was designed to engender popular identity with the Suharto regime. It transmitted the same developmental and sanitized cultural programs in every city across the country. The ambition to "build unity" through media was manifested most clearly in the "television enters the village" program. Televisions were placed in village halls throughout the nation and served by a network of terrestrial broadcast transmitters (and after 1976 by a domestic satellite) – all of which were under the control of the state (Shoesmith, 1994).

The urge to use telecommunications to foster identity with the proclaimed developmentalist pursuits of the state became so great that Indonesia, a so-called Third World country with a per capita income of US$125 (in 1976), became the third country in the world to launch its own communications satellite, the Palapa satellite, which cost US$160 billion. The reasons for launching the satellite revolved around the government's purpose to more "emphatically reach and mark the perimeters of national cultural space, to link the boundaries of the far-flung archipelago to the centre and to each other, thus enabling Indonesians throughout the nation to be able to more effectively 'imagine their community'" (Kitley, 1994).

Thus, in contrast to de Sola Pool's declaration that "satellites are technologies of freedom" (1983), the advent of satellite technology in Indonesia removed freedom from society by strengthening the centralized control of the state over it. For more than three decades, radio and television broadcasts in Indonesia were directly employed as tools of state propaganda. Print-based information sources, such as newspapers and magazines, though mostly privately owned, were also under state control. Censorship and the outright banning and closing of news media were common during the New Order era. The government, through its Ministry of Information and pervasive policing capacities, could easily ban or shut down publications that displeased it. The ban of *Tempo* magazine in 1982 due to its incisive coverage of the general election and again in 1994 for a second time because of its controversial report on one of Habibie's[1] pet projects, are obvious examples of how the state protected its legitimacy by quashing press freedom. Indonesia under Suharto could fit appropriately within the classic definition of the state defined by Max Weber (1919) as the set of institutions having the "monopoly of violence." As this example shows, violence was not always physical, but was nonetheless directed towards controlling thinking and, more deliberatively, to constructing the identity of a progressive developmental state to sustain the Suharto regime.

Through its control of media, the state controlled the building of a national identity by filling up the public sphere with production and manipulation of images, symbols, and ideas. Through its propaganda (national agenda), it tried to build and sustain what Castells calls a "legitimizing identity" needed to remain in power in an archipelago of great diversity and always in potential opposition to the state's hegemonic tendencies.

Giant billboards on the streets, big pictures in the newspapers and television kept telling the success stories of the New Order regime under Suharto. The people of Indonesia were thoroughly influenced by such media saturation. Those who were not had no option but to yield to the identity of "development" created by the state. The public sphere was fully embedded in the state propaganda machinery.

THE INTERNET ERA IN INDONESIA

The coming of the Internet soon became highly instrumental in ending this episode, and has proven to be far more powerful in scope than the printed page, the electronic voice or televised picture. It is revolutionary in how it potentially allows citizens – and corporations – to bypass, finesse, and resist attempts by the state to control its access and use. As such, it creates new cyber-terrains of contests over identity in a potentially renewed public sphere for civil society in Indonesia.

This section begins with a brief history of the Internet in Indonesia that explains chronologically how the Internet was developed in Indonesia, followed by a story of Indonesian Internet – the *warnet* (the Internet café).

The Internet was introduced to Indonesia for the first time in the early 1980s, via the first Internet connection made by the University of Indonesia, which also brought Indonesia into UUNET in 1984, thus making it among the first nations in Asia to enter the Internet world. However, because of a lack of infrastructure, there was no permanent Internet link until 1994 (Lim, 2001).

In the early 1990s, Indonesia formally welcomed the idea of the Internet and the information superhighway. Pushed by the issue of being globally networked, "Habibie's kids" (a reference to that generation of technocrats who benefitted from the largesse of oil revenues and political vision of a high tech Indonesia of Habibie (Shiraishi, 1996)), endorsed the state's building of the first Internet network in Indonesia, IPTEK-Net (Science and Technology Network). BPPT (Agency For Assessment and Application of Technology), via its project IPTEK-Net, made the first permanent Internet link from Indonesia in 1994, showing the supremacy of government in purposely pioneering this technology, as it had also done with satellite technology in 1976.

With the arrival of private commercial ISPs (Internet service providers), the Internet had attained a public presence by 1995. At the end of 1995, there were an estimated 15,000 Internet users in Indonesia being serviced by five commercial ISPs, in addition to IPTEKnet. Over the following six months the figures mushroomed (Hill and Sen, 1997). At the end of 1997, there were nearly forty ISPs in Indonesia. However, the boom of ISPs in Indonesia never led to the Internet being widely used. It was still used only by certain social classes, namely people who were able to pay both telephone pulse and Internet subscription fees, and who had access to telephone lines and personal computers.

The international issue of the digital divide pushed the Indonesian government to build a national Internet program through a loan from the World Bank. However, the low telephone penetration, low Gross Domestic Product, lack of stable infrastructure, slow growth of Internet subscribers, and the economic crisis in 1997 led to the collapse both of the commercial Internet and the government's project.

Thus, an alternative form of commercial Internet that survived the crisis was the *warnet*, or the Internet café, which could potentially reach even the lower classes as it offered low-cost Internet access. While it is arguable who was the founder of *warnet*, it is undoubtedly clear that the ones who popularized the technology were the young people from the Computer Network Research Group (CNRG) at the Institute of Technology Bandung (ITB), namely Onno Purbo with some ITB fresh graduates and students (Lim, 2001). In 1997, through their company, Pointer, these young people established numerous *warnet* throughout Bandung and Jakarta. They also gave free seminars on *warnet* business that resulted in the extensive growth of numbers of *warnet* in Indonesia, particularly in Java and Bali.

THE *WARNET*: EVERYDAY FORMS OF THE INDONESIAN INTERNET

The term "*warung*" is usually used to describe a simple place where people may buy some food and gather with friends or family while eating the food. The *warnet* or "*warung*-Internet" usually consists of one (or more) room(s) with several computers hooked to the Internet and rented on an hourly basis.

Unlike connecting from home, office, or public library, for Indonesian youngsters, accessing the Internet from *warnet* is a direct form of social rendezvous. Using the *warnet* does not only mean accessing the Internet but also interacting with other *warnet* users. Many *warnet* users enjoy accessing the Internet in a group; they often choose a *warnet* with private lounge where they can relax by sitting on the floor and sharing some interesting URLs or listening to MP3 songs. The users who are concerned about personal privacy can go to a *warnet* with spaces partitioned by bamboo curtains which block others from seeing what they are doing on the computers. This privacy is particularly sought by users who want to access either politically dangerous or pornographic information.

The most frequent online activity in *warnet* is chatting. The new privacy created in chatrooms is particularly important for the youth. In online spaces they can be more independent from their parents or older generations than in offline spaces, especially concerning social relations between the sexes (Slama, 2002) and social engagement in politically related activities (Hill and Sen, 1997). While the *warnet* facilitates online social relationships created in cyberspace, a number of *warnet* are also places for creating offline relationships.

By allowing for online and offline relations, the *warnet* all over Indonesia have become the new frontier where Indonesians create and mold their identities, searching for self-respect, belonging, and the confidence to engage with fellow citizens of Indonesia beyond the purview of the state and other authorities (e.g. parents). The rising popularity of *warnet* is a testament to the growing awareness of its capacity to offer an alternative means of creating personal identity through social interaction.

INTERNET AND THE EMERGENCE OF RESISTANCE IDENTITIES

While the Internet in Indonesia, particularly the *warnet*, developed free from the interference of state and corporate agendas, it should not be romanticized as a virtuous sanctuary of social good and harmony. Socially irresponsible acts, such as the encouragement of violence of one group against another, can and are promoted on the Internet. At the same time, resistance alone does not easily counter hegemonic tendencies of global capital or the state–corporate nexus. In other words, the flowering of the Internet within society is itself fraught with pitfalls and misdirection, antagonisms, and even violence.

In 1997, the national postal service PT Pos Indonesia, through its ISP, WasantaraNet, jumped into the *warnet* business by establishing *warnet* in post offices. This is an ambitious national strategy to supply Internet access in all of Indonesia's provinces via local nodes and *warnet*. This effort from WasantaraNet was an attempt to maintain national stability by controlling the flow of information at the point of access (Lim, 2001). This was seen by some Indonesian youths as an invasion of the state and implied that the Internet no longer belonged to the "people" as they imaged it. One of these young people, the CyberBug – a hacker from one prominent group of Indonesian hackers named *Kecoak* (cockroach) – responded by creating a kind of Robin Hood resistance identity by "hacking" the Wasantara *warnet* billing system so the *warnet* users could avoid paying the amount of money due per minute of Internet use. But why did these hackers just try to hack the billing system of Wasantara and not other *warnet*? And why did they publish the method for hacking on the web (CyberBug, 2000)? The answer is because they wanted to gain a reputation as leaders of resistance to the power of the state, a movement of a new generation of hackers:

> Almost all of the new-generation hackers are anti-establishment, anti-oppression. A tyrannical government like that of Indonesia is suitable to be perceived as an enemy by these hackers. In the end, no matter how harsh are the state's authorized party measures against these intelligent people, it will be impossible to stop the hackers. As quoted from the Hacker Manifesto: you may stop me but you will not stop all of us.
>
> (Torremendez, 1997; translation by author)

Another important example of individual resistance concerns the case of KlikBCA, the e-banking website of Indonesia's biggest bank, Bank Central Asia (BCA). In this case, Steven Haryanto used his own money to buy domain names similar to "klikbca" – www.klikbca.com. He bought www.klikbca.com, kilkbca.com, clikbca.com, klickbca.com, and klikbca.com, and then put the identical copies of the original website in these websites. His typo-error logic was proven right. From these websites, he got about 150 BCA customers to give their names and their personal identification numbers (PIN). However, he had not acted with criminal intent, as he never used the user names and PINs, and gave all of the data back to the BCA. He also registered his original name with a complete address as the owner of those websites. As he stated in his open letter to the public, his intention was only to "make the Internet banking users more aware about the security system" (Haryanto, 2001).

Haryanto had created a resistance identity, which could be seen as being destructive and as a misinterpretation of the freedom of the Internet through his notorious action. Yet, it also caused some to pause to think about such episodes in terms of how corporate actors occupy the Internet without considering the rights of consumers to the security of their accounts (S'to, 2001a, 2001b).

WARNET: THE VICTORY OF CIVIL SOCIETY – THE ASSOCIATION IS VIRTUAL, THE FIGHT IS REAL

While the above examples show how resistance identities can sporadically emerge, disappear and re-emerge within the context of the *warnet*, the final example below shows how resistance can be transformed into a social project through an organized political reform movement, marking the victory of civil society against the domination of the state.

What started as a mailing list (asosiasi-warnet@yahoogroups.com) became a virtual organization to discuss *warnet*-related issues. However, it developed later into a space for discussions on a wide choice of topics, ranging from technical computer-related problems to topics such as the monopoly power of the state-owned company and telecommunications regulations and policies. The list had its own motto: "The association is virtual, the fight is real." In May, 2000 the active members of this mailing list met and legally established their association, AWARI (AWARI, 2001 [Asosiasi Warnet Indonesia – Association of Internet Kiosks in Indonesia]). Although all agenda items were still arranged through the virtual space, resistance against the state monopoly (Telkom) accelerated through the discussions and conversations in the list. This led ultimately to the creation of a real world project of building an alternative to the state-run system. The project was manifested in a boycott against an increase in the telephone tariff, followed by a street demonstration, a boycott against the Ministry of Communications regarding licensing the Internet industry, and other resistance actions. Meanwhile, at the local neighborhood and city levels, unaffiliated *warnet* associations also began to emerge in response to two needs: to prevent price competition, and sharing of bandwidth (Lim, 2001). While perhaps modest or narrow in focus, this association reveals how the creation of an open-ended bulletin board was transformed into a successful project to resist state control and maintain alternative avenues of access to the Internet as a principal means for social interaction and identity formation.

THE INTERNET AND *REFORMASI*[2] (POLITICAL REFORMATION)

Although Marcus (1999) asserts that the political revolution in Indonesia was Internet driven, the Internet was not the sole driver for the reformation. Internet users in Indonesia numbered just 1 percent of the population (less than 2,000,000 in 1998), making it impossible for the Internet to create any major movement in Indonesia alone. Yet, in 1998 there was no other source of information other than the Internet that was free from the control of the state. It is important to note that for Indonesians there were two types of information that were forbidden: alternative politics or ideologies not in line with those of the state, and sex-related or pornographic materials. With the coming of the Internet, however, there was suddenly no barrier to accessing such information. The survey done by SCoT Research Group showed that about 90 percent of male *warnet* users access pornographic sites. Political information is not yet a competitor to pornography. However, at particular moments, accessing political information can become a major activity of *warnet* users in Indonesia. During the reformation struggle against Suharto's government, *warnet* was the major source of "forbidden" information, although there were other sources such as shortwave foreign news broadcasts, campus rumor networks, and faxed and photocopied underground bulletins.

With the ability to bypass the intervention of the state in connecting with the rest of the world, the Internet in the late 1990s provided the space for dialogs and information exchanges for people, especially for Indonesians who were suppressed under Suharto's regime. The global–local connection has undermined not only the ability but also the legitimacy of the state in controlling information. When citizens are made aware through the Internet of all sorts of alternative sources of information that are not dangerous to their sense of well-being, the idea of allowing the state to control these sources and the Internet is questioned and even rejected – either overtly by public acts of resistance or covertly through underground information networks using the Internet. Through global–local contacts and the building of discussion lists over the Internet during the reformation period, the Internet became the site of a renewed public sphere that allowed society to have dialogs without interference from the state.

A famous mailing list, *Apakabar*, is a perfect example to show the new social autonomy from the state. Started by an American, John McDougall, *Apakabar* forwarded Indonesian-related news and articles to its subscribers from all over the world. Most of the information/news it brought was not available in Indonesia. As it developed, it became one of the main sources for uncensored news and discussion on Indonesia. From 1996 to 1998, this list became a major irritant for the army and the Ministry of Information, and it helped to establish the Internet's reputation as a radically free medium (Hill and Sen, 1997).

Global–local relations among Indonesians who were in and out of the country generated massive amounts of previously banned information through the Internet. George Aditjondro,[3] an Indonesian professor who lives in Australia, was among the main sources of such information. He had been spreading thousands of email messages about the corrupt businesses of Suharto and his cronies. The list of the wealth of Suharto's family was typed on emails and spread to many places as free information. Indonesian students and youth abroad in Germany (through *Pijar*, an email-based newsletter and *Suara Demokrasi* [Voice of Democracy], a web-based newsletter) the US (through *Parokinet*, a mailing list) and other countries also made use of global–local contacts by their websites and mailing lists to infuse Indonesian society with information and provide Indonesians with the space for political discussions.

The Internet also has the power to create opportunities for people to speak and to create their identities freely. In addition to mailing lists created by young educated people, political parties also took advantage of the open information system of the Internet. The party in opposition to *Golkar* (Suharto's party), the Democratic People of Indonesia in Struggle (*PDI Perjuangan*) under Megawati Sukarno, put together a homepage about Megawati and her party to raise public sympathy for this repressed party (Wirantaprawira, 1998). The Indonesian Communist Party (PKI), which had been banned for more than thirty years, appeared again on the Internet, and no government official could effectively ban it (Komunis, 1999).

One instance of the capacity of the Internet to challenge the New Order cordons of police is the presence on the Net of the Democratic People's Party (PRD) (PRD, 1999), a small pro-labor, largely student-based party. Despite a government crackdown on the PRD, the trial and continuing detention of the party leadership and the harassment of the rank and file, the PRD continued posting on the World Wide Web and on *Apakabar*, maintaining its profile and openly challenging the government, and contributing to the downfall of the Suharto regime.

Because of suppression by the state, young people in Indonesia could not be exposed to alternative philosophies, beliefs, religions, or other ways of thinking. *Pancasila* was the only way of thinking.[4] Communism was seen particularly as a "latent danger" that could ruin society.[5] Many books related to communism and socialism never entered the country, and books of leftist Indonesian authors, such as Pramoedya Ananta Toer, were banned. Speaking about communism, or reading or owning a book about it could lead to years in jail. Through the Internet, however, Indonesian youth could show their resistance to the state. One group, The People's Resistance in Indonesia (CSVI, 2002), consisted of some young Indonesians in the Netherlands who defied the state by providing information about Marxism, leftist parties, and the Liberation Movement, East Timor, the Indonesian Communist Party, Pramoedya Ananta Toer, *Tapol*,[6] and other left-wing perspectives and information. These examples show how the Internet enabled people to circumvent the control of the Minister of Information or the authorized apparatus of the state upholding Suharto's rule.

THE *"REFORMASI"*: FROM REAL TO VIRTUAL AND BACK AGAIN

As noted above, the Internet has been crucial, but it is not the sole source of support for reformation. Megawati and PDI Perjuangan still had to go to the streets to get support. PRD still had to hold road shows at universities to obtain votes from students. Students and youth still had to make Internet-based information available for a wider range of society by transforming it to readable printed media (see Figure 7.1). This began to occur in early 1998, just before the fall of Suharto, when unprecedented amounts of information from the Internet became available on the street. As mentioned above, the most dominant information was the list of Suharto's wealth originally written by George Aditjondro. Students at the university

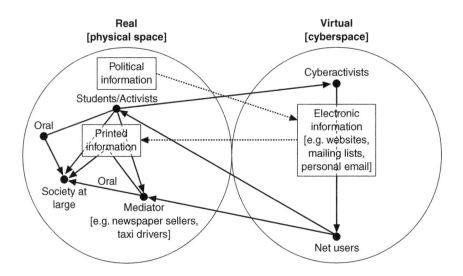

Figure 7.1 Flow of information: from real to virtual and back again

campus, *warnet*, and schools spread the printed version of this information. Newspaper sellers were selling photocopied versions of this information on the street. In Bandung, for example, one sheet of the list of
Suharto's wealth was being sold for just one US dollar. This information
filled a void for people who for so long had been trying to find "who is to
blame for the crisis." Upon learning that Suharto gained so much money
from his corrupt business, public opinion started to build against him.

As information reached more people, the resistance identity against
Suharto also spread, particularly among students and young people. As a
broad collective resistance identity was forming, the stage was set for it to
be transformed into a project identity. The "people" became collectively
self-empowered and the right moment to confront the state was born.
Using different kinds of communications technologies, including the telephone, fax, cellular phone, and particularly email, students mobilized
people to move to the streets and to occupy strategic places to challenge
the cordon of the authoritarian state. Finally, in May, 1998, thousands of
demonstrators representing diverse civil society groupings gathered at and
occupied the parliamentary building in Jakarta, ultimately forcing Suharto
– the President of Indonesia for thirty-two years – to resign from office.

The Internet played a crucial role in this process by providing otherwise
inaccessible information and thus challenging centralized information from
the government.

CONCLUSION

In the Preface of his book, *The Structural Transformation of the Public Sphere*, Habermas (1989) argues that the liberal public sphere is peculiar and historically unprecedented, as well as a non-transferable historical reality. Thus, we may ask whether cyberspace (the Internet) constitutes an authentic political or public sphere of this type. Yet, in the case of Indonesia, the Internet has clearly contributed a new space enabling the rise of civil society.

Will these public spaces become a beneficial public sphere that can contribute to the body politic in Indonesia? Will these cyber-communities help create the civil institutions that constitute a more democratic political reality in Indonesia? Will resistance identities emerging from these spaces become identity projects that lead Indonesia towards democratization? The cases of the *warnet* Association and *Reformasi* provide some answers to these questions. The virtual community has created a civil community that has been able to shift its action from resistance identity to project identity, thereby contributing to a more democratic society in Indonesia through fundamental political reform. But this is also only one particular case. No one can guarantee that all public spaces – or even all cyberspaces – will function as effectively as in the case of these examples. Resistance identities that emerge sporadically will not automatically transform themselves into project identities. The idealized public sphere will not just appear by the miracle of the Internet.

Habermas (1989) did not envision the Internet when he constructed his well-known model of the public sphere, and he might not believe that civil society could arise from electronic networks. As detailed in this chapter, however, it is clear that the Internet has contributed to the re-emergence of civil society in Indonesia. Moreover, the Internet is impacting all components of the public sphere – media, conversation, public opinion, action (Katz, 1997). Yet, contrary to utopian perspectives, which suggest that the Internet approximates an egalitarian world where equal distribution of information and conversation lead to a new and better democracy, in fact the Net can also create contrary outcomes. The fact that in Indonesia the Internet is available to only a small percentage of the population, such as the highly educated, shows that the Internet is at this point unequal, providing an overabundance of information for one group while it remains inaccessible for the majority. Moreover, it is entirely possible that the Internet can be used for factions of civil society to plot violence against others.

Recognizing the many possibilities of the Internet, this chapter is presented as an invitation to see that the Internet is powerful but is not neutral to power. By locating it within the triangle of state, corporate business, and civil society, it goes beyond the usual treatments of the Internet as only a technology by showing how the Internet and society shape and reshape each other. By inserting the question of democracy into the discourse, technology is given purpose beyond a socio-techno phenomenon, allowing an examination of the Internet as a means for political reform.

Pursuing the issue of social purpose reveals the drivers behind the shift towards more democratic practices throughout the world. The rise of an urban middle class demanding more freedoms from the state is an important element in this process. Others include the contradictory process of globalization, which both promises more freedom while enclosing the world into spheres of corporate monopolies over information, ideas, and knowledge. In both instances, the push for democracy is fundamentally a manifestation of the use of human agency to create meaningful identities beyond the grasp of state and corporate power. The Internet, in providing a new site for this struggle, has become a potentially vital public sphere. Will it continue to contribute to the actual material and social support for the better future of this country? This is the question now at hand in Indonesia.

NOTES

1 Habibie enjoyed President Suharto's patronage for more than twenty years, and was Minister of Research and Technology from 1978 to 1997; he was then appointed vice-president and became interim President when Suharto was ousted in 1998.
2 *Reformasi* which could be directly translated as "reformation" is a term to describe the period after the fall of Suharto in May, 1998.
3 George Aditjondro is a lecturer at the University of New Castle. He fled the country after his lecture about the oligarchy practices of Suharto and his cronies was claimed as politically dangerous.
4 *Pancasila* is the name of the foundation of Indonesia as a nation; directly translated as "five principle."
5 Suharto used the term *"bahaya laten"* (latent danger) for communism to emphasize that the communism that he had conquered (in 1967) had always existed and people had to be aware of it and see it as an enemy, a big danger.
6 *Tapol* is an abbreviation of *tahanan politik*, which is translated directly as *political prisoner*. During Suharto's era it had been taboo to talk about this issue, since most of the political prisoners were related to the Indonesia Communist Party (PKI).

BIBLIOGRAPHY

AWARI (2001) *Tentang Awari: Sejarah Asosiasi Warnet* (About Awari: the history of Internet Kiosk Association). Online. Available HTTP: http://www.warnet. or.id/1,01,4,07,00.html (accessed March 31, 2001).
Castells, M. (1997) *The Power of Identity: The Information Age – Economy, Society, and Culture*, London: Blackwell.
CSVI (2002) *The People's Resistance in Indonesia*. Online. Available HTTP: http://www.xs4all.nl/~peace/ (accessed July 1, 2002).

Cyberbug (2000) *Bobol WarPosNet* (Infiltrating the WasPosNet). Online. Available HTTP: http://www.k-elektronik.org/ezine/bobol-warposnet.txt (accessed July 1, 2002).

de Tocqueville, A. (1969) *Democracy in America*, ed. J.P. Mayer, Garden City: Doubleday.

Gramsci, A. (1971) *Selections from the Prison Notebooks*, London: Lawrence & Wishart.

Habermas, J. (1989) *The Structural Transformation of the Public Sphere*, trans. T. Burger, Cambridge, MA: MIT Press.

Haryanto, S. (2001) *Surat Permintaan Maaf* (The letter of apology). Online. Available HTTP: http://www.master.web.id/tutorial/wawancara/klikbca.htm (accessed July 1, 2002).

Hill, D. and Sen, K. (1997) "Wiring the Warung to global gateways: the Internet in Indonesia," *Indonesia*, 63: 67–89.

Katz, J. (1997) *Media Rants: Postpolitics in the Digital Nation*, San Francisco, CA: Hardwired.

Kitley, P. (1994) "Fine tuning control: commercial television in Indonesia," *Continuum: The Australian Journal of Media and Culture*, 8: 103–23.

Komunis (1999) *Partai Komunis Indonesia* (Indonesia Communist Party). Online. Available HTTP: http://www.geocities.com/CapitolHill/Lobby/9480/ (accessed March 31, 2001).

Lim, M. (2001) "The Internet in Indonesia: case study summary," in J. Barker, T. Argo, M. Lim, A. Rip and S. Yuliar (eds) *Social Construction in the Indonesian Context*, project number 95-CS-03, unpublished final research report, KNAW, University of Twente, Enschede.

Marcus, D.L. (1999) "Indonesia revolt was Net driven," in E. Aspinall, G. Klinken and H. van Feith (eds) *The Last Days of President Suharto*, Australia: Monash Asia Institute.

Pool, I.D.S. (1983) *Technologies of Freedom*, Cambridge, MA and London: Harvard University Press.

PRD (1999) *Partai Rakyat Demokratik* (Democratic People's Party). Online. Available HTTP: http://www.xs4all.nl/~peace/pubeng/mov/mov.html (accessed July 1, 2002).

S'to (2001a) *Peringatan Serius: Hati-hati Mengetikkan Klikbca.com* (Serious warning: be careful when typing klikbca.com). Online. Available HTTP: http://www.jasakom.com/Artikel.asp?ID=121 (July 1, 2002).

—— (2001b) *Perkembangan Lanjutan atas Kasus KlikBCA.COM* (Further development of the klikbca.com case). Online. Available HTTP: http://www.jasakom.com/Artikel.asp?ID=125 (accessed July 1, 2002).

Shiraishi, T. (1996) "Rewiring the Indonesian state," in D.S. Lev and Ruth McVey (eds) *Making Indonesia*, Ithaca, NY: Cornell University Press.

Shoesmith, B. (1994) "Asia in their shadow: satellites and Asia," *Southeast Asian Journal of Social Science*, 22: 125–41.

Slama, M. (2002) "Towards a new autonomy: Internet practices of Indonesian youth – conditions and consequences," paper delivered to the Third International Symposium of Anthropology Indonesia Journal, July 16–19, Denpasar.

Torremendez, C. (1997) *Situasi Perhackingan di Indonesia* (The hacking situation in Indonesia). Online. Available HTTP: http://www.k-elektronik.org/ezine/situasi.htm (accessed July 1, 2002).

Weber, M.M. (1919, reprinted in 1946) "Politics as a vocation," in H.H. Gerth and C.W. Mills (eds) *From Max Weber: Essays in Sociology*, trans. H.H. Gerth and C.W. Mills, New York: Oxford University Press.

Wirantaprawira, W.R. (1998) *Homepage Megawati* Soekarnoputri@Internet. Online. Available HTTP: http://megawati.forpresident.com (accessed July 1, 2002).

8 Malaysiakini.com and its impact on journalism and politics in Malaysia

James Chin

THE DEVELOPMENT OF MALAYSIAKINI.COM

Malaysia is widely regarded as a semi-democracy, with some of her harshest critics calling the Mahathir administration an authoritarian regime (see e.g. Case, 1992; Crouch, 1996; Alatas, 1997). The ruling coalition directly and indirectly controls all the mainstream media outlets in Malaysia, and media reporting cannot be described as fair or impartial. Information Minister Tan Sri Khalil Yaakob best summed up this policy by publicly declaring that:

> The Government pays for RTM's (Radio Television Malaysia) employees and the equipment used. So whoever is in the Government get to use RTM as their mouthpiece to air their manifesto and promises during a general election ... RTM is not interested in inviting any opposition party for interviews over its channels. This has been our practice.
>
> (*The Star*, July 3, 1999)

As a result of this policy, the mainstream media in Malaysia often will not cover articles critical of the government, the business interests of the political elite, and related stories of high-level nepotism, corruption, and cronyism. The most sensitive stories are those related to Mahathir and the royals. A prime example of this is the annual "10 Worst Enemies of the Press" list issued by the international NGO Committee to Protect Journalists (www.cpj.org). Mahathir is a regular fixture on the list but his name has never been printed when the list is published by the Malaysian mainstream press. In 2000, *Nanyang Siang Pau*, a leading Chinese daily, replaced Mahathir's name with the euphemism "a leader of Malaysia" when it published the list on one of the inside pages. Not surprisingly, none of the other English or Bahasa dailies in Malaysia carried the CPJ list or the report (*Nanyang Siang Pau*, May 3, 2000).

Besides outright censorship, this political climate has led also to self-censorship on the part of Malaysian journalists. Generally speaking, these journalists are conservative in reporting sensitive political stories, knowing full well the consequences of writing stories that would offend those in power. Many journalists simply do not file sensitive stories, as they fully expect that such stories would be "spiked" or, worse, they would be formally reprimanded by the "atas" (those at the top). In some cases, journalists who wrote stories that displeased the government or the media owners were transferred or put "on ice."[1] The end result is that political journalists in Malaysia write stories that reflect the government's view or, in some cases, simply reproduce the government's press statements. Those with political or career ambitions sometimes even distort the views of the opposition, hoping to gain favor with the ruling authority.

Within this environment, Malaysia offers an interesting case study of online newspapers and their possible niche as a source of alternative news, thereby breaking the regime's monopoly on the flow of news and information. Online newspapers in Malaysia are a relatively new phenomenon. The earliest online newspapers were the cyber version of "hard copy" dailies such as *The Star*, *The New Straits Times*, and their Bahasa Malaysia and Chinese counterparts. Because these papers are tightly controlled by the government through various restrictive legislation and ownership structures, they are widely regarded as an extension of the ruling regime and many dismiss their reportage. Genuine online newspapers (i.e. those without a hard-copy version) that target a Malaysian audience appeared only in 1999.

The first, most prominent and influential news portal is Malaysiakini.com (hereafter MK.Com). Malaysiakini.com ("Malaysia Now") was formed by two friends with a long history of social activism: Steven Gan and Premesh Chandran (*Asiaweek*, 2000). Both were student activists at the University of New South Wales in Australia in the mid-1980s. They were heavily involved in student politics and Gan was one of the first Malaysians to be elected to the UNSW Student Representative Council, the main student governing body. Together with other Malaysian students, they took a highly critical stand against the ruling Barisan Nasional (BN) regime back in Malaysia. During the 1987 crackdown in Malaysia, they criticized the use of the Internal Security Act (ISA), an instrument allowing authorities to detain persons without trial.

Upon returning to Malaysia, Gan pursued an orthodox career in the mainstream Malaysian press, working at several newspapers, including *The Sun*. Premesh Chandran spent a year at *The Sun* before he left for further studies in the Netherlands. Upon his return to Malaysia, he worked with the Malaysian Trades Union Congress (MTUC). Both remained active in the NGO/Human rights circle in Malaysia. In 1996, Gan was declared to be a prisoner of conscience by Amnesty International after he was arrested at the Asia Pacific Conference on East Timor (Apcet II) held in Kuala Lumpur. When his editors at *The Sun* refused to run his story on Apcet II, he resigned and moved to *The Nation*, a Bangkok daily.

The trigger for MK.Com's founding was the arrest of Deputy Prime Minister Anwar Ibrahim in 1998. By this time email and news groups were used widely by the *reformasi* supporters to exchange news and information, and to organize meetings and street protests. The setting up of an online newspaper was a natural progression. What the *reformasi* movement needed was a credible source of news to counter the government's propaganda in the mainstream media. Through Gan's contacts in Bangkok, MK.Com was able to secure US$100,000 (approximately RM380,000) in seed money from the Southeast Asian Press Alliance (SEAPA). SEAPA was founded in 1998 by journalists from Thailand, Indonesia, and the Philippines, to promote free media in the ASEAN countries. On top of the grant, Gan and Pramesh also invested their personal funds in MK.Com. MK.Com went "live" in October 1999, a year after Anwar's arrest.

Within a short time, MK.Com was able to draw other reform-minded journalists into its ranks. For example, Fathi Aris Omar, the Bahasa news editor, is a social activist with a long history of Islamic activism going back to his student days. He was editor of *Detik* (the Malay current affairs magazine banned in March, 1999) and *Perspektif* (a Muslim NGO publication), correspondent for *Utusan Sarawak* and occasional contributor to *Berita Harian, Utusan Malaysia, Harakah*, and *Massa*. Other senior journalists such as S. Vicknesan, Zakiah Koya and K. Kabilan worked for the *New Straits Times* for many years before joining MK.Com.

MK.Com's success in drawing surfers to its site was spectacular. Within months, its readership even surpassed the expectations of its founders, and within a context of declining news readership. Market research firm AC Nielsen in 2001 found that readership among Malaysia's Malay, English, and Chinese language newspapers had declined significantly over the period 1998 to 2000. The worst hit was the establishment English daily, the *New Straits Times*, which saw a 34 percent drop in readership. It was followed by the two most important Bahasa dailies, *Berita Harian* (down 30 percent) and *Utusan Malaysia* (down 27 percent). Even *The Star*, regarded by many as more independent in its coverage, lost 6.3 percent of its readership, while the leading Chinese daily, *Sin Chew Jit Poh*, lost 1.7 percent (AC Nielson, 2000).

This decline of print media coincided with a sharp rise in the popularity of Internet newspapers. Asian Media Report reported that MK.Com had 116,000 readers a day. MK.Com was so popular that over a week in July 2000, its server crashed due to the heavy traffic volume. Its regular readers immediately thought that the government had blocked access to the site. As a result, the ISP hosting MK.Com in North America demanded more money to handle the extra traffic. MK.Com refused to pay more and the North American site was closed on July 24 when MK.Com installed new servers in Malaysia. A new US mirror-site was later established.

MK.Com's success was not unique. Other *reformasi* and anti-government websites such as Harakah (Harakahdaily.com), the newsletter of the main opposition party, Parti Islam Malaysia (PAS), get more than 140,000 page views daily. Another popular site is Freeanwar.com. What was unique about MK.Com was its explicit selling point as an online newspaper with daily independent reporting of Malaysian affairs. All the other *reformasi* and anti-government sites do not have daily updates, nor do they claim to provide an independent source of Malaysian news. MK.Com's readership, however, reflected a very influential sector of society, as more than 90 percent of its readers are professionals and in senior management (Gan, 2002).

In its two years of existence as an online newspaper unfettered by the regulations of the state, MK.Com was an effective broadcast channel for alternative news stories and a home for more outspoken journalists.

MK.Com's image as an independent online newspaper providing an unbiased source of Malaysian news was significant, as many of the news items that appeared in MK.Com would not be carried by the mainstream media. This allowed MK.Com to claim several "exclusives" and "scoops."

In order to assess its political impact, it is helpful to review some of the major stories that first appeared on MK.Com. One of the most relevant of these examples occurred during the short campaign period in the 1999 general elections. *Sin Chew Jit Poh*, the leading Chinese newspaper in the country, published a front-page photo of all the BN leaders standing behind the Prime Minister, Dr. Mahathir Mohammed, an image that was meant to portray the unity of the BN coalition facing the elections as a single political unit. The event, unfortunately, had not occurred at all. The picture was real, but it was taken at an event a few years earlier. It had been modified electronically and Anwar Ibrahim (who was standing next to Mahathir) was digitally replaced by his successor Abdullah Ahmad Badawi. When MK.Com broke the story, the editor of *Sin Chew* was forced to make a public apology.

MK.Com also broke a story about how major mainstream English and Malay newspapers refused to accept paid advertisements by the opposition Barisan Alternatif (BA), in many cases without even looking over them. *The Star*, which later carried a few of the advertisements, refused to publish a BA advertisement which showed the infamous photo of Anwar Ibrahim sporting a black eye, the result of a beating by the Inspector-General of Police.

Moreover, MK.Com published a series of reports ("Bowman Papers") which alleged that Chief Justice Eusoff Chin[2] and V.K. Lingam, a prominent lawyer, were unusually close friends and this may have compromised the impartiality of the courts towards Lingam. The allegations include Lingam paying for Chin's holidays overseas and that Lingam even wrote the judgment for a case in which he was a litigant.

Another significant contribution which MK.Com made within Malaysia's political scene was the first news about rifts within a major opposition party. Just a month after the 1999 general elections, Marina Yusoff, KeADILan[3] vice-president, wrote a scathing letter attacking the conduct of Chandra Muzaffar, KeADILan's deputy president. The letter revealed in detail the deep rifts within the opposition party.

Moreover, it was not just the main political party that came under investigation, but MK.Com was also the first to publish allegations against the Sultan of Pahang. In March, 2001, MK.Com published a three-part article containing allegations by a Filipina nurse that she bore an illegitimate daughter to the Sultan of Pahang, a powerful figure in Malaysia, in what she claimed was a forced sexual affair. In Malaysia, stories about the excesses of the royal families, and especially the Sultans, are taboo. Although the full story is not known, it seems that the Filipina had used MK.Com to publicize her plight because secret negotiations between herself and the Sultan over maintenance and inheritance arrangements had broken down. Since there was no follow-up on the financial settlements, it appears that the tactic worked, suggesting that the Sultan's representatives were unwilling to risk further disclosure and gave in to her financial demands.

In all four cases, it is unlikely that any of the mainstream papers would have printed these stories. Certainly they did not do so, either before or after the story broke online, suggesting that there are still out-of-bounds areas for the mainstream media. However, there are also a number of examples where the mainstream newspapers ran otherwise-banned stories after they appeared on MK.Com. For example, when key office holders in the Malaysian Chinese Association (MCA) fought over the leadership of the party in early 2002, MK.Com reported that Prime Minister Mahathir had forced an agreement whereby both men would resign prior to the next general elections. While this agreement was well known among working journalists, no mainstream newspapers were able to print the story until MK.Com ran it. A day later, the story appeared in *The Star*, carrying a denial from Mahathir that there was such an agreement (*The Star*, March 27, 2002). The publication of these stories in offline mainstream papers is justified by the editorial argument that since the public had already seen the MK.Com story, it would look foolish if the mainstream papers did not cover it.

The greatest impact, however, of MK.Com's political reporting was during the 1999 general elections. Many in the opposition camp credited MK.Com (and the Internet generally) with giving them an opportunity to get their message across to the polity. Opposition political parties firmly believe that the Internet became the major medium to transmit their views to the public. The only complaint was that most of the readers were young, and may not be eligible to vote, or non-voters. During elections, it was common for the opposition to suffer a "blackout" in the mainstream media, in which only negative stories about them appeared (Commonwealth Observer Group, 1990).

During the 1999 elections, it was not uncommon for the opposition to print hard copies of MK.Com's news and to distribute it during *ceremahs* (political gatherings). These news items, especially those in the Bahasa Malaysia language, were widely distributed in the rural areas where most of the Malay population live. It is unclear if this helped the opposition to win any seats, but they certainly managed to break the monopoly of Bahasa news hitherto enjoyed by the mainstream Bahasa dailies such as *Utusan Malaysia* and *Berita Harian*.

By giving space to stories that would otherwise be "spiked" by the mainstream media, MK.Com succeeded in creating a bigger political space for the opposition in Malaysia. Traditionally, the Malaysian opposition are handicapped by an inability to get their views out to the public. Typically, the mainstream media within Malaysia, especially the broadcast media, run few positive stories about the opposition. Instead, they concentrate on negative stories, such as factional fights or infighting between and within opposition parties. Cases of deliberate misreporting to make the opposition look bad among the general public occurs, especially during electoral campaign periods or when the government comes under severe political pressure.

While most people see MK.Com as an independent media, many forget its role in promoting alternative voices or giving space to marginalized groups in society. Many of MK.Com's columnists are banned from the mainstream media and MK.Com provides them with a platform for a free market of ideas. Some of these columnists were contributors in the mainstream media before their columns were killed off for offending the government. An example is former *New Straits Times* columnist Amir Muhammad, whose popular "Perforated Sheets" column was apparently considered anti-establishment. When told that his column would no longer appear, he promptly defected to MK.Com where he writes the same themes under the new title "Counter Culture." Without the presence of MK.Com, Amir would have simply disappeared from the mass media and the only outlet for his writings would be a self-published book.

Another example is James Wong Win On. Wong, a former Member of Parliament representing the Democratic Action Party (DAP), who worked as a columnist and leader writer for *Sin Chew Jit Poh*, the bestselling Chinese daily in Malaysia. He resigned in protest over the sale of *Nanyang Siang Pau*, *Sin Chew's* main rival, to the Malaysian Chinese Association (MCA), the Chinese wing of the ruling BN. Wong resigned because he knew that he could still reach his readers through MK.Com. Together with MK.Com, he established Strategic Analysis Malaysia (SAM), a website that provides in-depth analysis of Malaysian politics. Other columnists such as Hishamuddin Rais, a former student activist, would likely not have been given a regular column in the mainstream press (at the time of writing, Rias was detained under the Internal Security Act (ISA), which allows for detention without trial).

Another area where MK.Com has been able to provide space to alternative voices lies in the letters section. Unlike mainstream media where "letters to the editor" are regularly discarded because of "sensitive" content, MK.Com publishes a wide range of letters on almost any topic. These letters regularly criticize both the government and the opposition. To the extent that MK.Com continues to take the lead in its role as a source of alternative news and to enjoy the readership it has developed, it seems that there may be a momentum of longer term effects initiated by MK.Com.

MK.Com and other online newspapers seem to have contributed to an atmosphere which will see a reduction in the level of self-censorship among working journalists in Malaysia. The practice of mainstream media running MK.Com's stories may be taken to reflect not just the online daily's influence in the news industry, but a relaxation of self-censorship among the media.

Since MK.Com's founding, half a dozen other websites providing independent news on Malaysia have appeared. The most important of these are AgendaMalaysia.Com, a Malay/English news portal, the Chinese news portals beritagenerasi.com, mytianwang.com, and freemedia.com, and Radigradio.com, a web radio station providing news bulletins and analyses in Bahasa Malaysia. With the exception of AgendaMalaysia.Com, all the other sites came online after mid-2000.

CHALLENGES FACING INDEPENDENT NEWS SITES

The case of MK.Com illustrates the potential of online news sites, but it also illustrates some of the pitfalls that face Internet sites which seek to be politically relevant. There are at least two types of threats: political and economic.

Political harassment

It is clear that many of the activities of MK.Com and other online news sites are critical of the Malaysian government. There are political and legal reasons why the government has not made any attempts to shut down MK.Com. In this case, the political reason may be traced largely to the establishment of the Multi-Media Super Corridor (MSC), a policy of turning the area between Putrajaya and Kuala Lumpur into Asia's Silicon Valley. Key pledges made to the MSC by Mahathir included tax holidays, no censorship of the Internet, and freedom of movement within the MSC. These were deemed necessary for the success of the MSC.

Because it is an online publication, MK.Com was not required to apply for a publishing license, an annual ritual that helps the government keep Malaysia's conventional print and broadcast media constantly in line, and is necessary to gain official press cards. Official press cards in Malaysia are issued by the Information Ministry and are available only to licensed media outlets. Under the Printing Presses and Publications Act (PPPA), and other legislation such as the Sedition Act, media outlets can be shut down immediately by the Home Affairs Ministry with little or no legal remedy. Thus, the site operates in a legal loophole.

Government officials have reacted, nevertheless, by using petty harassment, such as discrediting MK.Com by denying its legitimacy as a press outlet altogether. Some ministries and ministers regularly banned MK.Com's reporters from press conferences, claiming that they did not have the right to attend, as they did not possess a press card. MK.Com reporters cannot apply for press cards as MK.Com does not posses a publication license. Repeated attempts by MK.Com to apply for a press card were turned down. Nonetheless, MK.Com's popularity ensures that even if it is banned from official press conferences, its reporters are still able to access a number of news-makers, as some ministers and press secretaries (in order to reach a different audience and/or to correct MK.Com's view) want to get their press statements and views across to MK.Com.

There is little doubt that the government is aware of MK.Com's content. Ministers have referred to the site unfavorably, giving it free publicity in the process. Gerakan, a component party of the ruling BN, even wrote a letter to the editor regarding a news item. Outspoken UMNO Supreme Council member Shahrir Samad used to write articles critical of UMNO regularly on MK.Com.

Another form of petty harassment was to reprimand MK.Com reporters publicly. The Minister of Transport, Dr. Ling Leong Sik, unhappy with MK.Com's reporting of his son's business affairs and internal MCA squabbles, publicly rebuked MK.Com's reporters during a press conference (Malaysiakini.Com, May 24, 2000). Several other ministers refused to answer questions from MK.Com's reporters during press conferences.

The government has also attempted to discredit MK.Com by accusing it of being an opposition newspaper and biased in its reporting. RTM1, the official television channel, tried to discredit Steven Gan personally by accusing him of reporting falsely the deaths of immigrants in a detention camp near Kuala Lumpur when he was a journalist with *The Sun*. As things turned out, RTM1 had apparently muddled up reports done by Mr. Gan on two separate incidents and their respective outcomes, and found itself the one doing the bad reporting (*Straits Times* (Singapore), February 23, 2001).

A far more serious attempt to discredit MK.Com was the government's claim that MK.Com received secret funding from international financier George Soros, who was called a "moron" by Prime Minister Mahathir Mohammed and vilified widely in Malaysia for his alleged role in the Asian currency crisis in 1997 (Friedman, 1997). The government claimed that the SEAPA subsidy, which kept MK.Com alive in its early years, originated from Soros' Open Society Institute. Interestingly enough, the government used an external source, the *Far Eastern Economic Review*, a HK-based weekly with wide readership among the middle class in

Malaysia, to discredit MK.Com. The government also relied upon testimony from a former senior MK.Com journalist who said he resigned from MK.Com because of the Soros link. MK.Com steadfastly denied that it received any funding from Soros and suggested that the former staff who supported the government's allegations were doing it out of unhappiness with his salary.

Government criticism of the site often backfired, since, every time a minister or a senior official attacked MK.Com or other anti-establishment websites, traffic to the site immediately went up as people became curious about the content of these websites.

It is likely that legislation dealing with online content will be introduced in the near future. This legislation essentially makes defamation and printing false news online similar to offenses committed in offline sources, regardless of where the web server is located, as the law targets the source of the material, i.e. the person quoted, the writer, or the owner of the web page. Given the government's overwhelming majority in Parliament, the legislation will most likely be passed into law when it is introduced. When it becomes law it will likely affect the way MK.Com operates. Political news stories and readers' letters could easily be the subject of legal proceedings. It is almost certain that news articles and letters published online will undergo much greater copy-editing and legal scrutiny before they are published.

Another piece of legislation under consideration as of writing was to regulate the use of online content during elections. In August, 2001, the Singapore Parliament passed an amendment to the Parliamentary Elections Act to regulate political campaigning over the Internet (*Straits Times* (Singapore), August 14, 2001). The Malaysian government is almost certain to pass a similar law before the next general election in 2004.

While these laws will collectively make sites such as MK.Com much more cautious, it will still be difficult for the authorities to enforce them. The main effect of these laws will be to act as a deterrent for the writers and owners of anti-government sites not to go overboard with their criticism or exposés of government policies or wrongdoings.

Economic viability

Although political harassment does remain a problem for MalaysiaKini, the biggest problem in the long term, affecting a number of similar news portals, may not be the regime in power or censorship. Finance, or more precisely profitability, will be the biggest hurdle. Figures provided by MK.Com showed that in the first twelve months, it lost about RM31,786.[4] It managed to generate about RM190,000 from online advertising, a remarkable achievement given that online advertisements are new to the Malaysian marketplace. The bulk of its early income, RM375,000 of RM593,132, came from the Bangkok-based SEAPA. Like conventional newspapers, its biggest expense was salaries, which accounted for slightly more than half of its total expenditure of RM624,918.

At the time of writing, monthly costs were about RM90–100,000 to run its operations, and online advertisements generate less than 15 percent of that amount (Malaysiakini.com, February 27, 2002). Revenue from online advertisers is unlikely to cover MK.Com's operating expenses for some time to come. Although it is undoubtedly one of the most popular websites in Malaysia, many advertisers are reluctant to advertise on it for fear of offending the government, given its anti-government reputation. Most businesses in Malaysia simply cannot afford to offend the government and hence stay clear of MK.Com.

The financial squeeze has led to several attempts to generate new sources of revenue. Perhaps the most viable of these is the formation of Strategic Analysis Malaysia (SAM), a subscription-only site offering analytical reports on the Malaysian political economy. It is being led by James Wong Win On, a former DAP MP and *Sin Chew* journalist. Other potential revenue sources attempted by the company is the establishment-related companies that provide online media technology basic ISP services such as web hosting and web page design.

Non-corporate attempts to bolster funding have included establishing a voluntary donation vehicle called the "Malaysiakini Independent Media Fund," launched at the end of 2000. The fund, which aimed to collect RM330,000, only managed to collect RM13,000 by the end of March 2003. The company finally implemented a subscription system. This idea was resisted earlier because Malaysiakini wanted to create a large pool of readers in order to be a credible alternative news service. However, the implementation of a subscription system did not cover operating expenses, so, at the time of writing, the company is continuing to generate sponsorships. So far, none of these strategies appear to have succeeded.

In February, 2002, financial reality forced MK.Com to announce a subscription scheme, with five categories, from lifetime access (for a one-off payment of RM1500 or US$400) to all MK.Com content, to a simpler plan requiring RM10 (or US$2.50) a month. There is also an innovative subscription plan, whereby one can sponsor another reader who is unable to pay. Only selected news items and the letters section are free to the public without registration. In essence, MK.Com had decided to go half-way in terms of a subscription-based service. It allows free access to its letters section and the only areas where a subscription is needed are the news columns and the archives. It is still too early to see if this half-way subscription service will generate badly needed revenue. By the end of March, 2002, MK.Com was able to sign up only about a thousand subscribers.

The same month, MK.Com announced that it was selling 29 percent of its shares to the Media Development Loan Fund (MDLF) for RM1.3 million (Malaysiakini.Com, March 25, 2002), in a deal crucial to the company's long-term survival. The deal leaves a majority 61 percent stake in the hands of the company's founders, Premesh and Gan, with 10 percent allotted to an employees' share incentive scheme. The MDLF (www.mdlf.cz) is dedicated to assisting independent news organizations in developing democracies worldwide.

CONCLUSION

MK.Com's successes may be attributed to several key factors. First, it appeared at the right time and at the right place. The Anwar Ibrahim affair gave MK.Com a constituency hungry for news from outside the mainstream media. By going "live" immediately prior to the 1999 general elections, it was able to entice Malaysian readers who wanted news about the opposition campaign. They knew that MK.Com would give greater and fairer coverage to the opposition rather than the pro-government mainstream media.

The timing was also right given that, by the late 1990s, the number of Malaysians with access to the Internet in Malaysia had grown to a critical mass, about two million users. The government's promotion of a knowledge-based economy through schemes such as the Multi-media Super Corridor meant that access to the Internet was actively encouraged.

A second reason for the success of the site was that, from the beginning, the site had an image as a source of independent news. The political fallout from the Anwar Ibrahim affair had deeply divided the Malaysian polity. People were on the lookout for alternative news sources, especially those that were highly critical of the ruling regime. Mainstream media had lost almost all credibility due to its biased reporting and pro-government slant, and many suspected that the mainstream press is highly selective in its news coverage. MK.Com was able to fulfil their desire for news not covered in the mainstream media. It was widely seen by its readers as leveling a field dominated thus far by a very pro-government media. If the site had been promoted as an opposition site, it would have lost much of its credibility. Despite the fact that it gives much more space to opposition news than to government news, it has not lost any credibility, nor been seen as an opposition newspaper by the Malaysian public.

Moreover, the founders of the site, Steven Gan and Premesh Chandran, had reputations as idealists with long histories of social activism. They wanted to build a more democratic and open Malaysia and were willing to sacrifice their personal well-being. They also managed to recruit like-minded people to run MK.Com. Many of MK.Com's sub-editors and journalists are highly experienced journalists, who could easily command a much higher salary in the mainstream press.

A fourth reason for the success of MK.Com is the external funding from the SEAPA. Without the SEAPA subsidy, it is certain that MK.Com would not have survived its first two years of operation. Online advertisements simply cannot support MK.Com, or, for that matter, any other news portal in Malaysia.

MK.Com illustrates the potential of an online news site to reinvigorate politics and journalism. It has helped to level the playing field between the government and the opposition when it comes to access to the mass media. Prior to MK.Com, the opposition had a distinct disadvantage when it came to the mainstream Malaysian media. In terms of journalism, MK.Com has shown that it is possible to practice journalism without censorship, self or otherwise, in Malaysia.

In spite of its early success as an influential player in the Malaysian news scene, two ironies in the tale of MK.Com will continue to plague its effectiveness.

First, contrary to conventional wisdom, the biggest threat to the survival of an independent media outlet such as MK.Com may not be the wrath of an authoritarian government. Market forces will decide the survival of MK.Com. If MK.Com cannot generate enough revenue from online and offline sources, it will be in real danger of having its presence severely curtailed. While it is unlikely to be shut down, given the level of support in the Malaysian NGO community, inadequate funding means that it will not be able to provide the extensive coverage and daily news updates. In other words, it may not be able to function as an online daily. It will probably end up more like a weekly current affairs magazine with a large number of volunteer writers.

Second, and a bigger irony, is that MK.Com's continued success depends very much on its reputation as a purveyor of the free press. Malaysians visit MK.Com because they expect to read news that is not covered in the mainstream media. In a free media environment, MK.Com would be just another media organization and may not even survive the competition from other newspapers. If the press in Malaysia were like those found in regional neighbors such as Indonesia, Thailand, and the Philippines, it is likely that MK.Com would not be able to survive as an online newspaper, as many people still prefer a "hard" copy newspaper as opposed to a "cyber" or "virtual" newspaper.

A wider conclusion is that the Internet may not the "magic bullet" when it comes to the creation of an open and democratic society in less democratic countries and help foster a civil society. Like most things in a capitalistic society, financial viability is just as important as the commitment of individuals.

There are a number of interesting comparisons that may be made between MK.Com and Sintercom (short for Singapore Internet Community), a website promoting freedom of speech and alternative ideas in neighboring Singapore. Although Sintercom was never set up as a news portal, it also garnered widespread praise for its role as an independent voice in Singapore society. The site was shut down in late 2001 by its founder, Tan

Chong Kee, after about three years in operation, primarily because of the commitment of time and money to maintain the site. Despite strong praise from civil society promoters, Tan could get neither the financial backing nor volunteers to help maintain the site. The final decision to close the site was when the government requested that the site be registered as a political website, and that Tan sign an undertaking that he would be fully responsible for all Sintercom content (*Straits Times* (Singapore), August 26, 2001). Since the Singapore Broadcasting Authority refused to vet all content before it was posted on the website, Tan was legally responsible for all content, and thus could be held liable for any defamation or libel suit. In spite of the fact that all civil society activists praised the site, none of Singapore's major civil society groups (many had used Tan's site to propagate their ideas) offered to take over the site.

What this ultimately tells us is that while the Internet can lead to a free flow of information and ideas and help foster civil society, ultimately it has to abide by the laws of capitalism. In order for the Net to be used successfully, such as operating an alternative newspaper, keeping the operations in the black is just as important as the personalities' commitment to free exchange of ideas and news.

NOTES

1 "On ice" or "freezer" means that the offending journalist would never be promoted.
2 Chin has since retired as Chief Justice.
3 National Justice Party, the political party established by Anwar's supporters.
4 The Malaysian currency, Ringgit Malaysia, is pegged at a fixed exchange rate of RM3.80 = US$1.

BIBLIOGRAPHY

AC Nielsen (2000) "Mid year media index," September.
Alatas, S.F. (1997) *Democracy and Authoritarianism in Indonesia and Malaysia: The Rise of the Post-colonial State*, New York: St. Martin's Press.
Asiaweek (2000) "POLITICS.COM," February 25.
Case, W. (1992) *Semi-democracy in Malaysia: Pressures and Prospects for Change*, Canberra: Department of Political and Social Change, Research School of Pacific Studies, Australian National University.
Commonwealth Observer Group (1990) *General Elections in Malaysia, 20–21 October 1990: The Report of the Commonwealth Observer Group*, London: Commonwealth Secretariat.
Crouch, H. (1996) *Government and Society in Malaysia*, Ithaca, NY: Cornell University Press.
Friedman, A. (1997) "Soros calls Mahathir a 'menace' to Malaysia," *International Herald Tribune*, September 22. Online. Available HTTP: http://www.iht.com/ IHT/ECON/97/af092297.html (accessed January 29, 2003).

Gan, S. (2002) "Trials and tribulations of an independent press," MK.Com, April 20.

Malaysiakini.com (2000) "Reporter told he may have to leave PC," November 24.

—— (2002) "Ling, Lim sign PM-brokered 'deal' to step down before general election," May 24.

—— (2002) "M'siakini registers marginal loss for first financial year," February 27.

—— (2002) "Malaysiakini goes global," March 25.

Nanyang Siang Pau (2000) "The 10 worst enemies of the press," May 3.

Straits Times (Singapore) (2001) "Malaysia's net paper feels the heat," February 23.

—— (2001) "Amendments to parliamentary act," August 14.

—— (2001) "Sintercom fades out of cyberspace," August 26.

The Star (1999) "RTM 'only caters to Barisan'," July 3.

—— (2002) "Mahathir refutes article on 'MCA retirement pact'," March 27.

9 Who is setting the Chinese agenda?

The impact of online chatrooms on party presses in China

Xiguang Li, Qin Xuan, and Randolph Kluver

Much discussion of the rise of the Internet within the People's Republic of China focuses on the political consequences of the technology on China's Communist Party. A significant number of authors argue that the Internet is a "technology of freedom," which will lead to an increased democratization in authoritarian nations. Others argue, however, that new media technologies embody a potential to drastically inhibit democratic processes, because of the increased potential for surveillance, the commercialization of the Net, or even by facilitating anti-democratic sentiments, among other reasons. Researchers have posited various mechanisms of democratization, but one item of consensus that seems to be emerging is that the Internet, because it allows for a greater variety of information from global sources, increases the ability of Chinese to bypass the traditional mechanisms of news selection on the part of authorities, thus increasing their ability to think politically outside the parameters endorsed by the state.

Regardless of its ability to generate widespread political activism or not, the Internet has certainly opened the door to a flow of information that is historically unprecedented to the Chinese people. Online chatrooms, which are often referred to as *dianzi dazibao* (electronic big-character posters), are providing an open space for Chinese to exchange information freely and anonymously (Huang, 1999).[1] As a popular online activity of Chinese Net users (China Internet Network Information Center, 2001), chatrooms thus pose a significant threat to the government-controlled media by revising and reconstructing the agenda set by the Chinese official press. Agenda-setting theory holds that the mass media play a determinative role in establishing what is considered important, by leading newscasts with that story or printing it on page one, for example. When news gatekeepers no longer consider an item to be of importance, they allow it to slip off the public agenda (McCombs and Shaw, 1972). For decades, the Chinese mass media have served effectively in agenda setting for the People's Republic of China. But as globalization multiplies the number of news outlets, audiences gain the power to select new outlets, and thereby alter their media exposure.

For decades, both for political and technological reasons, the Chinese press has never become a forum for public discussion and debate. The official propaganda system has always tried to keep a one-way flow of information, from the government to the populace. New media, however, have provided new opportunities for political interaction that embody at least the following characteristics:

1   The ability to provide information anonymously.
2   Equal opportunity for political expression.
3   Open and unconstrained topics for discussion.
4   The ability to both read and publish.
5   Consumer-driven rather than propaganda-driven content.
6   A rapid media cycle that bypasses government censors.

China has indeed attempted to control the Internet, particularly as a political forum (Boas and Khalathil, 2001; Qiu, 1999/2000), but these efforts ultimately are more formal than they are real, as Chinese Net users have found various ways of bypassing official control. As a result, chatrooms in China are open to ideas and debates that are simply not accessible through traditional media, while the ability of readers to choose the content of online news reading threatens the power of the state to determine the media agenda.

It has been evident to observers of China that new media were directly affecting not only the business, but also the content of news presentations within China. Hachigian (2001) argues that by enabling access to stories of local scandal, for example, the public gains a new power over the government. She argues:

> The Internet's ability to provide a flood of new ideas makes it the most formidable challenge yet to a key source of power, one practiced by Chinese governments for centuries: the power to shape public opinion in a way that leads citizens to accept the CCP's [Chinese Communist Party] political legitimacy.
>
> (Hachigian, 2001)

Thus, there is a powerful indirect political consequence of the Net, which is that it undermines the ability of the government to self-legitimate through the tightly controlled press. In times of international conflict or crisis, such as the NATO bombing of the Chinese Embassy during the war in the former Yugoslavia, these forums have been especially significant as a means for China's population to express both "legitimate" as well as "illegitimate" public opinion.

The People's Republic of China boasts the world's fastest growing Internet network, with the number of users doubling approximately every ten months or so (CNNIC, 2001). Detailed analysis of Internet usage in

China is somewhat difficult to come by, as phenomena such as account sharing mask the true number of computer users within China. Further difficulties exist with self-reporting, in that there is incentive to mis-state or hide the nature of online participation, given both political and social pressures. Even with these difficulties, it is possible to make some generalizations regarding network participation. Computer usage is highest among university communities and among China's emerging middle class, largely professional workers.

The online networks and chatrooms serve several crucially important functions, both sociologically and emotionally. Liu (1999) argues that the virtual community serves not only to create emotional bonds with other Chinese, but also to provide opportunities for reflection and analysis of political and social life. In addition, the role of electronic networks in news distribution cannot be understated. In the first China Network Information Center survey of 2001, over 65 percent of respondents reported that the Internet was the primary source of information for news (CNNIC, 2001).

In terms of participation in online forums and chatrooms, the same CNNIC survey revealed that 37.53 percent of respondents reported using the networks for online chats and forums, and another 19.33 percent participated in news groups (CNNIC, 2001). Li (1990) argues that the Internet networks are not significant solely for their role as expressions of personal opinion and news dissemination, but also for transforming the community. Specifically, he argues that the presence of the electronic networks both provided a means of obtaining consensus on difficult political issues, and leverage for significant political action, something that could not possibly have occurred without the networks.

The most prominent of these sites is *Qiangguo* (http://www.qglt.com), sponsored by the *People's Daily* newspaper, China's most prominent news source, and generally accepted as the voice of the Chinese Communist Party. Not only does this forum have genuine prominence in national life, but it also represents the most heavily guarded sphere of online discussion within China. Unlike most other online forums, *Qiangguo* is constantly cleansed by employees of the newspaper and is closed when the responsible personnel go off-duty in the evenings. Moreover, the name of the forum, *Qiangguo*, literally translated, is "Strong Nation," illustrating the nation-building function of the site.

METHODOLOGY

In order to demonstrate our contention, we will focus on a qualitative content analysis of threads of discussion or "instances" in both the print edition of the *People's Daily* as well as the online *Qiangguo* forum. Denzin argues that the "messy texts" of online forums do not generate data that are generalizable, representative, or scientifically valid, but rather are oriented towards achieving a "strong reading," and hence an adequate analysis (Denzin, 1999). We have chosen this method because we believe that it presents a better opportunity to present fully the dynamics of agenda setting, which more quantitative analysis would obscure. Moreover, this quasi-rhetorical analysis is more in line with the nature of the forums we are examining, which are composed of argumentative, persuasive discourse.

In order to determine the impact of *People's Daily* news sites in online forums, we have coded offline articles in the *People's Daily* that speak of the events surrounding the crash and the subsequent political actions of the nations. We then searched for these key terms in the online *Qiangguo* forum to draw rough correlations between the content of the print edition stories and the greatest number of postings on the *Qiangguo* forum. We have included only news articles and forum postings directly related to the spy plane incident in our analysis.

Based on a close scrutiny of the content of the *People's Daily*, we have identified six different periods of coverage, and have chosen six dates (April 3, 9, 12, 14, 18, and 23) corresponding to significant developments during this period to examine postings on the *Qiangguo* forum. Accordingly, we divided the coverage of the *People's Daily* into six periods, and have identified the front-page stories and back-page stories during each of those periods as expressed through the coverage of the print version of the *People's Daily*. Of course, front-page topics refer to those articles appearing on the front page while *back-page topics* refer to those appearing on subsequent pages.

There were altogether eighty-nine related news reports and articles from April 1–30 in the *People's Daily* concerning the incident, and thirty-five of these articles appeared on the front page. The presentation of the issues within the pages of the *People's Daily* changed as the Chinese and US governments negotiated for a solution to the incident.

These two particular media channels are significant, since both have the *People's Daily* imprint, are overseen by the same governmental ministry, and are thus identified as officially sanctioned media. The difference between them is solely in the ability of readers to publish items on the electronic forum. By contrasting these two channels of official news, then, it is possible to ascertain the ways in which the Internet introduces new dimensions to political coverage in Chinese public life, within a bounded dataset. This incident provides an illustrative example of how the Chinese public can reconstruct and revise the official media accounts of events in ways that directly challenge the version of political reality presented by the mainstream press.

The April events, given their importance to Chinese–US relations, provoked a great deal of online response, including the "great hacker wars" (Zhou, 2001) as well as the use of forums for the expression of online nationalism (see e.g. Kluver, 2001), but we will focus our attention on the ways in which the Chinese public used the official forum to bypass the official version of events.

QIANGGUO AND THE SPYPLANE INCIDENT

In 1999, the *People's Daily*, China's most prominent daily, launched a chatroom called *Qiangguo* ("Strong Nation") forum to give readers a chance to react to the news, as well as to attract revenue. With newspaper sales plunging and chatrooms popping up on popular "portal" sites such as Sina.com and Netease.com, the *People's Daily* no doubt hoped the forum could drive Net traffic back its way. The forum is already one of China's most popular, averaging 70,000 page views a day, primarily among people aged 19 to 35 (Shaver, 2000). But most Chinese have used this system not only to discuss the news, but have also posted news stories which went unreported in the official media. The posting of news stories online, sometimes from unofficial sources, has drawn attention to issues ignored by the official press, thus making hidden agendas transparent. Due to economic, political, and ideological constraints, most traditional media have biases and are selective in news reporting. Chatrooms, however, not only enable people to look at events from different perspectives, using diverse sources, but also allow them to express their opinions freely. As a result, the "public agenda," or those topics to be discussed and debated in cyberspace, are often reconstructed items selected from both the Chinese and Western press sources.

In contrast to the days when China's party propaganda officials had a monopoly on news content, all newspapers waited patiently for stories from the *Xinhua* news feeds before laying out their pages. However, with the advent of new media, people in the chatroom are impatient. Most topics for discussion on the *Qiangguo* forum begin with the posting of the latest news reports taken from the Western press.

For example, at 5 p.m. on April 1, 2001, an *Associated Press* story about the collision of the US and Chinese military aircraft was posted on *Qiangguo*, at least two hours prior to the Chinese official press report. The posting of the *Associated Press* story immediately started a heated discussion on the web, and prompted an explosion of forum postings (see Figure 9.1).

The attention on the forums was most likely not prompted by the initial coverage by the *People's Daily*, however. In fact, in spite of the obvious importance of the story to China, *Xinhua* ran only seven stories on the incident in the first three days after the crash, compared with the Western agencies, which ran at least forty-seven stories each over the same period (see Figure 9.2).

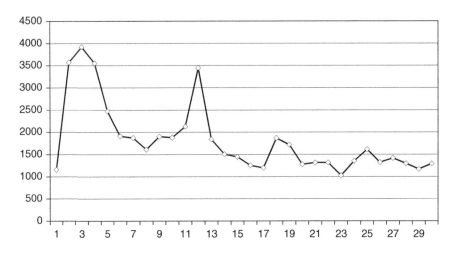

Figure 9.1 Postings on *Qiangguo* forum from April 1–30, 2001

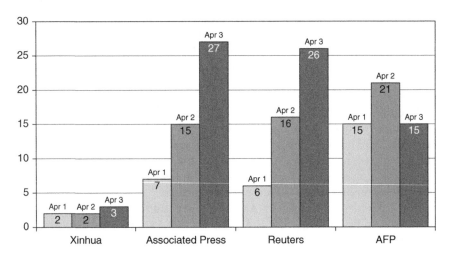

Figure 9.2 Number of articles by news source

EPISODES AND FORUM POSTINGS

Initial period (April 2–4)

A US EP-3E Navy Aircraft, on a surveillance mission over the South China Sea, collides with a Chinese fighter plane.

Front-page topics:

1 The Chinese people demand an explanation and an apology, and ask the US to take responsibility for it (keywords: explanation, responsibility, apology).
2 China has launched a search and rescue operation for a missing Chinese pilot (keywords: Chinese, missing, pilot).

During this period, there was a convergence between the issues as presented in the print paper and the online forum. Each of these issues received almost equal attention in the chatrooms. There is little difference between the contents of the front page and the forum postings (see Figure 9.3). All coverage in the *People's Daily* is on the front page.

Figure 9.3 Topics in *Qiangguo* forum on April 3, 2001

First negotiating period (April 5–11)

The US government says there is nothing to apologize for and demands the return of the crew and airplane. The Chinese government is not satisfied with the American government's response to the incident and demands an apology.

Front-page topics:

1 US must apologize (*dao qian*) to the Chinese people (keyword: apology).
2 Chinese people from all walks of life and every province are denouncing American hegemonic behaviors (keyword: hegemony).
3 Chinese leaders have expressed concern about the missing pilot Wang Wei, his wife Ruan Guoqin, and his fellow pilot Zhao Yu (keywords: Wang Wei, Ruan Guoqin, Zhao Yu).

Back-page topics:

1   President Bush and Secretary Powell say they "regret" (*yi han*) the lost Chinese pilot (keyword: regret).

During this period, there is again some convergence between the topics presented in the newspaper and those generated on the online forum. Postings related to the topic "demanding an American apology" generated far more activity to the forums than any other topic, and seem to have increased as a conversational topic since the first period (see Figure 9.4).

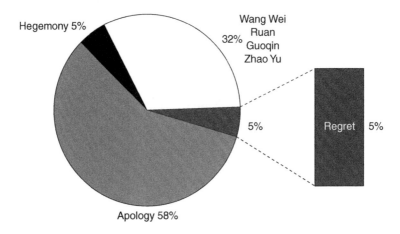

Figure 9.4 Topics in *Qiangguo* forum on April 9, 2001

Letter of regret (April 12)

The US ambassador presented a letter of regret (*zhi qian xin*) to the Chinese government and the Chinese government allowed the American crew to leave Hainan Island. The Chinese also demand an end to US surveillance flights near Chinese territories.

Front-page topics:

1   US present *zhi qian xin* to China (keyword: *zhi qian* letter, apology).
2   US must stop surveillance flights targeting China (keyword: spying).
3   China–US relations must be based on the three joint communiqués and the basic rules of international relations (key term: China–US relations).
4   The Chinese government allows the American crew to leave China (key term: American crew).

Back-page topics:

1 Chinese people throughout the country support the Chinese government's decision to release the crew (keyword: support).
2 Denouncing American hegemonic behaviors (keyword: hegemony).
3 Continuing search for missing pilot Wang Wei, but his hope of survival is little (keyword: Wang Wei).

Among these issues, the letter of regret and the American apology attracted the most attention on the online forum, generating 42 percent of the responses (see Figure 9.5). The topic the print edition relegated to the back page, the fate of Wang Wei, generated 27 percent, or the second largest number of postings in the forum. Meanwhile, the *People's Daily* front-page topics denouncing American hegemonism and the development of US–China relations are less frequent, suggesting that the drama of the story of Wang Wei was more important than the overt political issues. Interestingly, the release of the flight crew, which was intended to bolster China's international image, generated only a marginal 3 percent of postings, suggesting that Chinese posters assumed their eventual release.

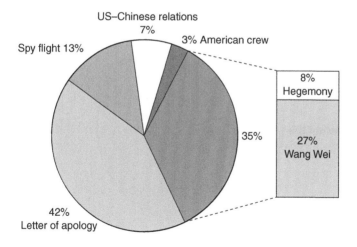

Figure 9.5 Topics in *Qiangguo* forum on April 12, 2001

The end of the initial negotiations (April 13–14)

After the American crew leaves China, a perception arises that both countries have made compromises.

Front-page topics:

1 The masses throughout China support the government's decision (key term: citizen support).

2   Masses throughout China are turning patriotic enthusiasm into a force to invigorate China (keyword: patriotism).

Back-page topics:

1   The search for Wang Wei continues (keyword: Wang Wei).
2   The Chinese government maintains national sovereignty and dignity (key terms: national sovereignty, national dignity).

During this period, it seems that the political issues have been resolved, and the most frequently discussed issue is Wang Wei (see Figure 9.6). The *People's Daily* seems to have lost all relevance to affecting the content of posts, as the Net posters completely ignored the front-page topic, the support of the masses for the Chinese government's decision. Similarly, there was virtually no response (1 percent) to the issue of national sovereignty and dignity, suggesting that Net posters did not pick up on the theme of the Chinese government safeguarding national dignity. At this point, online discussions had lost all political content, and were focused almost exclusively on Wang Wei's drama.

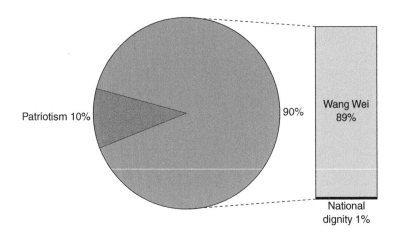

Figure 9.6 Topics in *Qiangguo* forum on April 14, 2001

The second round of negotiations (April 15–20)

China and the US begin a second round of negotiations over responsibility for the accident and the fate of the US plane, still on Hainan Island. China ends the search for Chinese pilot Wang Wei, and senior American government officials make verbal attacks on China.

Front-page topics:

1   Wang Wei is praised as a "Guard of Sea and Sky" (keyword: Wang Wei).

Back-page topics:

1   Criticism of American hegemony (keyword: hegemony).
2   China and US hold negotiations in Beijing (keyword: negotiation).

During this period, there is a clear contrast to the previous period in which Wang Wei was the primary issue. Efforts by the official press to prioritize Wang Wei as the main topic failed to gain any significant response. Rather, the back-page topic of the negotiations generated fully 78 percent postings, while American hegemony generated 6 percent (see Figure 9.7). What this suggests is that as the drama of Wang Wei came to a close, public attention moved on to the next step, as well as perhaps fatigue with the fate of Wang Wei. Again, it seems to suggest that front-page coverage by the *People's Daily* had little to do with shaping the agenda of the Net posting public.

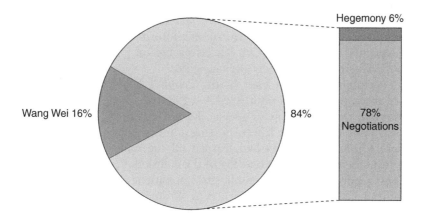

Figure 9.7 Topics in *Qiangguo* forum on April 18, 2001

Making concessions to avoid trouble (April 21–28)

The political fall-out from the accident seems to wane as China and the US hold further talks concerning responsibility and the fate of the plane.
   Front-page topics:

1   Wang Wei is honored as "Guard of Sea and Sky" (keyword: Wang Wei).

Back-page topics:

1   US must take full responsibility for the incident (keyword: respons-
    ibility).
2   International opinion supports the Chinese government's stand (key-
    words: international, support).

During this period, the print version of the *People's Daily* raised the
number of stories about pilot Wang Wei. There were five front-page
stories between April 21 and 25, with April 25 alone having three front-
page articles about Wang Wei. In spite of the increasing attention in the
print, however, less than 10 percent of the *Qiangguo* forum postings contained any reference to "Wang Wei." People were no longer paying attention to Wang Wei in spite of the prominence in the print paper.

It is clear that the official press lost control of public attention after
China released the American crew. The public no longer had any expectations from the government on this issue, and the *People's Daily* failed to
have a significant effect on agenda setting in the initial and final stages of
the coverage of the incident.

During the initial stages of the incident, the Chinese official press, led by
Xinhua News Agency and the *People's Daily*, failed to provide timely and
complete coverage of the incident, so as a result lost their role and function
as opinion leaders. Disappointed by the lack of meaningful news coverage
in the official press, the public had to seek information from the Internet.
Consequently, most of the news articles posted on *Qiangguo* forum were
from the Western news outlets and agencies.

For example, the front page of the *People's Daily* did not print any
stories about the collision until April 4, a full three days after the incident.
In addition, the Chinese news agency did not reveal the name of the lost
Chinese pilot until he had been missing for three days. In contrast, the
Chinese forum participants had learned all the names of the American
crew from the forum within one day of the collision.

Consequently, the Chinese public grew impatient and even distrustful of
the official Chinese press, and turned to Western sources for more complete information. Many Chinese websites and chatrooms were full of
information lifted and cross-posted from Western sources, giving these
Western sources an uncanny ability to set the Chinese political agenda.

One final example is particularly telling. On April 12, the *People's
Daily* printed Chinese President Jiang Zemin's statement concerning the
"letter of regret," which indicated that the letter served as an apology to
the Chinese side. But the Chinese public disagreed with Jiang's interpretation of the letter, and a full 55 percent of postings on the forum argued
that, in fact, the American government had not apologized to China,
which was a formal precondition set by the Chinese government for the
release of the American crew (see Figure 9.8). On the same day, a CNN

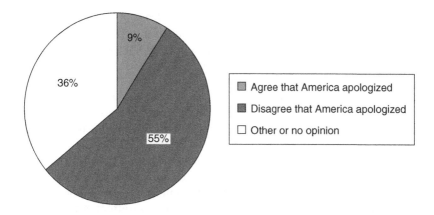

Figure 9.8 Attitudes towards US letter

story was posted on the forum which reported that the US President denied that he had apologized. Later, another article from the American press was posted on the forum, again reporting that Secretary of State Powell said that the US did not apologize. The participants in the forum, then, trusted Western media as to the intentions of the Western leaders, and the consequences for China's policy, more than they did either the Chinese government or the official Chinese media. Only 9 percent of postings supported Jiang's interpretation of the meaning of the letter.

The attitudes expressed on the forum, then, were more in line with American public opinion over the meaning of the letter than with the official Chinese press. In fact, the US had gone to great lengths not to apologize, and released the letter only in English, rather than in English and Chinese, so there could be no confusion over translations, and this letter pointedly omitted use of the word "apology." In fact, Colin Powell argued that "[T]here is nothing to apologize for. To apologize would have suggested that we have done something wrong or accepted responsibility for having done something wrong. And we did not do anything wrong. Therefore, it's not possible to apologize" (Pan and Pomfret, 2001).

This example illustrates that participants on the *Qiangguo* forum had taken a stand directly opposing the government's position in this crucial issue. This development must be worrisome to China's leaders, as it could lead ultimately to a loss of confidence in government. One posting on the forum said that the official press coverage of the incident was a self-proclaimed "spiritual victory" on the part of the Chinese government that ultimately demeaned China: "We're betrayed by those sons and daughters of high officials who are making money in US and Chinese–US trade" (http://bbs.people.com.cn/bbs/, April 13, 2001).

Some Chinese specialists in China–US relations believed that the acceptance of the American letter of regret and the release of the American crew would benefit both countries. A healthy relationship between the world's largest developing country and the world's only superpower is also important for world peace. The Chinese press thus tried to mobilize public support for the government's decision. However, due to new sources of information not previously available in China and a transparency of information brought by the Internet, it will become increasingly difficult or even impossible for the government to use traditional propaganda mechanisms for political mobilization.

One important consideration of this incident is that it is not only possible, but it is probable, that people outside of China logged on to the *Qiangguo* forum and contributed to the online debate. These overseas Chinese likely had access to a wide variety of news sources, and were able to contribute these items to the forum, and thus had a direct impact on the public agenda even while outside of China. Although data are not available to determine the extent to which this occurred, it underscores the point we have been making, which is that the Internet has seriously undermined the ability of the Chinese government to define the political agenda, and in many ways has internationalized the news flow into China in unanticipated ways.

CONCLUSIONS

Online forums and chatrooms such as the *Qiangguo* forum have changed the fundamental flows of news in China, and, with them, the ability of the state to establish interpretive frameworks for understanding events, especially those of international concern. Whereas the official press has always sought to "correctly guide public opinion," the Chinese authorities are losing the battle to control information and limit individual expression via the Internet. Chinese news websites and forums have displayed a liveliness not found in traditional media within China. The Internet is changing China, exposing the nation to ideas and debates that are simply not accessible through traditional media.

This analysis demonstrates that a vibrant civic discourse exists in the chatrooms and forums of China and overseas Chinese that often does act within both imposed and agreed-upon constraints, such as the continued dominance of the Chinese Communist Party. In spite of the fact that the *Qiangguo* forum is sponsored by and bears the imprint of the *People's Daily* newspaper, the forum has become a significant place for the expression of competing frames by which to explain current events to Chinese web users.

In their eagerness to develop the Net, China's top leaders appear willing to tolerate a certain amount of frankness that would otherwise be stamped out. The Internet has become a powerful and popular channel for both the government and ordinary Chinese to hear and to be heard. But this incident reveals something far more meaningful for scholars of the Internet in Asia. Citizens of a variety of nations now have the ability to find alternative sources of news and information, if they grow distrustful of their national news media. In this instance, Chinese citizens turned to the news sources of the very nation with which they were in conflict for information on how to interpret events. Setting the press and public agenda for another country through media and the Internet has become a new form of "soft power" in international politics (Li, 2001). The more trust international media gain with Internet users, the more pronounced will be this effect.

For China, the lessons are quite clear. The official press in China cannot expect that the traditional role of Party-controlled presses in setting the public agenda will go unchallenged. In the age of globalization, without immediate and profound press reforms, Western media will eventually set the agenda for the Middle Kingdom.

NOTE

1 *Dazibao*, or big-character posters, have historically been an important part of political communication in China, as they were used to galvanize public opinion around critical political issues (see Chu, 1977).

BIBLIOGRAPHY

Boas, T. and Kalathil, S. (2001) "The Internet and state control in authoritarian regimes: China, Cuba, and the Counterrevolution," Carnegie Endowment for International Peace Working Paper no. 21. Online. Available HTTP: http://www.ceip.org/files/Publications/wp21.asp (available as of January 29, 2003).

China Internet Network Information Center (CNNIC) (2001) "Semiannual survey report on the development of China's Internet." Online. Available HTTP: http://www.cnnic.net.cn/develst/rep200107-e.shtml (available as of January 29, 2003).

Chu, G. (1977) *Radical Change through Communication in Mao's China*, Honolulu: University of Hawaii Press.

Denzin, N. (1999) "Cybertalk and the method of instances," in S. Jones (ed.) *Doing Internet Research: Critical Issues and Methods for Examining the Net*, Thousand Oaks, CA: Sage Publications.

Hachigian, N. (2001) "China's cyber-strategy," *Foreign Affairs*, 80, 2. Online. Available HTTP: http://www.rand.org/nsrd/capp/cyberstrategy.html (available as of January 29, 2003).

Huang, E. (1999) "Flying freely but in the cage – an empirical study of using Internet for the democratic development in China," *Information Technology for Development*, 8, 3: 145–62.

Kluver, R. (2001) "New Media and the end of nationalism: China and the US in a war of words," *Mots Pluriels*, 18. Online. Available HTTP: http://www.arts.uwa.edu.au/MotsPluriels/MP1801ak.html (available as of January 29, 2003).

Li, T. (1990) "Computer-mediated communications and the Chinese students in the US," *The Information Society*, 7: 125–37.

Li, X. (2001) "Globalization and soft power," *Globe Journal*, January, Beijing.

Liu, D. (1999) "The Internet as a mode of civic discourse: the Chinese virtual community in North America," in R. Kluver and J. Powers (eds) *Civic Discourse, Civil Society, and Chinese Communities*, Stamford, CT: Ablex publishing.

McCombs, M. and Shaw, D.L. (1972) "The agenda-setting function of mass media," *Public Opinion Quarterly*, 36: 176–87.

Pan, P. and Pomfret, J. (2001) "Detained Americans freed, leave China for Guam: US 'very sorry' for unauthorized landing, death of pilot," *Washington Post*. Online. Available HTTP: http://www.washingtonpost.com/wp-dyn/world/issues/chinatensions/ (available as of January 29, 2003).

Qiu, J. (1999/2000) "Virtual censorship in China: keeping the gate between the cyberspaces," *International Journal of Communications Law and Policy*, 4: 1–25. Online. Available HTTP: http://www.ijclp.org/4_2000/ijclp_webdoc_1_4_2000.html (available as of January 29, 2003).

Shaver, S. (2000) "Jiang Yapin's chatroom springs to life during big events like Taiwan's election," *TIME*, 155, 14.

Tang, R. (2001) "Air incident sparks China chat attack." Online. Available HTTP: http://www.cnn.com/2001/WORLD/asiapcf/east/04/02/china.crash.chat/ (available as of January 29, 2003).

Zhou, J. (2001) "China hackers declare 'war' in cyberspace," *South China Morning Post*, April 26.

10 Clicking for votes

Assessing Japanese political campaigns on the web

Leslie M. Tkach-Kawasaki

INTRODUCTION

The growth of the Internet over the past seven years in advanced demo-cratic countries has prompted widespread speculation regarding its use as a means of political communication. The Internet, as the most popular flagbearer for this new wave of ICTs (information communications tech-nologies), has received a great deal of attention for its potential as a demo-cracy-enhancing information and communications channel. However, as Internet diffusion continues to spread throughout the world, we are becoming increasingly aware that its use varies widely in different social, cultural, and political environments.

As discussed in the Introduction to this volume, many Asian nations have only recently seen widespread ICT diffusion within their borders. Boasting user figures that comprise nearly one-third of the world's Internet user population, Asian nations face numerous challenges which are important to their future economic, political, and social development (Hachigian, 2002). In the political arena especially, political actors within these nations are cautiously making forays online, yet are concerned about the long-term political impact of the Internet on their existing power struc-tures and political cultures. Mindful of the potential of the emergence of new political actors, one-party political regimes that have been politically stable for a long period, such as Singapore and Japan, have been especially cautious regarding the political Internet.

One outgrowth of the rapid expansion of the Internet since the early 1990s has been initiatives on the nation-state level to regulate various aspects of Internet content within national borders. These initiatives range from blocking certain content on WWW (World Wide Web) sites, as done in China, to requiring third parties that create politically oriented websites during election campaigns to register with the appropriate government authorities, as is the case in Singapore. The Japanese government has taken steps to deal with the Internet as a medium for political campaign activities as well but in ways that are quite different from those in other countries. Since a small number of politicians and political parties first experimented with providing political campaign information through their websites in 1995, the Japanese government has applied existing media-use legislation in the form of the POEL (Public Offices Election Law) to political content that is aimed at the electorate during official election campaign periods. In the fall of 2001, the government established a review committee to study the application of the POEL to political campaign activities involving the Internet. The committee's deliberations resulted in an announcement in late June, 2002 that the government plans to submit a bill to the Japanese Diet in 2003 to revise the POEL to allow the use of the Internet for election campaigning.

This chapter addresses two main issues: first, the development between 1995 and 2002 of the government's interpretation of the POEL with regard to the use of the Internet as a political campaign medium, and, second, the ways in which Japanese political actors have been using the Internet to create a new, web-based relationship with voters. Japan's experience to date with the political Internet provides an interesting study in the integration of traditional campaign practices and institutional regulations with new media technologies. In order to examine how the Japanese political Internet has evolved over time, especially during election campaign periods, the website contents of major political parties and a number of candidates were archived during election campaign periods in 2000 and 2001. Through examining how the Internet has been used practically in Japan's political, legislative, and media environment during political campaigns, this chapter demonstrates that although political actors face a number of challenges in practically applying new media technologies to political activities, they can also be used strategically to promote certain political agendas.

Within this chapter, I will discuss how the Internet has been used for political campaigns by tracing its early development as a political media tool primarily in the US and the UK in the mid-1990s and pointing out the gap between the "theoretical" possibilities of the Internet and the reality of how it is being used in political campaigns. I then turn to a brief description of the Japanese political environment, including the political culture, institutional practices such as the POEL (in terms of how it has been applied to the use of the Internet to date), and the overall political media environment in Japan. I will argue that as the Internet continues to diffuse and become part of "everyday life," it is simultaneously reinforcing and altering traditional relationships among political actors. The Internet can be a valuable political communications and information platform, but its value rests not on the technology itself but how it is exercised. Consequently, in the concluding portion of this chapter, I will suggest some changes that may take place in the Japanese political landscape in the future due to the introduction of the Internet to the realm of politics.

ENTER THE INTERNET

Many positive interpretations of the Internet's potential as a democratic political communications medium during the early 1990s tended to focus on its potential rather than practical experience. As democratic nations experienced declining voting rates and widespread political apathy, many observers viewed the Internet as a panacea for reinvigorating political participation and interest. It was suggested that the provision of more political information and faster communications capabilities could lead directly to a more informed citizenry willing to participate actively in politics (Grossman, 1995; Rash, 1997; Rheingold, 1994). As a result, the potential advantages of the Internet, such as its speed of communications, unlimited capacity for storing and retrieving information, and control by the user over content (Abramson *et al.*, 1988), were emphasized more than its practical use. While mindful of its possibilities, some scholars pointed out that before dreams of a "digital democracy" through the Internet could be realized, access, and the desire to seek political information through the Internet were necessary prerequisites (Delli Carpini, 1996; Hill and Hughes, 1998; Selnow, 1998).

In response to expanding online populations in the mid-1990s, the American elections in 1996 and 1998 drew a wide range of political actors to the Internet. During the 1996 US general election, political parties appeared online with sophisticated websites offering links to state organizations and candidates. The ranks of candidates and politicians with their own websites also swelled, with many sites offering features such as email addresses, profiles of candidates, and campaign platforms (Davis, 1999; Kamarck, 1999). However, given the difficulty of assessing the impact of this new medium, as well as the cost involved in getting online, many candidates were wary of investing in online campaign activities. Trent and Friedenberg (2000, pp. 343–4) note that in the 1998 American election:

> 43 percent of 270 campaigns surveyed had already spent, or soon expected to spend, less than US$500 "designing, building, and maintaining" their Internet site. An additional 38 percent had already spent, or soon expected to spend, between US$500 and US$2000 to develop their Internet site, and an additional 17 percent had already spent, or soon expected to spend between US$2000–US$10,000 to design, build and maintain their Internet site. Only two percent expect to spend in excess of US$10,000 on their Internet site.

Political parties and candidates were also joined online by a number of non-traditional political actors. Interest groups used their websites as a means to get their message across to the public, simultaneously saving money and bypassing traditional media channels (Hill and Hughes, 1998). Mainstream media channels such as newspapers established online versions that included political news with up-to-date election coverage. One particularly interesting development was the creation of political portal sites as an exclusively online presence. Non-partisan in nature, sites such as www.vote.com and www.election.com offered instant polls, non-partisan voting information, and direct links to a wide variety of candidate and party sites.

Noting the American experience with the political Internet, political actors in other countries as well soon started to incorporate the Internet into their political campaigns. During the 1997 UK general election, at least eighteen major and minor parties constructed websites featuring functions ranging from email communications to party platforms (Gibson and Ward, 1998). With widespread attention being paid to the impact of this new medium in many different areas, political researchers sought to clarify the relationship between the Internet and political activities, especially political campaigns, from a number of different perspectives.

The results of empirical research conducted in the US and UK indicate that political actors initially took a "politics as usual approach" to the use of ICTs for political activities (Gibson and Ward, 1998; Margolis and Resnick, 2000). Quite possibly unfamiliar with this new medium and concerned with investing campaign resources such as funds and volunteers, parties tended to use the Internet in the same fashion as other media channels. However, as time progressed and they became more familiar with the Internet, new online strategies appeared such as targeting and directed email campaigns. Yet, in their website content analysis focusing on major and minor parties in the UK in 1997, Gibson and Ward found that hopes for the World Wide Web to be "a level playing field" for cross-party competition were not being realized in actual practice. Larger parties were more proactive in providing mainly election-related information through their websites and offered more communication opportunities than smaller parties; moreover, website contents tended to be aimed at top-down information flows rather than bottom-up communications from the electorate (Gibson and Ward, 1998). In addition, studies conducted in the US during the 1996 and 1998 elections suggested that rather than transform democratic activities, the Internet may be used for internal party organizational practices such as recruiting new members, communicating with party activists, and promoting candidates and platforms (Gibson and Ward, 1998; Margolis *et al.*, 1997). Comparisons of party websites in the US and the UK demonstrate that although British parties seem to have more presence on the Internet, generally speaking, there were no apparent differences in terms of site features and communications means designed to enhance the party–voter relationship (Margolis *et al.*, 1999).

These studies seem to point to a rather wide dichotomy between conceptions of the Internet's potential as a democratic information and communications channel among political actors and its practical application in political life. As user populations continue to grow, allowing researchers more opportunities to study not only how political actors are active on the Internet but also how the electorate responds to their efforts, new possibilities for the strategic use of the Internet are starting to appear. Foot and Schneider (2002) found that political actors in the 2000 US election exhibited increased sophistication in their use of the Internet for organization and mobilization practices compared to earlier campaign efforts. Rather than focus solely on the potential merits of Internet use, its evolution as a medium for political communications in different political environments and cultures is becoming increasingly important.

POLITICAL CAMPAIGNS IN JAPAN

Analyzing how the Internet can be integrated into different political milieu requires an understanding of the conditions under which it is used. During the mid- to late 1990s, the practical connection between the use of the Internet and political activity tended to focus on elections and campaigns as conducted by political actors, especially since elections are intense periods of political activity that demonstrate a convergence of political forces. However, evaluating the Internet's long-term potential as a political communications medium requires assessing how it is used in different political contexts and identifying the factors that influence its use. Consequently, relating these factors to the use of new media technologies allows for a more intensive study on how the Internet is being integrated into political life.

The first factor is the actual political environment itself. While the multi-party systems in the US and UK provided a playing field for intense party and candidate competition, the situation in Japan was quite different. Japanese political actors were uncertain as to how to use the Internet most effectively in a socio-political environment of a single dominant party that was being challenged by newly established political parties. The Liberal Democratic Party (LDP), which had been in power for most of Japan's postwar period, was facing extremely low approval ratings in the polls and a rising percentage of non-aligned or "floating" voters throughout the 1990s. A surprise vote of non-confidence in the government briefly brought a coalition government of eight small parties to power in 1993 that in turn was able to effect major revisions in the electoral system. This was a particularly significant development in Japanese postwar politics. Revisions to the electoral laws changed the nature of political campaigns by allowing parties to nominate only one candidate per constituency and also allowed opposition parties to provide real political competition.

The brief period of victory over the LDP revitalized traditional opposition parties with strong ideological or traditional support bases such as the JCP (Japan Communist Party), the New Komeito Party (formerly the Komeito Party), and the SDP (Social Democratic Party of Japan), and stimulated the formation of new political parties. Among these new parties, the most serious challenge to the LDP since 1994 has been from the Democratic Party of Japan (DPJ). Led by Kan Naoto and Hatoyama Yukio and established in September, 1996, it has enjoyed some popularity among the electorate in subsequent elections. Given an economy mired in recession throughout the 1990s, wide public reporting of scandals involving a number of LDP politicians, and the emergence of new political parties, Japan's political world was in a dynamic state.

A factor in the "playing field" in which these political parties competed was Japan's political culture. Each nation, through its history, has a set of historical and cultural values, expectations, and institutions that permeate its society either directly or indirectly, establishing a framework for conducting certain social activities, including political activities. Verba and colleagues (1978) define political culture as "consisting of the system of empirical beliefs, expressive symbols, and values which define the situation in which political action takes place ... [it] refers to the system of beliefs about patterns of political interaction and institutions." Political culture also comprises the institutional and regulatory framework that establishes the necessary infrastructure for how political activities are conducted, shapes political decisions and activities, and, as pointed out by Martin and Stronach, essentially "sets the parameters of the political game" (1992).

Political culture in Japan is related to Japanese social behavior, which anthropologists have described as emphasizing group orientation, hierarchic social levels, and personal relations, especially at the local level (Doi, 1973; Nakane, 1972). The emphasis on these local ties has often been cited as particularly strong in Japanese political culture (Curtis, 1971; Flanagan, 1996; Richardson and Flanagan, 1984). Once the decision has been made to run for public office, candidates establish local support groups, or *koenkai*, charged with "the function of organizing large numbers of the general electorate on behalf of a particular Diet candidate." These local organizations assist in the day-to-day management of the campaign, distributing leaflets, and volunteering in the local campaign office. Local politicians rely on a combination of support from their *koenkai* as well as backing from local community leaders or elites. Once successful, candidates are expected to reciprocate this support by using their political office to benefit the community on the whole: not doing so would cost them the support of the community. In this sense, close ties to cultural values that emphasize human relationships, deeply rooted conservative practices, and strong group loyalties are reflected in a number of campaign practices that are still in place today.

The electoral system in place prior to 1993 also contributed to the local-level orientation of Japanese political campaigns. Under the multi-member district system that was in place from 1948 until 1993, candidates vied for office in many constituencies by competing with other candidates backed by the same party for a limited number of seats. With few ideological or issue-related differences, campaigns were often waged among individual candidates on the basis of each candidate's reputation and support network within the community. With support bases firmly centered at the local level, very few political campaigns are conducted nationally. This traditional style of mobilizing local campaign support among the electorate has led to the characterization of Japan's political environment as one of weak party ties and strong individual candidate organization (Curtis, 1988; Stockwin, 1987).

One further reinforcement of the local-level nature of Japanese campaign practices has been the provisions set forth in the POEL regarding campaign practices, including campaign finance regulations and the distribution of campaign-related political information. Because of the POEL and its wide range of regulations, in contrast to other nations that have few restrictions on political campaign media advertising, Japan's electoral system has been described as "one of the strictest in the world in terms of electioneering" (Curtis, 1988).

Established in 1950, the POEL's original intent was to lessen the financial burden that campaigns place on individual candidates, especially in terms of political campaign advertising. Provisions within the POEL limit the type, amount, and means by which candidates are allowed to distribute political information and advertising through the mass media and other channels. Means included in the "other channels" range from campaign posters (which must conform to a certain size) and paper lanterns to placards and pamphlets (*Senkyoseido kenkyuiinkai*, 2001). The POEL was originally aimed at "words or text" contained in political advertising; however, with the advent of television as a political campaign medium in the early 1960s, the scope of political advertising was revised in 1964 to include images (Section 142). The following section of the POEL, Section 143, also itemizes the appropriate formats and limits for campaign-related information such as posters, signboards, electronic lighting, and billboards (*Jichisho senkyobu*, 1995).

In addition to the physical composition, distribution, and availability of campaign-related information, the POEL also contains provisions for an "official campaign period," ranging from seven to twenty days that is set aside immediately prior to any national, prefectural, or local election held in Japan. Within this time period, the POEL distinguishes between two types of politics-related activities: "political activities" (*seiji undo*) are those activities that are undertaken for political education purposes and "campaign activities" (*senkyo undo*) are political actions undertaken expressly for the purpose of obtaining votes or influencing the electorate during the period immediately before any public election. The "official campaign period" was originally established to prevent candidates from directly influencing voters before an election.

The provisions in the POEL regarding media use during election campaigns are also supported by the non-partisan stance of the Japanese broadcasting and print media (Flanagan, 1996). During election campaign periods, news programs scrupulously avoid direct mention of candidates, and individual politicians are not allowed to directly purchase political advertising in either the broadcast or print media. Alternatively, each candidate is allowed one television appearance on the national television network and must adhere to strict guidelines with regard to commercials and print advertisements prior to the officially designated campaign activities period. Political parties, on the other hand, have enjoyed relatively greater freedom in political advertising through the media. Yet here as well, parties are restricted in actively promoting individual candidates or targeting constituencies during the campaign activities period. These restrictions have led to suggestions that the mass media plays a less crucial role in forming political impressions than in other countries (Flanagan, 1996). This type of media environment in turn enhances the local, networking nature of each candidate's or potential politician's local networking organization (Akuto, 1996).

The final factor that Japanese political actors have contended with in terms of integrating the Internet into their campaigns was the actual Internet user population in Japan. In 1996, Japanese Internet users comprised less than five million people, or about 4 percent of the total population, compared with the US user population of close to 10 percent (Japan Internet Association, 1998). Even by 1998, Internet users in Japan comprised only 7 percent of the population, compared to approximately 23 percent and 10 percent in the United States and the United Kingdom, respectively (Japan Internet Association, 1998, 2000).

Although Japanese political actors – especially political parties and candidates – have had a certain amount of experience with other media channels such as television, figuring out how to use the Internet most effectively within their political campaigns has been rather challenging, given the above factors. In a political culture that relies on local networking and relationships, how does a political party or candidate establish a potentially "voting" relationship through a website or through email communications? Another potential serious issue concerned whether websites fall within the restrictions contained in the POEL regarding the format of political campaign advertising. While the answers to these questions continue to be addressed by political actors in any country, integrating the Internet with Japan's political culture, legislative, and media environment has proved to be particularly interesting.

WEBSITES AND THE POEL: 1995 TO 1999

Japanese political actors first started experimenting with the Internet during the summer of 1995 when a small number of candidates created websites to promote their platforms for the 1995 Upper House election.

Their online efforts quickly drew the attention of the Ministry of Home Affairs (currently the Ministry of Public Management, Home Affairs, and Posts and Communications, or MPMHAPC). Concerned about election platforms posted on individual politicians' websites, the Ministry requested candidates to remove their websites.

The issue resurfaced shortly before the October 1996 Lower House election when approximately forty candidates constructed websites as part of their election campaign activities. By this time, all major Japanese political parties had established websites, the majority of which contained party platforms and candidate and constituency listings. Decreeing that the "text and images" contained within websites constituted a form of political advertising that was viewable by an "unspecified number of people," the Ministry warned of potential infringements of Section 142 of the POEL (Sato, 1996). Although a number of politicians withdrew their websites, opposition political parties challenged the government's interpretation of the use of the Internet.

In early October, the now-defunct New Party Sakigake submitted a public inquiry to the Ministry arguing that websites, "being of a different nature than materials such as pamphlets or posters, fall within a grey zone" (Kojima, 1996). The party also asked the Ministry to distinctly clarify the boundaries between "political activities" and "campaign activities" (*Sakigake kaitogan*, 1996). The Ministry replied by issuing a statement that "Internet [use] notwithstanding, if candidates conduct activities with the goal of getting elected and thereby influence voters, those activities are deemed to be 'campaign activities' and violate the POEL" (Sato, 1996). In response, all political parties complied voluntarily with the Ministry's directives and removed their candidate listings and public platforms from their websites prior to October 8, the start of the official campaign activities period. A further statement issued by the Ministry at the end of the month upheld the government's application of the POEL to the contents of websites established by political parties and candidates (Miyoshiki, 1996).

After the 1996 general election, the furore regarding the use of websites for political campaigning subsided until the following spring, when the DPJ convened a study group composed of nine representatives from three political parties (the LDP, Shinshinto, and DPJ) to discuss how the Internet could be used for political activities. Although no consensus was reached, the following year, a month prior to the 1998 Upper House election, the DPJ submitted a proposal for reforming the POEL to allow websites to be used for election campaign activities. As in the 1996 general election, a number of parties provided lists of candidates on their sites, but removed them prior to the official campaign activities period. Even though the use of the Internet was discussed among the LDP, New Komeito, and Jiyuto parties at a party secretaries' conference in early December, 1999, it remained the only point on which the parties could not agree, and the LDP in particular was opposed to the use of the Internet for campaign purposes (Oniki, 1999).

During this initial period of compliance with the POEL, it was clear that opposition parties and their respective candidates took a positive attitude towards the use of the Internet for political campaign purposes. For newer political parties, the use of the Internet offered an inexpensive means for proposing election platforms, publicizing their party policies and candidates, and communicating with the electorate. Yet the strictures of the POEL constrained them from actively campaigning on the Internet throughout the official election campaign activities period immediately prior to elections.

THE FIRST "WEB" ELECTION: 2000

With a general election set to be called prior to October 2000, Japanese political actors took to the Net in earnest. Since 1998, Japan had experienced an "Internet boom," as the user population quadrupled to close to twenty million people by early 2000 (Japan Internet Association, 2001). Furthermore, American and British examples of how the Internet could be used in political campaigns provided impetus for political parties and candidates to emphasize their campaigns through the Internet.

The pro-Internet stance taken by newly established but smaller parties continued into early 2000. The main opposition party, the DPJ, was particularly proactive. In a February, 2000 magazine article, DPJ leader Yukio Hatoyama emphasized the practicality of using the Internet in communicating with and eliciting opinions from the electorate (Netbrain, 2000). Other parties also followed suit as the New Komeito Party established an internal "Internet committee" that concentrated on website development.

In spite of the fact that other parties were embracing the Internet, LDP politicians were slow to embrace the use of the Internet. Although Prime Minister Mori actively encouraged potential candidates and current politicians to establish websites in March, 2000, only 33 percent of LDP candidates had sites, compared to more than 80 percent of DPJ candidates and 50 percent of New Komeito Party candidates. As partial compensation for the lack of self-produced websites, the main LDP party site offered individual profile pages of its candidates.

In May, the government announced that a general election would be held on June 25, and political parties and candidates started to focus on the election in their website contents to varying degrees. A website content analysis conducted over May, June, and July, 2000 (incorporating periods before, during, and after the official campaign activities period) demonstrates that parties experimented with different uses of the Web through targeting certain voting populations and communicating with the electorate while at the same time complying with the POEL.

As with their past efforts to legally integrate the use of the websites in political campaigns, the DPJ demonstrated the most proactive stance towards using the Internet. At the end of May, it established an election-specific website, with a separate domain name to focus attention on the election. The site contained statements from prominent party members, results of an interactive poll that had been placed on the main party website, and various articles regarding democracy in Japan written by noted researchers. The New Komeito Party also took a dynamic approach to the election by creating a similar election-oriented section on its site, with candidate statements and links to candidate sites.

Three parties – the LDP, DPJ, and New Komeito – used their websites to strategically target certain voting populations. Click-through banners on the top pages of their websites allowed users to access sections aimed specifically at certain demographic voting groups such as women, youth, and urban-dwelling professionals. The DPJ and LDP sites also prominently featured daily updates of national, regional, and party-related news. The DPJ focused attention on the former Prime Minister by placing a banner on its website emphasizing his popularity ratings with the electorate. In addition, the DPJ and New Komeito parties offered the most varied range of communicative functions through their sites. In additional to email addresses (which all parties listed on their sites), the DPJ offered audio messages from candidates, replays of its TV commercials, and instant interactive polls. The DPJ also participated in live broadcast events and was the first party to offer both HTML-based and cellular telephone or i-mode[1] versions of its main party website.

Mindful of the restrictions of the POEL, although the refresh dates of the websites showed that parties updated their sites daily, the sections of the websites that dealt specifically with the election were not updated. The DPJ and LDP parties continued to post current events and news-related links on the top pages of their sites through the official campaign activities period (June 13–25). In contrast, the New Liberal Party featured a banner prominently on its website stating that it was refraining from updating any sections of its website during the two-week period immediately prior to the election.

Given current data, it is impossible to link campaign activities conducted through the Internet directly with voting results. However, it is still possible to discern important trends from the experiences of these parties on the Web. First, as was the case in the US and UK during the late 1990s, information flows tended to be top-down in nature. Except for the instant polls that were updated weekly on the DPJ site, none of the major parties offered direct interactive features on their sites designed to communicate with the electorate in real time. Although the parties were aware of the advantages of the Internet, they demonstrated a certain caution in incorporating an Internet strategy within their standard campaign media mixes.

Second, in addition to competing with other parties and candidates through the Internet during this election period, non-traditional political actors and individuals emerged in the campaign milieu. Political interest groups and individuals produced email newsletters, bulletin-board services, and chat groups to engage in Internet-based political dialogue. Ideologically neutral political portal sites such as *senkyo de go* (makepeace.tripod.co.jp) and election.co.jp (www.election.co.jp) offered political information, links to major political parties and candidates, and Internet-based surveys. "Anti-candidate" (*rakusen*) websites were also launched as politically concerned individuals used the Internet as a means for evaluating individual candidates and politicians and engaging in political dialogue. Although the POEL was often cited as one reason why parties and candidates felt restricted on the WWW, the emergence of these new "Internet-based" political actors signaled an important trend. These sites circumvented the POEL, which had heretofore been applied only to the website contents of political parties, candidates, and politicians.

THE SECOND "INTERNET CAMPAIGN": 2001

In the one-year period between the June 2000 general election and the July 2001 Upper House election, the Internet continued to gain popularity in Japan. By mid-2001, the number of people with access to the Internet through either PC-based or mobile telephone devices rose to over thirty million, or approximately 25 percent of the Japanese population (Japan Internet Association, 2001).

Although most of the attention to date had been focused on the use of the Internet specifically during election campaign periods, two important events during this year demonstrated advantages and disadvantages in using it for political activities. Late in 2000, LDP faction leader Kato Koichi, spurred by thousands of anonymous messages pledging support received through his website, made an unsuccessful internal attempt to unseat former Prime Minister Mori Yoshiro. This turn of events led to speculation among politicians concerning the use of the Internet as a means of gauging political support, as it became obvious that the anonymous nature of email messages did not translate into real political support. However, this event also focused attention on the use of websites and Internet-based communications in non-election periods, which were again not covered within the POEL.

Yet the most significant manifestation of the Internet as a political tool was the skillful way in which current Prime Minister Jun'ichiro Koizumi used his website to successfully win the party's internal leadership race. By appealing directly to party members at the local levels through his website, Koizumi was able to gain enough popular support within the LDP to secure the nomination. Continuing his championing of the Internet as a political tool, in late May the Prime Minister started distributing a weekly email newsletter through the official Prime Minister's Office website that quickly proved highly popular, garnering a subscription base of two million within two months of its inception (Video Research, 2001). As the newsletter was distributed through the Prime Minister's Office, it successfully avoided the POEL's jurisdiction. Heralded as the first email newsletter produced by a major world leader and disseminated directly to the electorate, this strategic use of the Internet signaled an important turning point in using the Internet to establish a relationship between political actors and the Japanese public.

As a result of Koizumi's successful non-campaign use of the Internet, a new attitude towards the Internet permeated the 2001 Upper House election campaign. If the trend in Internet-based political activities in 2000 focused on parties and websites, the 2001 campaign placed an emphasis on personalities and email campaigns. In turn, the 2001 campaign versions of the websites produced by almost all parties reflected these trends by prominently featuring party leaders and regularly distributing email newsletters through various formats. The LDP, DPJ, New Komeito, and JCP also experimented with cellular phone-based versions of their websites with some disseminating email newsletters through cellular phone messaging systems.

CONCLUSION

We have seen that, in locating the political use of the Internet within Japan's political culture, legislative, media, and Internet environments, a number of important trends have been highlighted.

Returning to the first question posed at the beginning of this chapter, the above discussion indicates that the POEL proved no match for the reinvigorated political Internet on a number of fronts. From 1995 to 2000, the period in which the Internet was used mainly as a broadcast medium, there was some possibility that it could be restricted under the POEL. However, when the communicative functions of the Internet were employed, it became a more individually oriented, communicative medium. Despite being applied initially to the contents of websites, specifically those produced by political parties and candidates, the POEL made no provision for email communications. Political parties and a select number of candidates continued to distribute email bulletins to subscribed members throughout the official election campaign period in July, 2001. Moreover, the convergence of fixed PC-based Internet applications and cellular phone-based messaging systems complicated the relationship between "text and images" widely available through the Internet and those that are viewable on individual cell phones. These factors, combined with the upsurge in the numbers of non-traditional political actors on the Internet, led to the establishment of a review committee in the autumn of 2001 to investigate the relevance of applying the POEL to the new uses of the Internet.

This study of how the Internet was used within the political environment in Japan has also demonstrated that the strategic use of the Internet possibly creates new relationships, not only among voters, politicians, candidates, and political parties, but also with other political actors. This points to the need for a longer term and more analytical study to assess the voter–political actor relationship as mediated through the Internet. In the future, the initial trend of political actors' superseding mediating political influences such as the mass media or political parties in possibly two-way communicative situations may become more prevalent.

Although the promise of a "digital democracy" or "e-democracy" may be many years away, and may take forms different from what have been suggested by scholars, it remains a possibility. Only comparative and intensive study concerning the political uses of the Internet in cross-national environments can truly reveal the potential of the political Internet.

NOTE

1 Docomo's "i-mode" is a proprietary instant-messaging protocol introduced in 1999 and available through cellular phones by subscription and is similar to "short-messaging systems" (SMS) provided by European telecommunications carriers. Docomo is a subsidiary of Nippon Telegraph and Telecommunications (NTT).

BIBLIOGRAPHY

Abramson, J.D., Arterton, F.C. and Orren, R. (1988) *The Electronic Commonwealth: The Impact of New Media Technologies on Democratic Politics*, New York: Basic Books.

Akuto, H. (1996) "Media in electoral campaigning in Japan and the United States," in S.J. Pharr and E.S. Krauss (eds) *Media and Politics in Japan*, Honolulu: University of Hawai'i Press.

Curtis, G.L. (1971) *Election Campaigning Japanese Style*, New York: Columbia University Press.

—— (1988) *The Japanese Way of Politics*, New York: Columbia University Press.

Davis, R. (1999) *The Web of Politics: The Internet's Impact on the American Political System*, New York: Oxford University Press.

Delli Carpini, M.X. (1996) "Voters, candidates, and campaigns in the new information age: an overview and assessment," *Press/Politics*, 1, 4: 36–56.

Doi, T. (1973) *The Anatomy of Dependence*, New York: Kodansha International.

Flanagan, S.C. (1996) "Media exposure and the quality of political participation in Japan," in S.J. Pharr and E.S. Krauss (eds) *Media and Politics in Japan*, Honolulu: University of Hawai'i Press.

Foot, K.A. and Schneider, S.M. (2002) "Online action in the US 2000 political campaign," in V. Servaty (ed.) *L'Internet en Politique, Des Etats-Unis A L'Europe* (Politics on the Internet: The United States and Europe), Strasbourg, France: University of Strasbourg Press.

Gibson, R. and Ward, S.J. (1998) "UK political parties and the Internet: 'politics as usual' in the new media?" *Press/Politics*, 3, 3: 14–38.

Grossman, L. (1995) *The Electronic Republic*, New York: Penguin Books.

Hachigian, N. (2002) "The Internet and power in one-party East Asian states," *The Washington Quarterly*, 25, 3: 41–58.

Hill, K.A. and Hughes, J.E. (1998) *Cyberpolitics: Citizen Activism in the Age of the Internet*, Lanham, MD: Rowman & Littlefield, Inc.

Japan Internet Association (1998) *Intanetto hakusho 1998* (Internet White Paper 1998), Tokyo: Japan Internet Association.

—— (2000) *Intanetto hakusho 2000* (Internet White Paper 2000), Tokyo: Japan Internet Association.

—— (2001) *Intanetto hakusho 2001* (Internet White Paper 2001), Tokyo: Japan Internet Association.

Jichisho Senkyobu (Ministry of Home Affairs) (1995) *Koshokusenkyoho* (The Public Offices Elections Law), Tokyo: Gyosei.

Kamarck, E.C. (1999) "Campaigning on the Internet in the elections of 1998," in E.C. Karmarck and J.S. Nye (eds) *democracy.com*, Hollis, NH: Hollis Publishing Company.

Kojima, N. (1996) "*Sakigake, intanetto no homupeji ni kokoku, kosenho kitei nashi* (Sakigake advertises on its website: No regulations exist)." Online. Available HTTP: http://www.mainichi.co.jp/eye/sousenkyo/article/internet/1996/1010. html (accessed May 9, 2000).

Margolis, M. and Resnick, D. (2000) *Politics as Usual: The Cyberspace Revolution*, Thousand Oaks, CA: Sage.

Margolis, M., Resnick, D., and Tu, C.C. (1997) "Campaigning on the Internet: parties and candidates on the world wide web in the 1996 primary season," *Press/Politics*, 2, 1: 59–78.

Margolis, M., Resnick, D., and Wolfe, J.D. (1999) "Party competition on the Internet in the United States and Britain," *Press/Politics*, 4, 4: 24–47.

Martin, C.H. and Stronach, B. (1992) *Politics East and West: Political Culture in Japan and Britain*, Armonk: M.E. Sharpe.

Miyoshik, Y. (1996) "*Denpa senkyo' ni jichisho ga 'no,' homupeji ha kosenho no kisei taisho* (Ministry of Home Affairs says 'no' to 'electronic elections,' aims at regulating web sites)." Online. Available HTTP: mainichi.co.jp/eye/sousenkyo/article/internet/1996/1030-1.html (accessed May 9, 2000).

Nakane, C. (1972) *Japanese Society*, Berkeley: University of California Press.

Netbrain (2000) "*Giin kaikan kara akusesu kano, kojin saito wa seito de notan* (Access from the Diet made possible, parties focus on individual sites)," April, p. 21.

Oniki, H. (1999) " '*Homupeji de no senkyo undo' jijiko goi kara hazusareru* (LDP, Jiyuto, and New Komeito disagree on using websites for election campaign activities)." Online. Available HTTP: http://www.mainichi.co.jp/eye/sousenkyo/article/internet/1999/1204.html (accessed May 8, 2000).

Rash, W.R. (1997) *Politics on the Nets*, New York: W.H. Freeman & Co.

Rheingold, H. (1994) *The Virtual Community: Finding Connection in a Computerised World*, London: Minerva.

Richardson, B.M. and Flanagan, S.C. (1984) *Politics in Japan*, Boston, MA: Little, Brown & Company.

Sakigake kaitogan (1996) (New Party Sakigake, public enquiry) October 2. Online.

Available HTTP: coara.or.jp/~sakigake/etc/renketu.html (accessed December 28, 2000).

Sato, H. (1996) *"Jijitsujo no 'kaikin' jyotai: seisaku senden ya kaihyo sokuho* (The reality of lifting the ban: political advertising and the latest election results)." Online. Available HTTP: mainichi.co.jp/eye/sousenkyo/article/internet/1996/1008-2.html (accessed May 9, 2000).

Selnow, G. (1998) *Electronic Whistle Stops: The Impact of the Internet on American Politics*, Westport, CT: Praeger.

Senkyoseido kenkyuiinkai (2001) *Senkyo seido no shikumi* (Japanese elections), Tokyo: Senkyoseido Kenkyuiinkai.

Stockwin, J.A.A. (1987) "Japan: the leader–follower relationship in parties," in A. Ware (ed.) *Political Parties: Electoral Change and Structural Response*, Oxford: Blackwell.

Trent, J.S. and Friedenberg, R.V. (2000) *Political Campaign Communication: Principles and Practices*, Westport, CT: Praeger.

Verba, S., Nie, N.H. and Kim, J.O. (1978) *Participation and Political Equality: A Seven-nation Comparison*, Cambridge: Cambridge University Press.

Video Research Ltd. (2001) *"Intanetto oodeiensu sokutei: shushokanshi saito/merumaga hakkou kaishi-de akusesu kyuuzou (2001.6.25)* (Internet Audience Survey: Access to the Prime Minister's website rapidly increases 2001.6.25)." Online. Available HTTP: http://www.vrnet.com.co.jp/webm/web6/index.html (accessed December 15, 2001).

11 The Tamil diaspora, Tamil militancy, and the Internet

Shyam Tekwani

Every new innovation in communication technology since the printing press has worried governments about the resulting impact on sovereignty, but these worries have been misplaced, as these governments have been able to use the technology to strengthen their hold on public opinion (Perritt, 1998). The Internet may yet, however, prove to be the exception. Perhaps the most distinguishing feature of the Internet that makes it more threatening to governments than earlier advances in technology is that it is not susceptible to the same physical and regulatory controls as print, telegraph, telephone, radio, and television technologies.

Overseas ethnic diasporas have traditionally formed networks to exchange goods and services, including news and information, with other members of the diaspora. Even before the advent of mass communication technologies and the mass media, members of these diasporas always found ways to communicate with the home country and to keep abreast of the community in the host country, either through the post and telegraph, telephone, or the newspaper or radio and television. However, the spread of the Internet has added significantly to the ability of the diaspora to create and sustain such networks. Although these networks have used every available mode of communication through the ages to maintain the networks of trade and communication, the Internet is particularly suited to their needs, as it is relatively inexpensive and allows for almost instant, one-to-one communication. Online media, unlike other forms of capital-intensive media such as broadcast media which follows a top-down and hierarchical model, allows easier access and is non-linear, largely non-hierarchical, and relatively inexpensive (Karim *et al.*, 1998).

Karim (2002) documents how diasporic communities have become extensive users of online services such as email, Internet Relay Chat, Usenet, Listserv, and the World Wide Web. As the number of language scripts and translation capabilities of online software grows, an increasing number of non-English speakers are drawn to the medium (Karim, 2002), thus increasing the potential impact of the Internet on these communities.

Activist groups, within ethnic diasporas, have the potential to become a strategic asset their home countries and territories can draw upon to help them achieve regional politico-military objectives. A study by the Rand Corporation (Nichiporuk, 2000) describes the role diasporas are increasingly playing in the political/militant movements in their home countries, through extensive fund-raising activities, and international public relations campaigns:

> The growing web of information, communications, and mass media links, including the Internet, international TV news networks, and global banking nets, increases opportunities for globally distributed ethnic Diasporas to play a key role in military campaigns involving their home state or territory. This can be done through extensive fund-raising for the purchase and transfer of arms, an international public relations campaign to demonize opponents of the home state, or the exertion of pressure upon governments in host countries to turn against the enemies of their home state or territory.
>
> (Nichiporuk, 2000)

The report cites as a tangible example the Tamil diaspora in Canada and Western Europe that has been active in funneling financial support to the Tamil insurgents fighting Sinhalese government forces in Sri Lanka. It predicts that with time, key diasporas would acquire even more influence upon the military balance in their home regions. The report warns that diplomatic, intelligence, and defense policy-makers would have to consider ever more carefully the impact of ethnic diasporas upon regional wars in the next ten to twenty years, as they become more involved in supporting the military standpoints and campaigns of their home states.

DIASPORAS ON THE NET

While several researchers have seen in the Internet a potential to strengthen democratic processes (Rheingold, 1993; Zekos 1999), some commentators have seen in the Internet a threat to governments' ability to maintain political and ideological power. Political and other groups hostile to traditional governmental functions and policies are perceived as using the Internet to strengthen their respective causes and to increase the perceived threat to national integration and sovereignty. The Internet, which functions as a network rather than an institution, unlike other forms of traditional mass media that are fairly institutionalized in both their structure and their politics, is ideally suited to social/militant movements, and is clearly an ideal tool in a "netwar." Militant movements operate without the support of institutional power, usually seeking alternative forms of power to compensate for those held and used by the institutions they seek to change (Cooper and Nothstine, 1992). For many militant groups, the Internet is increasingly the alternative form of power. In recent years, almost all known and several unknown rebel groups fighting for separate homelands across the globe have expanded their zone of conflict to the Internet. Many of these sites are hosted on servers thousands of miles away from the zone of conflict. While local guerrillas are fighting unconventional wars at home, their supporters and political think-tanks comprising both active militant cells and their diasporic brethren overseas are busy drawing international attention to their side of the story in cyberspace.

While some of these sites are created and maintained by the "political" representatives of militant groups abroad, as in Tamilcanadian.com, or by the militants themselves, such as that of the Moro National Liberation Front (http://mnlf.net//), many others are hosted and maintained by members of ethnic diasporas who have settled in the West and use the Internet to maintain links with the homeland and other members of the diaspora, while simultaneously drawing the world's attention to the plight of their ethnic or religious group in their home countries.

For example, the Zapatistas' activist supporters in the US have been rallying support for the guerrillas online (http://www.ezln.org/) since their 1994 uprising. Burmese expatriates have several networked sites on the Internet that draw the world's attention to the pro-democracy movement in Burma and counter the restricted political and social environment that exists within the military junta's Burma. East Timor's National Council for Maubere Resistance, the main body of resistance to Indonesian rule, ran a website (http://www.uc.pt/Timor/TimorNet.html) which was hosted on a server at Portugal's University of Coimbra. The *Organisesi Papua Merdeka* (*OPM*, the Free West Papua Movement), agitating for the separation of the western half of the island of Papua New Guinea from Indonesia, ran a website (http://www.converge.org.nz/wpapua/) from New Zealand. The BFM, or the Bougainville Freedom Movement, of the Bougainville Revolutionary Army, fighting the Papua New Guinea government for a separate homeland, ran a website (http://www.magna.com.au/~sashab/BFM.htm) that was hosted from Sydney to mobilize support from sympathizers from all over the world.

Among terrorist groups, defined here as groups with a political agenda engaged simultaneously in a violent armed struggle including attacks on civilians, the Revolutionary Armed Forces of Colombia (FARC) fields press inquiries through electronic mail (http://www.resistencianacional.org/). Peru's primary terrorist organization, Shining Path (http://www.csrp.org/) and (http://www.blythe.org/peru-pcp/), broadcast their Marxist-Leninist propaganda online. In South Asia, the Liberation Tigers of Tamil Eelam's site (http://www.eelam.com) is one of the several sites reflecting the view of Sri Lanka's Tamil Tigers, fighting a bloody war for a homeland for minority Tamils in Northeast Sri Lanka, and vigorously supported by the Tamil diaspora. Kashmiri militants fighting for independence along the Himalayan borders of India have sites maintained from Britain (http://www.kashmir.demon.co.uk/ and http://www.ummah.org.uk/kashmir/). Middle Eastern groups such as the HAMAS have extensive networks on the Internet and are linked to an intricate web of supporters among diasporic communities across the world.

As the Internet expands to include more users and encompass wider, more interconnected networks linking Asia to such resistance movements, terrorist groups have been just as quick as their counterparts in more developed societies to appropriate the new technologies to their own use. The LTTE in fact has been a pioneer in this regard, using the Internet to overcome government controls on media to reach out to the Tamil community settled outside Sri Lanka.

Asia's encounter with the Internet takes on a unique and particularly fascinating dimension when looked at from within the context of how militant and political groups opposed to their governments use the Internet to reach out to the international media to disseminate propaganda, recruit, train, and solicit funds and influence international public opinion and, most importantly, to network with members of the diaspora across the globe. The website even provided samples of Canadian and US passports, presumably put online to aid militants in the fabrication of false identities.[1]

As Karim (2002) has noted, a number of post-colonial diaspora groups, as well as older groups such as Europe's Roma, are using online networks to communicate. The content of their messaging consists largely of cultural, heritage, genealogical, and religious information, as the sites contain discussions of traditional lore, festivals, and recipes and worldwide locations of community members and institutions to community publications, local activities, news from home, or the home country. Current events and developments in the diaspora are discussed regularly on online news groups. Individuals from respective diasporas use the Net to create online resources about their cultures, often in collaboration with cross-cultural research teams, as well as using the Internet to create directories of community members and services. Karim concedes that while a cyber network does not allow for the same level of interaction as a real community, it facilitates communication to a much greater extent than has been previously possible for diasporic groups.

In addition to all the social, cultural, and economic networking that the Internet enables, the ongoing communication revolution enables diasporic communities to have more rapid and visible means of calling attention to issues of interest in their home countries, as well as to correct what are considered misperceptions by outsiders and mobilize political support. In a study of nationalist websites from Kurdistan, Macedonia, and Armenia, Bakker (2001) found that "the aim of these websites is to (re)construct a true nation and to create counter-knowledge about a specific region." All these websites, some of which have registered over a million hits, are hosted in the Western world. According to Bakker, "the diaspora is very visible, members of the (virtual) nation can be found everywhere."

Diasporas are also using the Internet to overcome restrictions imposed by borders and national regulations. Karim (2002) gives the example of several online services catering to Sindhis, an ethnic group originating from the Indian subcontinent whose members were dispersed by the partition of colonial India and by migration patterns outside the subcontinent. These services help to electronically re-create the community, which has no homeland in the offline world. A Hong Kong-based website provides Sindhi history, culture, literature, directories, and recipes and, along with a host of other interlinked sites, seeks to reunite the dispersed community in cyberspace.

Given the globalization of these local resistance movements, several questions arise. One of these is: How and why do social/militant movements use the new communication technologies? In other words, what are the particular characteristics of the Internet which make it prone to use by these groups? Moreover, how do diasporic communities use the new communication technologies to actively support homeland wars in the country of their origin? I will use as a framework Arquilla and Ronfeldt's definition of "netwar," and seek to illustrate my arguments by examining the use of new communications technology by the Tamil rebel group, the LTTE in Sri Lanka, and the Tamil diaspora scattered around the globe.

NETWAR AND THE ORGANIZATION OF SUPPORT

In a ground-breaking work on conflict in the Information Age, Arquilla and Ronfeldt (1997) analyze what they refer to as "netwar." Their thesis focuses on how the information revolution causes shifts in how societies may come into conflict and how they will wage war:

> Netwar refers to information-related conflict at a grand level between nations or societies. It means trying to disrupt what a target population "knows" or thinks it knows about itself and the world around it. A netwar may focus on public or elite opinion, or both. It may involve public diplomacy measure, propaganda and psychological campaigns, political and cultural subversion, deception of or interference with local media, infiltration of computer networks and databases, and efforts to promote dissident or opposition movements across computer networks.
>
> (Arquilla and Ronfeldt, 1997, p. 28)

The term "netwar" draws more on the word "network" rather than "Net" as in Internet, connoting that the information revolution is as much about organizational prowess as it is about technological prowess, and that this revolution favors whoever masters the network form. The key defining characteristic of a netwar is that it "consists of a web (or network) of dispersed, interconnected 'nodes' (or activity centers)" (Arquilla and Ronfeldt, 1997). These centers may be individuals, groups, formal or informal organizations, or parts of groups or organizations. The sectors, cells, or nodes may differ in size, level of integration, membership, appearance, and specialization.

The success of such a netwar actor then depends on the strength of the underpinning ideology or common goal that binds the nodes or cells together, despite their disparate locations or functions, and enables them to work autonomously towards one common strategic or ideological objective.

The experiences of diasporic activist groups give them a unique position to wield the advantages offered by the information revolution. They have, even in the pre-Internet era, been masters of the network form out of necessity. With the Internet, itself a structure of networks, they are now reaching out to their militant brethren, as much as the militant groups themselves have sought them out in the past for their support and their funds. Militancy and activism in the information era then becomes a matter of merging existing networks, or linking them to form newer, wider networks that are more effective and less penetrable.

The framework set by Arquilla and Ronfeldt helps to demonstrate how the networked structure of the Internet has attracted the mass migration of social and militant movements to the Internet, and how the traditionally networked diasporic groups have been able to adapt the information revolution to extend and deepen their links with each other and with their homelands, and in many instances to act as independent nodes of the militant network, pursuing a common ideological or strategic goal.

MILITANT MOVEMENTS AND NEW COMMUNICATION TECHNOLOGIES

Computers and the new media technologies offer tremendous advantages to ethnic diasporas and the political groups that sometimes emerge from them, in much the same way that they benefit business corporations. Primary among these is quick and easy communication and increased access to established networks, and access to international media and an international audience. The primary use of the new technology for such politically motivated groups is the dissemination of political propaganda, to aid in recruitment and fund-raising and, most importantly, to draw international attention and support. The Internet strengthens these groups by allowing them to reach a much larger pool of potential recruits, solicit funds and raise awareness, all at a low cost with low risk of detection or interception. Most of their websites are hosted on foreign servers, usually in the West, and are usually published in English to directly reach an international audience. Many of these sites are sophisticated in design and intricately networked, with extensive links and video and audio clips. They are often updated on the same day that events in the offline world occur, and some are even updated on an hourly basis. The invisible nature of these electronic associations means that terrorist groups and their support networks can now develop and expand without attracting the attention of intelligence agencies, and can form strategic alliances with one another in cyberspace, posing a more significant threat than their predecessors who hid in relatively more traceable terrain in the physical world, and used communication technologies that could be blocked or intercepted easily (Joyce-Hasham, 2000).

Another major advantage of the Internet for political/terrorist groups is that it allows them to reach their target audience when other outlets and media are denied them, either by distance, expense or, in many cases, government censorship. It also allows them to reach new and previously inaccessible audiences, particularly the diaspora. For example, Kashmiri extremists overcame local newspaper resistance to cover their terrorist campaign against India by using the Internet to reach international media and their target audiences within the international Muslim community. Likewise, the Mexican Zapatistas very quickly acquired a global audience and international attention to their cause and struggle because of the sophisticated use of the Internet by their NGO supporters in the United States (Castells, 1997). Wright (1991) identifies three target audiences for terrorist propaganda: the uncommitted, the sympathetic, and the active. The uncommitted audience includes the general public in the country of operation and international public opinion. The sympathetic audience comprises those who already have a broad historical or ideological sympathy with the terrorists' expressed political aims and often includes significant portions of the diasporic community. The active audience comprises self-confessed members of the terrorist organization. The Internet and other new technologies provide clear and unprecedented advantages to terrorists in reaching out effectively to all three audience groupings. Group websites and publicity sites put up by sympathizers reach out beyond national boundaries and government censors to the international media and diasporas abroad, providing a counterpoint to government-controlled media as in countries such as Sri Lanka, Cuba, and Burma.

In the case of Sri Lanka, a hostile international press is one of the factors affecting the morale of Sri Lankan troops fighting the rebels in northeast Sri Lanka, leading to the highest desertion levels in that nation's history. A hostile press abroad also hampers an economically vulnerable government's ability to successfully counter-insurgency where it may be justified to protect civilian life and property. In the case of Mexico and the EZLN, too, the military's image suffered at the hands of international media. The military was restrained, on the one hand, by activists and journalists who mounted media campaigns to tarnish its image, and, on the other, by indecisiveness on the part of Mexico's civilian leaders (Arquilla and Ronfeldt, 1997).

Gunaratna (1999) writes of emerging trends in international terrorism driven by the spread of new communication technologies:

> Due to the sweeping changes in the international environment in the late 1980s and throughout the 1990s, the dynamics that drive terrorism as well as the nature of terrorism itself has changed. Traditionally groups received external support either from a neighboring government or a political party but increasingly Diaspora, migrant, and co-ethnic communities have begun to play more assertive roles.... Further, increased travel, communication and migration mean that post-Cold War conflicts galvanize greater co-ethnic support, draw international NGO (particularly human rights and humanitarian) assistance, and generate greater Diaspora/migrant support. As a result, many post-modern conflicts have greater staying power.

Viewed within this context, diasporas function as actors in the netwar waged by militant groups. Activist groups within the diasporic community are using the networks, now greatly facilitated by new technology, to function as autonomous nodes of the militant network.

Functionally independent of the group engaged in war in the homeland, these nodes, which may vary in the intensity of their involvement, with some restricted to spreading propaganda or drawing attention to the "sacrifices" of their men waging war against the government, others actively raising funds or soliciting recruits, share a deep commitment to the professed goals of the militants. This commitment may stem from an ethnic bond, a shared belief in the "justness" or inevitability of the war being waged, or a conviction that the militants represent their own ethno-political goals.

THE SRI LANKAN TAMIL DIASPORA

The Tamil diaspora exists in nearly all of the world's richest countries, and in recent years has shown exponential growth in the interrelated economic, financial, and educational sectors. Tamils began leaving Sri Lanka in 1956, when Sinhalese was made the official language of the country, with many of these emigrants leaving for greater opportunities in the UK and North America. The numbers increased in the 1970s, but it was in 1983 that the real exodus began, as thousands of Tamil refugees fled ethnic riots which rocked the island in July of that year. The British colonial policy of divide and rule unleashed historical tensions between the Sinhalese and Tamil communities after independence in 1948. Tamils, although well educated, were given a disproportionate number of powerful positions in the Civil Service by the British. The Tamil minority was seen to have received preferential treatment. Since Sri Lanka became independent in 1948, the Sinhalese majority has dominated the country. The growth of an assertive Sinhala nationalism fanned the flames of ethnic division. Politicians sought to redress the balance with populist but discriminatory policies against Tamils. By the mid-1970s, Tamils were calling for a separate state in the north and east of the country. In 1983, the country erupted into full-scale communal violence after thirteen soldiers were killed by Tamil militants and civil war erupted between Tamils pressing for self-rule and the government.

The earlier emigrants are now settled in their countries of domicile, and are beginning to play a growing role in the economic, political, and cultural life of these countries (Wijemane, 2000). In the UK alone, where more than 80,000 Tamils live, the numerical and economic strength of the community is significant enough for local politicians to pander to its votes by criticizing the actions of the Sri Lankan government, and on occasion lobbying for the rights of the Tamil movement and its representatives with the British government. The annual per capita income of the Tamil diaspora is now estimated, on the most conservative basis, at around US$20,000, or about twenty-two times greater than the annual per capita income of the population of Sri Lanka (Wijemane, 2000).

Even before the Internet boom, the Tamil diaspora was networked and used these networks to form cohesiveness, such as during the 1983 riots in Colombo, spreading the news and attracting world attention to the plight of Tamils in Sri Lanka. Descriptions of the riots by international news media evoked widespread sympathy for Sri Lanka's Tamils, which was exploited by many Tamils already living abroad, including propagandists for the many fledgling militant groups that then existed, and militant groups benefitted from donations by members of the already large and rapidly growing Sri Lankan Tamil diaspora (Richardson, 1999). Today, the growing financial strength and international power of the Tamil diaspora is the new reality, and a vital third factor in the economics and politics of Sri Lanka that the government cannot ignore. The Sri Lankan government has no control over it at all and many believe that this strength will have a significant role to play in determining the final military outcome on the island (Wijemane, 2000). For example, many of the estimated 700,000 Tamils living outside Sri Lanka left in the aftermath of the 1983 anti-Tamil riots, and are believed to be die-hard *Eelamists*, willing to settle for nothing less than a separate state for Tamils. Eelam is the name of the independent homeland, comprising the north and the east of Sri Lanka that the Tamil rebels are claiming. This emigrant community contributes an estimated US$2 million monthly to the LTTE's war chest (Subramanian, 2000).

Until 1987, Tamils outside the country were able to keep track of events in the Tamil northeast on a daily basis, through community organizations, the Church, and non-government agencies. With the Indo–Sri peace accord of 1987, many more of these groups shut down their operations in the belief that peace was at hand. But when violence resumed in

1990, most of their news sources had dried up. By then, the Internet was fast filling in the vacuum.

Ironically, the development of the Internet has coincided with the escalation of the ethnic war in Sri Lanka, which first erupted into violence in July, 1983. Today, even as local and international media are kept away from the actual war zone by the Sri Lankan government, daily reports on events related to the war are available from many sources on a day-to-day basis, to anyone with a computer and modem.

THE WAR IN CYBERSPACE

Internet access is far from widespread within Sri Lanka. Less than 10 percent of households in the country are connected to the telecommunications network, though under the current liberalization-privatization policies the network is believed to be growing at around 30 percent per year (Samarajiva, 1998). Sri Lanka has one dominant carrier, six facilities-based data communication operators, and two non-facilities-based data operators offering Internet connectivity. Most web pages put up in Sri Lanka though, according to Samarajiva, are still vanity pages, and most Internet use is for email and browsing of foreign web pages. It is the use of the Internet by Sri Lankans living outside Sri Lanka that is significant.

In spite of the low usage rates within Sri Lanka itself, the Sri Lankan Tamil diaspora is among the most networked group of expatriates, linking through email lists, chatrooms, and discussion groups that are active, vocal, and passionate. A prime example is Talking Point, a discussion group hosted on the Tamilcanadian.com site, where a broad spectrum of expatriate Tamils from across the globe comment on and discuss a variety of issues pertaining to the politics of Sri Lanka and the outcome of the ongoing war (Subramanian, 2000).

There are several pro-Tamil newspapers with names similar to popular European and US papers such as the *Tamil Tribune* (http://www.geocities.com/tamiltribune) and *Tamil Guardian* (http://www.tamilguardian.com), a pro-LTTE newspaper covering Tamil affairs in Sri Lanka and abroad. It has been widely reported that Tamils living in Sri Lanka also prefer to get their news of the war in the NE from the Internet and satellite radio stations based abroad (Majumder, 2000). Satellite radio plays an important role in the diaspora's quest for news and helps feed the data going out on the Internet as well. There are three satellite radio networks in Europe alone which cater to the Tamil community. The networks, which are independent, source their news from correspondents spread across northern Sri Lanka. Information out of Jaffna, the heart of Tamil country, and the center of the war zone, and which has no working telephone lines, is passed through word of mouth, ham radio and via the Tamil Tigers' clandestine radio station (Majumder, 2000).

Besides a network of general sites that link Tamils across the globe such as Tamilcyber and Jaffnatamils online or colombotamils online, expatriates have several well-developed sites putting out their take on the ongoing war and its implications and outcomes. Equally numerous are sites on Tamil history, culture, and politics, and information archive sites putting out the latest "news" from the war zones. Some of the more political sites are Tamilcanadian.com, tamiltigers.net, Tamilnation.org, Eelamweb.com, and sangam.org.

Many of these sites clearly set out their agendas on the website, leaving little doubt as to the purpose of the site. Tamilcanadian.com describes itself as a site for the "History and culture of Tamils of Tamil Eelam." Eelamweb.com states the following in the "About us" section:

> Eelam web is aimed at rebuilding Tamil Eelam, the traditional home land of the Tamils, which has been ravaged by the genocidal policies that have been undertaken by successive Sinhala dominated Sri Lankan governments. The mass human rights abuses committed by the Sri Lankan government and its forces are done so in the cover of a complete censorship of all information concerning Tamils in Tamil Eelam. Due to the sufferings that Tamil people are facing in their own homeland, we, at EelamWeb have found this page a necessity to expose the terror of the Sri Lankan government and its forces. Culture is the heart of any civilisation and it gives us a great responsibility as Tamils living outside of Tamil Eelam and free of suppression by the Sri Lankan government, to take the initiatives to showcase the rich culture and tradition of Tamil Eelam.
>
> (http://www.Eelamweb.com/aboutus/)

The Internet offers expatriate Tamils and Tamil rebels a cheap, convenient, and powerful medium with which to counter government propaganda and keep aloft the Tamil cause. Sites representing the Tamil movement in Sri Lanka, particularly the LTTE, are among the earliest and most sophisticated rebel sites on the Net. For example, Sangam.org, one of the major pro-Tamil sites on the Internet, describes itself unambiguously as an "organization of expatriate Tamils to promote the right to self-determination of the Tamil nation." While many of these sites are perceived as being fronted by those with real links with the LTTE, there are an equal number which are independent but still subscribe to and propagate the same political line as the militants.

For example, Tamiltigers.net, a pro-LTTE site operating out of Canada, in its "Disclaimer," has the following to say:

> This page has no connection, other than an ideological one, to the Liberation Tigers of Tamil Eelam. We are not, nor were ever, members of the LTTE. This page does not secure funds for the LTTE, nor is it

funded by the LTTE. This site exists only as an informational database. This page represents an expression of our views and as far as we know the Canadian government still allows for the freedom of expression.

(http://www.Tamiltigers.net/about.htm)

The "disclaimer" goes on for another three or four paragraphs describing in sarcastic terms why the LTTE is banned in Canada and stating that Canada supplied arms to the Sri Lankan government which uses these arms against Tamil civilians. It also mentions US military support to the "Sinhalese" Sri Lankan government and even cites the US policy turnaround on the Kosovo Liberation Army (KLA), which was listed as a terrorist organization in 1998 but became allies against Serbia in 1999! Clearly no space is to be wasted when it can be used for propaganda.

In the face of this formidable online onslaught, the Sri Lankan government, which is seen widely as losing the battle on the ground, is clearly far behind in the propaganda war as well, lacking both the resources and the passion that keeps the formidable Tamil diaspora alive and networked on the World Wide Web.

THE LTTE ONLINE

The LTTE is especially reliant on electronic propaganda disseminated via the World Wide Web and news groups (Usenet), and has established a prominent presence on the Internet, with many of its websites fully documented and indexed in popular search engines. In a study for Canadian Intelligence, academic Peter Chalk (1999) commented on the LTTE's considerable use of the Internet as a communications tool. He notes how the group has established several well-run websites with "hot links" and other "jump-off points" that are cleverly networked to internationally renowned humanitarian and development agencies. These include the World Council of Churches, the International Educational Development Inc., and the Robert Kennedy Memorial Center for Human Rights, among others, as well as citations of the teachings of Mahatma Gandhi.

The group's official website, http://www.eelam.com, provides a long list of features, including the latest "news" from the front, audio speeches of the group's leader, and songs glorifying the Tamil cause and the LTTE's campaign. Indeed, the LTTE's version of the Tamil struggle has been packaged and marketed in much the same way as a mainstream newspaper's online version, with various sections including news, analysis, history, and a media press kit.

Despite the clear propagandistic intent of the site, the Sri Lankan government, unlike others in Asia and elsewhere which have acted to block politically threatening websites, has done nothing to block access to

LTTE sites within Sri Lanka. Perhaps realizing the difficulty in doing so, the Sri Lankan government put up its own site giving the government's point of view on the ongoing war. The army's website is the latest attempt to take the battle to the enemy camp, of keeping pace with technology, and war in the cyber era. The military website (www.slarmy.org) was launched last year to carry the "official" account of the fighting. The army website provides up-to-date information on various regiments and units of the army and its version of the current situation in the combat zone. The army's advent into cyberspace has been long overdue in a battle that has been fought as much with propaganda as with conventional weapons.

One of the most significant effects of the cyberwar so far has been the ability of the LTTE and the Tamil diaspora to keep the international media and international public opinion focused on the Tamil cause, thereby applying pressure on a politically weak Sri Lankan government vulnerable to such pressure. The pro-Tamil movement has been effective in countries with a significant Tamil population, such as the UK, Canada, Europe, and Australia, as well as other countries where the group does not have a substantial or well-established ethnic presence, such as the United States.

Perhaps the most important propagandistic function is to define the group and the struggle in a way that has the most impact on public opinion. According to Arquilla and Ronfeldt (1997):

> Netwar means affecting what the opponent knows, or thinks it knows, not only about its challenger but also about itself and the world around it. Among other things, this may mean trying to shape images, beliefs, and attitudes in the social milieu in which both are operating.

The LTTE has been quick to see how the new medium could be used to shape an online image of the movement and its leadership, quite distinct from the violent terrorist actions of its cadres at home in Sri Lanka. The Tamil websites accomplish this by constantly drawing attention to the "injustices" committed against the Tamil minority by the Sinhala majority, as represented by the Sinhala government, and the "atrocities" committed by the Sri Lankan Army against Tamil civilians. Pro-Tamil websites are frequently saturated with accounts of Tamil suffering, often graphic video images of "army atrocities" or the aftermath of military action. Many of these pro-LTTE sites reproduce material and images put up on the official sites of the LTTE, thus acting as an extension of the LTTE's official propaganda machinery, even while disclaiming affiliation with the LTTE.

The LTTE, always known for its powerful propaganda machinery, has successfully transferred many of its tactics of the pre-Internet era to its websites. The LTTE songs and speeches of leader Prabhakaran that blared from loudspeakers in LTTE-controlled territory in northeast Sri Lanka in the 1980s and 1990s are now available, some free and some for sale as cassettes on the numerous pro-Tamil sites.

The graphic videos of victorious battles and suicide attacks which were shown to the Tamils and international media as well as used in LTTE training camps are available online also for sale and often for free downloading, serving both as revenue generators and propaganda tools.

The posters of LTTE cadres slain in battle with the Sri Lankan Army which were plastered all over NE Sri Lanka are now available as digital postcards on websites. The LTTE website offered such digital postcards, featuring pictures of "martyred" Tigers from the elite Black Tigers and the women's squad.

In the aftermath of the September 11, 2001 attacks on the US, there have been some major changes to these sites, as, for example, the pictures of passports mentioned earlier have all been removed. It seems clear that these websites were altered so as not to be included in the sweep of terrorist organizations that occurred soon after. LTTE funerals, however, which in the offline world were once lavish affairs that included the entire local community and were a major propaganda event, still manage to draw some mileage online with extensive coverage given to the dead cadres, their exploits and their sacrifices (Tekwani and Kimmelman, 2003).

The effectiveness of the pro-Tamil propaganda campaign may be gauged by the high degree of legitimacy the group enjoyed right up to the late 1990s among many Western nations, which is the main focus of Tiger international publicity activities. For most of the 1990s, the LTTE was regarded as a legitimate liberation movement engaged in a struggle, and, as such, was permitted to establish representative offices in several Western countries from where they engaged in lobbying and fund-raising activities. This network of international bases provided the LTTE with a launching pad for its international propaganda offensive, which was simplified and simultaneously intensified with the entry of the Internet. In recent years Western and Asian governments moved to ban the LTTE in response to its terrorist activities, and the group was forced to close down its international offices, but business continued as usual on the Internet. By the time the landlines were cut off, the LTTE Internet operations were sufficiently in place for the group to continue without so much as a break in stride.

In a recent departure, influenced by the advent of the new technology and the hardening stance of populations and governments against terrorism, the LTTE has been toning down its official image. Even as the website of the groups and its supporters highlight in graphic detail the harsh actions of the country's military, and glorify the violent struggle of their compatriots, the LTTE has softened and modified its own image online. While the early LTTE sites posted gory photographs more violent than those of current militant Islamic sites, it has since evolved into a moderate (for its genre) well-organized, and sophisticated site, appealing to the international community with references to international law, the right to self-determination, and even quoting the teachings of Gandhi. By appealing to non-violent methods, the group makes a concerted effort to distance its separatist goal and international lobbying from the violent activities of the insurgency. Thanks to new technology, the site achieves a subliminal appeal to credibility and for the uninitiated and the unaware; this aura of legitimacy could well clinch their support.

CONCLUSION

As Arquilla and Ronfeldt (1997) have argued, in a netwar such as the one waged by the Tamil diaspora on behalf of the LTTE and by the LTTE itself, the "battle" is mainly about "information" – about who knows what, when, where, and why. The pro-Tamil movement across the globe has used the Internet to make sure that this information was made available to Tamils outside Sri Lanka to help in the tremendous fund-raising effort that has sustained the LTTE's violent campaign for nearly two decades. This web presence has been crucial in the "sophisticated international revenue-generating operation" that draws heavily on diaspora contributions (Chalk, 1999). The propaganda campaign online is a key player in keeping the uncommitted members of the diaspora focused on the "struggle" and ensuring the flow of funds. The Internet campaign has also focused on the international media, and through it brought to bear on international public opinion a very Tamil version of the war in Sri Lanka.

In Sri Lanka's environment of tight governmental control of media output (in different phases of the war against Tamil militancy, controls have been imposed on foreign media reportage from the island as well) the emergence of the Internet offered the militants and the Tamil community an opportunity to provide their own version of the war and the situation in Sri Lanka. Over the past six years the Internet has emerged as the single most important weapon in the arsenal of Tamil militants and is clearly a significant means for the Tamil diaspora to keep abreast of events and people in the homeland in which many Tamils have not set foot in decades.

In an essay on the societal implications of the information revolution, Nichiporuk and Builder (1997) posit the following:

> [N]ation-states will increasingly find their powers curtailed by the availability of information to those who reside both within and outside their borders; and those powers that remain will increasingly have to contend with non-state actors who are acquiring power through the availability of information.

Diasporas are functioning increasingly as non-state actors in international conflicts, and governments dealing with terrorist groups and insurgencies within their borders are finding out that power balances are shifting away from their favor. Across the digital world, virtual diasporas are being created, bringing to cyberspace all of their immigrant experiences, fears, hopes, recipes, directories, and, most of all, their politics.

The use of the Internet by militant separatists and their supporters is a new reality which governments will have to acknowledge, especially at a time when developing countries across the globe, and Asia in particular, are caught in the vortex of frenzied ICT development. The Internet has immense democratizing potential. It can empower whole communities; it can fill the void of information created by repressive governments, such as in Nigeria during the Abucha regime; it can link communities across continents, as it has the Sri Lankan Tamils or the vast Indian diaspora. However, just as it lends itself to constructive ends, it has immense potential for the destabilization of nations, and for the proliferation of terrorist activities and the dissemination of misinformation and propaganda.

Given the difficulty in censoring the Internet, and the ethical and political issues that accompany any form of censorship, the solution lies in providing more information, rather than in preventing or blocking access to information. Internet access blocking, as countries such as Canada and Cuba have found, can often be a futile effort, which consumes precious resources (Perritt, 1998). What governments can do is to become more Internet-savvy themselves. Diasporas, militant groups, and activists are often far better prepared and maintain more interactive websites and proactive networks than governments and government agencies net-wide. Governments need to rectify this situation first.

Sri Lanka is both a lesson and a warning for the cyber era. It is a lesson for the dispossessed on the tools of technology and its ability to empower; and for governments, a warning that propaganda can now be of the people, for the people, and by the people. While it is unreasonable to assume that all or even most members of a diaspora support or encourage militant movements in their homelands, as the Rand report (Nichiporuk, 2000) suggests, the increasing role of the Internet in social and militant movements across the world is a development to be studied and understood in an international climate where technology and conflict seem inextricably intertwined.

NOTE

1 These illustrations have been removed from the web subsequent to the terrorist attacks on the US on September 11, 2001. Archives are in the possession of the author.

BIBLIOGRAPHY

Arquilla, J. and Ronfeldt, D. (1997) *In Athena's Camp: Preparing for Conflict in the Information Age*, Rand Corporation.

Bakker, P. (2001) "New nationalism: the Internet crusade," paper prepared for the 2001 International Studies Association Annual Convention. Online. Available HTTP: http://www.users.fmg.uva.nl/pbakker/VN/InternetCrusade.pdf (accessed July 14, 2002).

Castells, M. (1997) *The Power of Identity*, Cambridge, MA: Blackwell.

Chalk, P. (1999) "Liberation tigers of Tamil Eelam's (LTTE) international organization and operations – a preliminary analysis," Commentary n. 77, Canadian Security Intelligence Service Publication.

Cooper, M.D. and Nothstine, W.L. (1992) *Power Persuasion: Moving an Ancient Art into the Media Age*, IN: US Educational Video Group.

De Silva, K.M. and May, R.J. (eds) (1991) *Internationalization of Ethnic Conflict*, London: Pinter.

Gunaratna, R. (1994) *Indian Intervention in Sri Lanka: The Role of India's Intelligence Agencies*, Sri Lanka: South Asian Network on Conflict Research.

—— (1997) *International and Regional Implications of the Sri Lankan Tamil Insurgency*, London: International Foundation of Sri Lankans.

—— (1999) "Dynamics of diaspora-supported terrorist networks: factors and conditions driving and dampening international support for PIRA, LTTE, PKK and Kashmiri groups," unpublished doctoral dissertation, University of St. Andrews, Scotland.

Joyce-Hasham, M. (2000) "Emerging threats on the Internet," The Royal Institute of International Affairs, Briefing Paper no. 15. Online. Available HTTP: http://www.ciaonet.org/pbei/riia/jom01.html (accessed January 8, 2001).

Kalathil, S. (2001) "The Internet and Asia: broadband or broad bans?" *Foreign Service Journal*. Online. Available HTTP: http://www.ceip.org/files/publications/internet_asia.asp (accessed August 14, 2001).

Karim, H.K. (2002) "Diasporas and their communication networks: exploring the broader context of transnational narrowcasting (DRAFT)." Online. Available HTTP: http://www.nautilus.org/virtual-diasporas/paper/Karim.html (accessed June 10, 2002).

Karim, H.K., Smeltzer, S., and Loucheur, Y. (1998) "Online access and participation in Canadian society," SRA Papers. Ottawa: Canadian Heritage.

Majumder, S. (2000) "Tamil diaspora surfs for news," BBC News Online. Available HTTP: http://news.bbc.co.uk/1.hi/world/south_asia/762664.stm (accessed September 9, 2001).

Nichiporuk, B. (2000) "The security implications of demographic factors," Rand Corp. Online. Available HTTP: http://www.rand.org/publications/MR/MR1088/MR1088.html/ (available as of February 6, 2003).

Nichiporuk, B. and Builder, C.H. (1997) "Societal implications," in J. Arquilla and D. Ronfeldt (eds) *Athena's Camp: Preparing for Conflict in the Information Age*, Rand.

Perritt, H. Jr. (1998) "The Internet as a threat to sovereignty? Thoughts on the Internet's role in strengthening national and global governance," Indiana University School of Law, Bloomington, Written Symposium on The Internet and the Sovereign State: The Role and Impact of Cyberspace on National and Global

Governance. Online. Available HTTP: http://www.law.indiana.edu/glsj/vol5/no2/4perrit.html (accessed March 7, 2000).

Ramasamy, P. (2000) "The Tamil diaspora's quest for Eelam." Online. Available HTTP: http://TamilCanadian.com (accessed July 22, 2000).

Reuters (1998) "Propaganda to the people." Online. Available HTTP: http://www.wired.com/news/news/history/politics/story/11363.html (accessed March 2, 1999).

Rheingold, H. (1993) *The Virtual Community: Homesteading on the Electronic Frontier*, HarperPerennial. Online. Available HTTP: http://www.rheingold.com/vc/book/ (accessed July 13, 2002).

Richardson, J.M. (1999) "Problems of a small state in a big world – how global economic trends and great power politics have impacted Sri Lanka," *History and Politics: Millennial Perspectives*, Colombo: Law and Society Trust.

Ronfeldt, D. and Martinez, A. (1997) "A comment on the Zapatista netwar," in J. Arquilla and D. Ronfeldt (eds) *Athena's Camp: Preparing for Conflict in the International Age*, Rand.

Samarajiva, R. (1993) "Institutional reform in Sri Lanka's telecommunication system: regulation, corporatization, and competition," *Asian Journal of Communication*, 3, 1: 37–63.

—— (1998) "Media policy and law: global challenges, a Sri Lankan response." Available HTTP: http://composite.uqam.ca/videaz/docs/rosaen.html (accessed August 18, 2001)

Subramanian, N. (2000) "Tamil diaspora for nothing less than Eelam?" *The Hindu*. Online. Available HTTP: http://www.sysindia.com/forums/Eelam_Tamil/posts/122.html (accessed September 5, 2000).

Tekwani, S. and Kimmelman, K. (forthcoming 2003) *Impact of New Communications Technologies on Insurgency*, Tokyo: UNU Press.

Weiner, M. (1992) "Security, stability, and international migration," *International Security*, 17, 3: 91–126.

Wijemane, A. (2000) "War and the new realities." Online. Available HTTP: http://www.news.tamilcanadian.com/news/2000/10/20001009_4.shtml (accessed November 22, 2001).

Wright, J. (1991) *Terrorist Propaganda*, London: Macmillan.

Zekos, G. (1999) "Internet or electronic technology: a threat to state sovereignty," commentary, *Journal of Information Law and Technology*, 3. Online. Available HTTP: http://elj.warwick.ac.uk/jilt/99-3/zekos.html (accessed September 10, 2002).

12 Construction and performance of virtual identity in the Chinese Internet

Karsten Giese

Rapid economic, social, and cultural changes have been taking place in China for about twenty years, a result of China's economic reforms, integration into the world market, and the globalization and distribution of technological innovations have had a great accelerating effect on the change of life spheres in Chinese cities. The omnipresence of commercials for foreign lifestyle products and the guiding role taken by TV soaps from Taiwan or pop music from Hong Kong in urban day-to-day life are a few signs of a deep-rooted structural change that creates the basis for the phenomena described here. As China's markets became liberalized and a profit-orientated entrepreneurship took hold, economic units and social institutions such as the *danwei* (work unit) faced pressure to minimize their formerly extensive social tasks (You, 1998). By the end of the twentieth century there was not much left of the *danwei* (Hebel, 1997) that once regulated all parts of life for its members and which for generations had integrated individuals into society (Shaw, 1996).

The erosion of such urban and national enterprises has implications for the members of Chinese society, as individuals have had to adjust from being an object of planning and patronization in an alimentary and welfare system with the *danwei* as the normative social institution (see Shaw, 1996) into autonomous subjects of a pluralized life sphere, organized by means of the market. In the process, the individual obtains greater autonomy in decision-making and planning in a number of spheres. Whereas the *danwei* had provided the employee with a safe and irrevocable work contract, social security, and leisure activities, individuals in today's China have to compete with others by offering their skills and know-how. The individual now also has to choose the social groups he wants to belong to and can act in. By undermining structures of affiliation and paternalism, a loss of social and psychic security and stability comes within formerly unified communities which were tied to certain locations, and from which individuals drew their values and identity. In its place, individual free space for development and fields for experiment and social or economic action is created, with space for different ideals, allowing plural identities to be constructed.

Within this context, modern mass media have increasingly taken on a role as a framework for interpersonal reference, offering the sense of identity the *danwei* had previously offered. In particular, the role of television is demonstrated by the fact that by 1987, more than half of the respondents asked in a representative survey in the Greater Shanghai region reported their most important family activity was watching TV (Chu and Ju, 1993). With liberalization, the entry of foreign media products in television has led to a more diverse content broadcast over national stations (Dong *et al.*, 1998; Guan, 1998). Representations of alternative lifestyles as widely watched series from Taiwan or Hong Kong, or game and music shows provide alternative or new sources of influence on ethnic, cultural, and national identity in Mainland China. With the growing influence of regional and local TV programs using local dialects, regional and local identities are expected to develop alongside, or even in place of, national identities. The growth of personal communication technologies[1] such as the mobile phone and pager might be expected to reinforce the construction, confirmation, and consolidation of these new identities.

As a result of these social processes of change, the term "identity" is moving from the periphery into the centre, at both the personal and social level. China thus, perhaps more than any other nation, illustrates the ways in which computer-mediated communication interacts with larger social processes to being the process of reconstruction of personal and group identity. The uncertainty arising from social change causes individuals to seek out common features, such as acceptance, understanding, and emotional security. This search for psychological and emotional security has normally occurred in interpersonal communication, usually geographically bound, a so-called "great good place" (Oldenburg, 1997). This demise of *danwei*-based identity in turn creates opportunities for the development of new "good places" that are not defined by obligatory membership in a certain group, but are established through private values and institutions, such as family structures and shared interests.

Social psychology understands identity as a combination of features and role expectations marking the individual. In this case, identity is viewed as a complex of characteristics attributed to the individual from the outside, and what distinguishes individuals is their particular specific combination of traits. Collectives and social systems form social identities through the same process. However, this concept of crediting qualities of identity from outside remains incomplete, as long as the aspect of self-perception is not added. The concept of reflexive identity formulated by Frey and Haußer (1987) takes subject and object within one person into account. In this way, the bearer of certain features and the person of assigned features are one and the same person. In this case, identity is represented by the view the person takes of himself.

According to the theory of social identity, individuals themselves relate to groups within specific contexts when they are able to identify with the other members of that group. Relations to groups can change in correspondence to certain situations. Any context bears a specific identity, however. The individual unites multiple identities; hence the individual identity is fragmented, multiple, aspect-related, and ultimately imperfect in character (Döring, 1999; Gergen, 1990, 1991; Haraway, 1991; Markus and Wurf, 1986; Turkle, 1996a). By examining the content of group communications, it is possible to identify how both individuals and groups perceive themselves.

Thus it may be possible to discover the transformation of Chinese identity by examining these social groups. As consensual themes and ideas emerge, they can be identified as specific patterns of thought. By examining a range of groups and their thematic discourses, it is possible to identify a range of consensual patterns of thinking that illustrate the emerging group identities in China. These themes are referred to as *identity clusters*. These constituents may later affect the development of self-image within China.

Information technologies such as the telephone and the Internet may take on the potential for integrative bridging of groups across spatial boundaries. Since the entry of the Internet into China in 1995 (Sautédé, 1996), this medium supplies people from different social and geographical backgrounds with a virtual "good place" or better said "third place" (Debatin, 1996; Rheingold, 1994; Turkle, 1996b) in cyberspace. Because due to the anonymity provided by this new medium, the fear of social sanctions as well as the sense of shame are very much reduced among the participants. A much more open and controversial discussion and a more courageous positioning of individuals than in the traditional social settings are the result. The Internet therefore provides an experimental field which focuses the search for identity and support unleashed by social change.

GROUP AND IDENTITY IN THE INTERNET

Despite the short history of the Internet as a medium, contemporary usage parallels the use of mobile phones in the People's Republic of China, and represents an integrated leisure activity of urban middle classes (Bu and Guo, 2001a, 2001b; China Internet Network Information Centre, 2000, 2001, 2002). As of mid-2002, over forty-five million users go online for an average of 8.3 hours per week (China Internet Network Information Centre, 2002). The most recent CNNIC survey asked people for their motivation of logging into the Internet, and by mid-2002 – as in all previous CNNIC surveys – the respondents' Internet activities were related closely to their leisure activities. Usage of the Internet in China is dominated strongly by interpersonal communication, as the primary use for 92.9 percent of respondents is to receive and send emails. For 45.5 percent of users in China, socializing in chatrooms represents the most frequent activity, while almost 19 percent use bulletin board systems (BBS) most often. Communicative online games are the primary Internet activity for 18.6 percent of users (China Internet Network Information Centre, 2002).

As this usage pattern demonstrates, the Internet is an alternative medium to spread information and opinions to the national information domain monopolized by traditional media (Bu and Guo, 2001a, 2001b). The decentralized and fragmented structure of the network promotes self-determination and provides spaces for self-realization through myriad interests and topics. As the example of Falun Gong shows (VirtualChina.Com, 1999), new informal social trend-setters use this space for their own agendas, such as distributing their ideas and values, and promotion of their particular interests.

The Internet thus simultaneously acts as an indicator, catalyst and agent of an accelerated socio-cultural change in mainland China, by constructing, performing, and reproducing multiple identities. Forced by commercial competition between ICPs (Internet content providers) and by the dynamic development of the medium itself, content has to be up to date, innovative, and closely related to the social reality of users. The Internet fulfills the function of an *indicator* of trends, developments, and materializing potentials. In addition, because it provides a new social space and field of experimentation, supplying access to global models, points of view, and practices, the Internet serves as a *catalyst* with the potential to focus and strengthen socially established tendencies in China. Finally, because of its dynamic development and technological characteristics, the Internet itself turns an *agent* of accelerated change: participation in IRC, BBS, and other communication platforms require the learning of computer-mediated synchronous communication that triggers other communicative innovations. These communication styles have repercussions for the contents of communication, and the creation of participant identity and their orientation to "real life" (Dabiri and Helten, 1998).

Anonymity in an atmosphere free of "real life" social sanctions makes public articulation of even controversial and nonconformist individual standpoints easier (see Döring, 1999; Dubrovsky *et al.*, 1991; Kiesler *et al.*, 1984). In a limited public community these problems become topics of discussion that usually get expressed only in the private sphere. Participants in hundreds of communication platforms on the Chinese Internet help each other with practical advice for living that other institutions are seldom if ever able to manage. In addition, participants use this space to perform individual identities. Those platforms, representing various lifestyle orientations, such as fashion, music, literature, friendship, partnership, and marriage to sexuality, parenthood, education, software, sports, gender issues, consumer's protection, or Chinese foreign policy. Thus, these platforms create virtual "identity workshops" for a huge number of users in China (see Bruckman, 1992). Within these virtual "identity workshops" people experiment with alternative lifestyles, and experience community/inclusion or demarcation/exclusion. These platforms serve to determine and construct individual, cultural, social, regional, ethnic, or national standpoints. Users therefore support discussions of changed subjective views and values as well as exploration of innovative forms of interaction – in other words, chatrooms and BBSs serve to facilitate the search, determination, and performance of identities (see, in a different context, Bruckman, 1992; Sandbothe, 1998).

METHODOLOGY

Although there are a number of platforms that provide the spaces for community building and identity formation in synchronous (chat, IRC) or asynchronous form (news groups, mailing lists, BBSs), this study focuses primarily on bulletin board systems. BBSs generally appeal to a broader Chinese public due to their user-friendly design and their greater topical openness. From the researcher's point of view, BBSs normally show two additional advantages: first, every part of the communication process is publicly accessible, and, second, the individual postings are usually stored for a longer period of time, thus providing a kind of collective memory for the participants and at the same time a valuable communication archive for the researcher.

BBSs in China are mainly operated by a wide range of providers such as universities, state institutions, and companies. The majority, however, are maintained by commercial Internet providers (ISPs/ICPs) and are usually hosted on their main portals. There has always been a varying degree of censorship and active intervention by BBS providers, but increasingly, self-organized and liberal BBSs are also accelerating the degree of moderation, due to the respective state laws and regulations (Giese, 2001). A number of BBSs now also function as platforms for discussions with a variety of experts and subjects chosen by the provider, as is the case with the popular *People's Daily* Strong Country Forum (*Renmin Ribao Qiangguo Luntan*).

For this study, about sixty Chinese BBSs were monitored for a period of two months in mid-2001. In addition, the content of the popular BBS Jin Yong's Inn (*Jin Yong Kezhan*) was analyzed for two entire weeks. Findings from these spot checks have to be verified by enlarging the basis for interpretation in the framework of a following long-term survey. Due to these limitations the discussion in this chapter has to be confined to a number of general findings valid for the majority of Chinese BBSs and Jin Yong's Inn. Our interpretations, though not overly generalizable at this point, do help to illustrate the themes emerging in the creation of identity.

Jin Yong's Inn[2] was selected primarily because of its popularity among Chinese users. During July 2001, it ranked second to fourth consistently among some 400 BBSs listed by topforum.com, a site that provides dynamic daily rankings based on popularity (traffic). One other decisive aspect was the close connection to the Chinese literary genre of Kungfu novels, which is very popular in China, but not very commonly known in the West.

To examine this issue, a content analysis was conducted on postings to this BBS, to discover the ways in which themes, values, and attitudes are expressed, which might be expected to play a role in developing individual and collective identities. Based on the assumption that consensual patterns of thought act as constituents of multiple identities, this research sought to uncover answers to the following central questions:

1　What kinds of themes are most prominent in bulletin board systems?
2　Which attitudes and values are expressed?

In order to move to the more critical issue of how the bulletin board systems help to establish identity, it was necessary to develop a methodology which would identify significant interactions from incidental ones. We sought to identify *clusters of identity*, or consensual statements that seemed to serve as indicators of emerging self-perception. Thus, a third question was also examined:

3　Which statements are capable of establishing consensus within or beyond a specific group and constitute clusters of identity?

The basic instrument in this study is a qualitative analysis of contents and discourse (Oevermann *et al.*, 1983). In the framework of context-reduced computer-mediated communication (Debatin, 1998; Reid, 1994) in a BBS, the danger of misconceptions is reduced to a minimum due to the fact that all information which is passed to the participants is also open to the researcher and virtually no nonverbal aspects of communication (except, perhaps, for emoticons) exist that otherwise might be missed. In order to identify and eliminate possible distorting influences of subjective or ethnocentric biases, a German-Chinese team engaged in a continuous process of analysis over the interpretation of the recorded data. Careful attention was given to consensual statements made within individual discourses, because they help to draw sequences that signify collective patterns of thought and self-perception, and therefore serve as constituents in clusters of identity.

Our analysis followed a sevenfold process:

1　Isolation of different topical threads. In a BBS, several discussions take place frequently at the same time, so it is necessary to identify and isolate single threads as well as individual contributors in order to better analyze the contents.
2　Documentation of controversial discussions. This involves the thorough chronological documentation of the thematic discourse.

3 Identification of attitudes with the potential for consensus. Archives are created of exact discourses so as to avoid interpretive distortion.
4 Reduction of consensual statements to their central thoughts.
5 Synthesis of consensual patterns of thought. In summarizing and clustering consensual central ideas, it is possible to abstract these out to specific patterns of thought and constituents of identity.
6 Summary and assessment of preliminary results. Partial results and thematic threads are compiled as clusters of identity and then evaluated as indicators of social development.
7 Evaluation and adaptation of methods.

FINDINGS: BULLETIN BOARDS IN CHINA

The BBSs tend to demonstrate great differences in regard to the number of active users. This active core actually tended to be extremely small in a number of cases. Furthermore, "full-time" contributors affiliated with the respective ISP or ICP quite often dominate the discourse. Instead of being widely used public spaces for free discussion, some of the forums are used by this group of individuals to act as public stages for self-presentation and self-promotion.

During the period of observation, a number of boards showed a large number of postings by many individual participants, but with virtually no interaction between contributors. Statistics generated by these BBS may show long verbal contributions and a large amount of traffic, but this is confined largely to sending and reading of postings, but not to commenting and interacting. A number of BBSs, however, had a high volume of two-way communication between the participants. Moreover, the demarcation between asynchronous and synchronous communication broke down, since participants used the BBS as a *de facto* chatroom. They tended to express themselves as in a conversation instead of a conventional written form normally used in communication in BBSs. Communication generally lacked longer statements and consisted mainly of short messages in the style of SMS or IRC. The intervals between individual postings of one thread tended to be extremely small, and participants in a respective thread were usually gathering online. As far as thematic discussions arose beyond small talk and socializing, they tended to be very short-lived and often died down after only a few minutes.

One interesting phenomenon which may be observed in virtually every Chinese BBS is the exchange of arguments and viewpoints on specific topics via the headers of the postings while the body remains empty. This seems to be a universal pattern, as this characteristic is gaining ground all over virtual China. In addition, it seems that this growing tendency of "chattification" is resulting in a general shift towards socializing and small talk and a decreasing volume of thematic discourse within the majority of Chinese BBSs.

Perhaps the most outstanding phenomenon in Chinese BBS is the use of unusual linguistic features which may be observed all over the (Chinese) Internet. These can act as an essential element for creating collective identities and for community building within the virtual space. One of these phenomena is the strategy of circumventing censorship measures by using homonyms, such as using 发论工 (*fa lun gong*) or similar nonsense combinations in place of the correct characters for 法轮功 (*Falun Gong*). In this way, the software applied in virtually all Chinese BBSs (Giese, 2001) for filtering out incriminated keywords is useless and allows meaningful discourse without interference. These BBS-specific language features make understanding and analysis an even more challenging task.

Regardless of censorship issues, the use of homonyms is especially widespread and is very often applied in a playful manner. The phenomenon basically derives from the specific characteristics and problems of Chinese language computer input. The system that is most commonly used in the PRC works with alphabetical keyboard input of *Hanyu Pinyin*, the standard phonetic transcription for Mandarin Chinese. Normally, Chinese computer users type syllables or words (that consist of more than one syllable) without tone marks. Accordingly a list of homonymous Chinese characters for each syllable is displayed, the user chooses a character by typing the respective number from the list, and the character or word is inserted into the text. In many of the monitored BBSs, keywords that are specific to the general topic or internal discourse are widely replaced by terms which are from different contexts or by groups of characters which do not have any meaning at all. In many cases, a playful BBS-specific nonsense slang develops that makes sense only to the informed participant. This creates a constantly shifting virtual context and common ground for discourse heavily influenced by this slang and the resulting metaphors.

Another widespread phenomenon in Chinese BBSs is the inclusionary-exclusionary function of language use. Questions of participants supposedly revealing a general lack of understanding for the basics of a given BBS are very often ignored by other participants or are responded to with verbal sanctioning. The virtual community obviously expects all its members to share a common knowledge of the basics of the respective BBS – the collective memory. Normally this can be acquired only by studying the BBS history documented in archived threads of communication or by observing the virtual interaction of participants for a longer period. Visitors by chance are excluded and ignored by their obvious lack of basic knowledge.

These universal phenomena may also be observed in Jin Yong's Inn. Superficially this BBS addresses fans of the Chinese literary genre of Kungfu novels, as indicated by its very title. By this fact, the framework for identification is also made up already which is constitutive for the virtual community inside the Inn. But discussion in this BBS is not confined to Kungfu novels, but rather all kinds of everyday conversation focusing on the latest real-life incidents as well as on self-reflection of the community itself are present.

The topical preoccupation with Kungfu novels is reflected primarily by the literary style and the terms used in conversation, and especially by the nicknames some of the participants choose for their virtual *alter ego*. In addition, we observed manners of individual participants that were obviously created to fit the ideals typically propagated in Chinese Kungfu novels. A few participants actually seem to mask themselves by copying certain characters and types from well-known novels of this genre. They create online identities to a degree that normally can be observed only among the players in MUDs. Nevertheless, the majority of users do not participate in this kind of extensive role-play, though it is a widely accepted behavioral pattern.

The choosing of the nickname and verbal appearance is essential for the creation of one's personal identity within the group. For example, one participant named himself "Little Shark" (*xiaohao shayu*). In his postings, he creates an image of himself that corresponds clearly with the behavioral patterns of rebellious youths and the characteristics ascribed to sharks. Consequently, he also uses metaphors from the context of the oceanic life of real sharks. Although he basically respects the virtual "elders," he tries to improve his own standing by constantly provoking them in a playful and humorous battle of wits as a way to achieve upward mobility in the social hierarchy of the Inn. In one conversation, for example, he changes the name of the senior "class" of knights from Kungfu novels (*xia*) into the homonymous shrimps. Respondents picked up this language play, and conversation continued in this new underwater environment.

Many participants also choose nicknames related to characters or functional types of Kungfu novels, such as political monk, noble bandit, heroic beggar, frustrated official, and so on. These participants also act in conformity with the chosen models. However, in spite of this adherence to the theme, real-life and contemporary phenomena are not excluded from the virtual discussions. On the contrary, many real-life events are discussed in the BBS, and modern urban attitudes and values prevail in the discussion. Political and social topics are of great relevance to the participants in this communication platform and shape the sphere of discourse.

One of the basic structures within this virtual community is the principle of seniority. As the premise of the BBS is that of a lodge, guests who have stayed in the Inn for a long time acquire a more senior status within the community. They are normally addressed with respect (though quite playful from time to time) and often in a way men with higher status were addressed in pre-modern China, and in Kungfu novels. But the individual standing is dependent also upon frequent active participation by sending postings and responding to others' postings. In this way, participants who only recently entered the Inn and do not belong to the inner circle of doyens can acquire position and reputation by sending postings of high-quality content and style. The participants in this virtual Inn judge the (verbal) behavior of the participants according to their position in the community. The higher the rank, the better the reputation of an individual participant, the stricter the moral standard that is applied – quite obviously following traditional Confucian ethics. Participants respond to verbal behavior that is potentially destabilizing or destructive to the community by verbal sanctions, loss of reputation, and, in some cases, serious social exclusion as well.

The title of the BBS and the characteristic language and style practiced by the participants create clearly visible obstacles for newcomers. Entry to this virtual community is not acquired easily. Although they know everything is ambiguous, everything and everyone in this virtual environment may well prove the opposite of what it-he appears to be in real life, and although they know there are no means of checking statements or identities of their fellow occupants, participants seem to be emotionally tied to this virtual good place.

The familiarity, attachment, and relations built up over time make this a difficult place to leave as well. During the time of observation, participants who wanted to leave the group felt themselves obliged to announce and to justify this step. Others replied to these announcements, discussed this individual behavior, its potential consequences for the group, and reflected on the development of the group itself. In direct responses to the "desertion" other participants tried to convince or persuade those about to leave by appealing to them, morally judging their behavior, exerting verbal pressure, and so on. It was made very clear by the participants that they shared a fear of losing long-time activists and with them the basis for further existence and development of the group. Reflecting on the virtual community itself, they discussed the basis for its existence, what or who is central to it, and what kind of behavior is destabilizing and therefore to be sanctioned. With its barriers to entry and leaving, the existence of emotional bonds, and the participants identifying themselves with each other, Jin Yong's Inn shows all the relevant characteristics of a social group (see Heintz (2000) for a different context).

This description indicates the complexity and diversity of the social structure inside this virtual community. Different groups fulfill different social functions. There is the inner circle of long-time residents of the Inn who act as the center of gravity for the community by frequently initiating discussions and replying to a large number of postings. There are other, less active, long-time participants who act as social memory and moral authority. These are the *Éminences Grises*, senior participants who stay in the background but intervene in specific situations they perceive as important for the development of the community. Their omnipresence, though very often only anticipated by the other participants, obviously has stabilizing effects on the group as a whole. Both functional subgroups set the virtual framework for identification with the group that is constitutive for all participants. Normally, newcomers accept this, are called to order and obey, or leave.

As in real-life social groups, participants integrate slowly into and advance in this virtual social group. Every member is expected to learn the constitutive basics of the group. Normally they will do this by participating passively as lurkers for some time and/or by studying the archived communication files. New participants are also expected to show active interest in the group and its maintenance.

To analyze the virtual construction and performance of identities, we differentiate between several different spheres of discourse. First, there is the virtual identity of the social group, which is negotiated by its members (on the basis of the given setting) in a continuing evolutionary process. Second, there are the individual identities of more or less pronounced virtual roles. These can be related explicitly and exclusively to the virtual life in Jin Yong's Inn (those related to characters of novels) or web identities that are not confined by the Inn's virtual space (from participants that use the same nickname in different virtual contexts). Last but not least, the individual statements of participants also reflect their real-life individual identities. This last point becomes important as soon as real-life issues are discussed. They are reflected clearly in the individual's statements related to the meta-level of social life in the virtual community as well, because this virtual environment obviously forms an inseparable part of the social life to the guests of the Inn. Making any clear cut between online and offline and creating a dichotomy between virtual life and real life hence seems merely to be a kind of scientific fiction and – on the top of everything – one of rather questionable analytical value.

DISCUSSION

In the introduction, three issues were raised: (1) the tension between individual and group; (2) the role of new media for culture and identity; and (3) the process of identity construction. These issues will be discussed in the light of the preliminary data collected.

The individual and the group

From our observations, it seems that language is certainly one of the clearest indicators of the changing role of the individual versus the state or group in China. Language is a vehicle for self-articulation and, at the same time, a manifestation of a given social order, power structure, and ideology. Therefore, structural changes in the relationship between the individual and the state or group become most visible in the changing usage of language. Until the mid-1980s standard Chinese (*putonghua*) as well as various technical terminologies were basically decided upon by central

government institutions, and enforced by publishing authoritative diction-
aries and by the linguistic conventions used in the party paper *Renmin
Ribao*. Since the early 1990s, a gradual undermining of this kind of terminological, linguistic, and grammatical standardization may be observed
everywhere in Chinese society. Manifestations of this process are numerous: from the borrowing of linguistic-terminological patterns from Taiwan
and Hong Kong, changes in technical terminologies influenced by local
dialects, or the growing tendency to incorporate vocabulary or even grammatical structures of colloquial English into the spoken and written
Chinese language, to linguistic innovations by individual artists or social
groups.

Similarly, in the majority of the BBSs we monitored as well as in Jin
Yong's Inn, many linguistic hints for a stronger position of the individual
versus the state or group may be found. However, in contrast to the slow
and gradual organic process of language change in the offline world, the
language of the BBSs seems to be breaking with established rules with the
expressed intention of provoking linguistic innovations. As in informal
groups, individual creations are incorporated into the language of the
group and support the evolution of specific group slang. Here, more so
than in the offline world, every individual experiences his or her own influential word power. In contrast to the offline world, in the context-reduced
setting of a BBS, the style and content of every individual message is much
more decisive for self-expression and perception by others. Creative use of
language seems to be one of the main means of improving one's individual
position in a given social group. The example of "Little Shark" from Jin
Yong's Inn is clear evidence of this feature.

There are a number of other manifestations of the importance of a new
individual freedom of choice in terms of choosing the community with
which one wants to interact. A phenomenon that seems to be very widespread is the simultaneous "trial membership" in quite a few communities
– an option not possible in the offline social world. The individual looks
for a suitable virtual social group according to his or her personal likings
and interests, participates for some time and leaves if unsuitable, and
sometimes even tries to initiate and "design" his or her own BBS. Such
opportunities are seldom present in the real world.

On the other hand, this individual online freedom is also constrained by
the requirements of virtual membership. It is obvious in Jin Yong's Inn
that everyone who wants to lodge in the Inn is expected to respect the
rules and conventions the group considers fundamental, and code violations will be enforced by sanctions. Although there is a basic consensus,
the degree of acceptance of basic rules and values differs from individual
to individual. We observed passive acceptance, active constructive participation, and isolated revolt in specific cases. All of these are obviously
manifestations of an individual's active integration into the chosen
community and his subordination under the given rules. However, the

power of sanctioning and the hurdles a participant must face to leave the community are obviously not based on external force but on internalization through individual free choice and emotional bonds.

As a result, tension between the individual and the virtual group does exist. However, the individual has an upper hand in the virtual world, since membership is more likely to be based on the free personal decision to be a member of a given virtual group than in the real-world setting. In the real world, externally enforced membership and/or the lack of alternatives act as constraints to the individual in terms of his or her membership of the group. In virtual worlds, the individual freedom to escape the pressure or sanctions by the group simply by leaving whenever one wants weakens the group's hold on the individual. In this way, Chinese virtual communities have the potential to support individualization and fragmentation of the social linkages of modern Chinese individuals. However, the individual's search for a social group to integrate with, the acceptance of rules, values and sanctioning power of a group are evidence of the individual's need for a sense of belonging and for models for identification, not only in times of accelerated socio-cultural change.

The role of new media for culture and identity

The Internet does not function as a one-way influence on the individual, in contrast to traditional radio and television. Cultural and identity patterns are acquired on the Internet via communicative group-based processes, especially within BBSs. The findings of this study indicate that virtual communities of the Chinese Internet seem to strengthen certain tendencies which for years have been immanent to the pluralization and commercialization of electronic mass media in China. While there is evidence of choice of BBSs and the freedom of individual expression, some qualification needs to be expressed. For example, the visual appearance of the primarily commercial portals and their BBSs show a tendency towards uniformity and the number of alternative topics of BBSs is quite limited. In total, the vast majority of Chinese BBSs exemplify less than thirty thematic categories. Similarly, the variety of topics discussed within individual BBSs is also restricted. Moreover, discussions within a given BBS often tend to be thematically narrow and related closely to relevant topics of the offline environment at the time. Consequently, the diversity of points of views and opinions communicated during our observation proved surprisingly limited, as well. But because this study is limited to a short period, further research over a longer period might lead to different results.

Earlier, we noted that the commercialization and diversification of Chinese TV and radio programs has led to the strengthening of patterns of identification based on locale and dialect. The same effect occurs on the Chinese Internet as a large number of BBSs cater to a given region or city intentionally or as a result of a dominating group of participants all based in or originating from the same geographical region. Because there are no strict linguistic rules to be followed as in mass media, BBSs provide an even larger space for the construction and evolution of subcultures and group identities based on dialect, regional slang, and common elements of regional culture. Therefore we may draw the conclusion that Internet and BBSs can add to the process of cultural and regional diversification and growing heterogeneity of Chinese society on the basis of dialect, region, and subculture.

However, a number of BBSs have no strong ties to a given locale. Jin Yong's Inn is an example of this, and the linguistic and terminological borrowings from Hong Kong and Taiwan were very obvious. As a consequence, participants from these parts of Greater China may be able to add to the variety of patterns for identification by offering some non-Mainland perspectives, although these are certainly filtered through Hong Kong, Taiwan, or overseas Chinese eyes. The case of Jin Yong's Inn may suggest that linguistic or ideological reservations against accepting foreign behavioral patterns or value orientations may be greatly diminished in the longer term.

In addition, the analysis of verbal conflicts and striving for consensus in this study indicate that BBSs with their context-reduced communication are able to offer alternatives to the relevant patterns, structures, and processes that are prevalent in the offline reality of the PRC. Social groups and processes seem to be more open, self-determined, and liberal than their offline manifestations. The Internet, and especially BBSs, as new media obviously provide a public space for the construction of a primarily self-organized, interest-based virtual civil society. Although Chinese laws theoretically limit online freedom, the virtual space is far less sanctioned than Chinese offline reality. BBSs as virtual communities or social groups become an experimental field for the testing of behavioral patterns and strategies; and not least for solving conflicts and reaching consensus. All this happens exclusively by exchanging arguments and counter-arguments, since there are no institutionalized or structural power imbalances, apart from the position of the *banzhu* (moderator), which is perhaps the most important difference with Chinese offline reality. The significance of this feature of BBSs on influencing the construction of individual social identities of participants and on social groups and the whole Chinese society is most tantalizing.

Identity construction

As far as the construction of identities is concerned, we found that this question is more complex than anticipated. It is important to make a clear-cut division between the construction of individual and collective identities.

First of all, findings from this study show that BBSs can function as stages for self-realization, as well as for experimenting with the ideal self or alternative patterns, playing Clark Kent and Superman or Dr. Jekyll and Mr. Hyde. The findings indicate the existence of several different patterns of identity construction. One group of participants seem to strive to translate their dominating offline identities into their online *alter egos*. These individuals try hard to act convincing in different online contexts. Other netizens obviously use BBSs for the creation of an idealized self. A third group of users intentionally construct virtual identities, which fit into the thematic contexts of given BBSs. In other words, they create their own ludic, or playful, identities in a kind of role-play. Because the individual actors in the context of Jin Yong's Inn borrow primarily from a few given role models of well-known Kungfu novels, their construction of ludic identities proved most convenient for observation and analysis. In several cases, identities were constructed, which were not limited to only one BBS. In these cases, participants usually show extroverted verbal behavior, providing evidence for the analytical reconstruction of their online identities. But for those participants who are obviously not interested mainly in role-play or the construction of ludic identities, longer observation seems necessary to draw any conclusion.

On the other hand, there is clear evidence that the construction of individual and collective identities is influenced greatly by the public discourse within a given BBS. Although superficially occupied with playing role games, communication in Jin Yong's Inn often focuses on identification patterns, behavioral norms, and value orientations; yet it is no unprecedented utopia that is created here. On the other hand, the adoption of certain aspects of Confucian social ethics, though mostly only borrowed from Kungfu novels, is by no means a backward orientation towards a pre-modern ideology. On the contrary, articulations of participants indicate that the ideal of the "noble person" (*junzi*) within this virtual community means consciously disassociating from the growing "Social Darwinism" they experience in other virtual contexts as well as in their everyday real life.

Members of Jin Yong's Inn themselves choose a code of conduct which is perceived as Confucian in terms of its values. In this way, the borrowing of specific linguistic patterns strengthens the self-consciousness of the group and its identity, and serves to highlight the contrast between members and outsiders. There is ample evidence of consensual patterns of thought in this group in regard to this code of conduct. However, the discourse also clearly indicates a modern urban value orientation that does not quite fit into the picture of Confucian teachings of morality. In the end, it seems that the participants of this BBS wantonly borrow pieces from diverse Chinese and foreign value systems and put them together in a postmodern patchwork: materialism, consumerism, *Spaßgesellschaft* (living only for fun) seem to be some of the relevant keywords in this setting. It will be most interesting to observe further if and how this may develop into a new value system and model for identification.

There is a great deal of diversity in orientations among virtual communities in the Chinese Internet. Therefore, we may draw the conclusion that a new plurality of identification models has also developed within this medium. Unfortunately, so far as the impact of this pluralization of orientations and patterns of identification on Chinese society as a whole is concerned, we have to leave this to future studies.

NOTES

1 By 2000 more than sixty million people were using pager services (Zeng, 2000). In the same year the number of mobile phone users had grown to more than forty-five million (National Bureau of Statistics, 2000), and reached 144.7 million by the end of 2001 (Ministry of Information Industry, 2000).
2 The case study of Jin Yong's Inn is part of a larger study involving a survey of six major Chinese BBSs and will take two years (2002 to 2004) to complete. Research progress will be documented on the project's website: http://www.chinaBBSresearch.de.

BIBLIOGRAPHY

Bruckman, A. (1992) *Identity Workshop: Emergent Social and Psychological Phenomena in Text-Based Virtual Reality.* Online. Available FTP: ftp://ftp.cc.gatech.edu/pub/people/asb/papers/identity-workshop.rtf (accessed July 26, 1999).

Bu, W. and Guo, L. (2000a) "2000 nian Beijing, Shanghai, Guangzhou, Chengdu, Changsha hulianwang shiyong zhuangkuang ji yingxiang de diaocha baogao (chengren bufen)" (Survey report on the state of usage and the impact of the Internet in Beijing, Shanghai, Guangzhou, Chengdu and Changsha 2000 (Adults)). Online. Available HTTP: http://www.chinace.org/ce/itre/ (accessed July 25, 2001).

—— (2000b) "2000 nian Beijing, Shanghai, Guangzhou, Chengdu, Changsha qingnian hulianwang shiyong zhuangkuang ji yingxiang de diaocha baogao" (Survey report on the state of youth usage and the impact of the Internet in Beijing, Shanghai, Guangzhou, Chengdu and Changsha 2000). Online. Available HTTP: http://www.chinace.org/ce/itre/index_.htm (accessed July 26, 2001).

China Internet Network Information Centre (CNNIC) (2000) *Semi-annual Survey Report on the Development of China's Internet.* Online. Available HTTP: http://www.cnnic.net.cn/develst/e-cnnic200007.shtml (accessed November 15, 2000).

—— (2001) *Zhongguo hulian wangluo fazhan zhuangkuang tongji baogao.* Online. Available HTTP: http://www.cnnic.net.cn/develst/rep200107-1.shtml (accessed July 19, 2001).

—— (2002) *Statistical Survey Report on the Development of Internet in China.* Online. Available HTTP: http://www.cnnic.net.cn/develst/2002-7e/ (accessed October 8, 2002).

Chu, G.C. and Ju, Y. (1993) *The Great Wall in Ruins. Communication and Cultural Change in China,* State University of New York.

Dabiri, G. and Helten, D. (1998) *Psychologie & Internet. Psychologische Grundlagenstudie zum Phänomen Internet Relay Chat*, Diplomarbeit am FB Psychologie, Freie Universität Berlin. Online. Available HTTP: http://userpage.fu-berlin.de/~chlor (accessed January 20, 2000).

Debatin, B. (1996) "Elektronische Öffentlichkeiten. Über Informationsselektion und Identität in virtuellen Gemeinschaften." Online. Available HTTP: http://www.uni-leipzig.de/~debatin/english/Articles/Fiff.htm (accessed October 20, 2000).

—— (1998) *Analyse einer öffentlichen Gruppenkonversation im Chat-Room. Referenzformen, kommunikationspraktische Regularien und soziale Strukturen in einem kontextarmen Medium*. Online. Available HTTP: http://www.uni-leipzig.de/~debatin/German/Chat.htm (accessed January 10, 2000).

Dong, Q.W., Tan, A., and Cao, X.B. (1998) "Socialization effects of American television and movies in China," in D. Ray Heisey and Gong Wenxiang (eds) *Communication and Culture: China and the World Entering the 21st Century*, Amsterdam: Editions Rodopi.

Döring, N. (1999) "Sozialpsychologie des Internet," dissertation, Göttingen, Hogrefe.

Dubrovsky, V., Kiesler, S., and Sethna, B. (1991) "The equalisation phenomen: status effects in computer-mediated and face-to-face decision making groups," *Human Computer Interaction*, 6, 2: 119–46.

Frey, H.P. and Haußer, K. (1987) "Entwicklungslinien sozialwissenschaftlicher Identitätsforschung," in Hans-Peter Frey and Karl Haußer (eds) *Identität. Entwicklungen psychologischer und soziologischer Forschung*, Stuttgart: Enke.

Gergen, K.J. (1990) "Diskussionsforum. Die Konstruktion des Selbst im Zeitalter der Postmoderne," *Psychologische Rundschau*, 4, 1: 191–9.

—— (1991) *The Saturated Self: Dilemmas of Identity in Contemporary Life*, New York: Basic Books.

Giese, K. (2001) "*Big Brother* mit rechtstaatlichem Anspruch. Gesetzliche Einschränkungen des Internet in der VR China," in Benno Engels and Olaf Nielinger (eds) *Elektronischer Handel in Afrika, Asien, Lateinamerika und Nahost*, Schriften des Deutschen Überseeinstituts Nr. 50, Hamburg.

Guan, S.J. (1998) "The prospects for cross-cultural communication between China and the West in the 21st century," in D. Ray Heisey and Gong Wenxiang (eds) *Communication and Culture: China and the World Entering the 21st Century*, Amsterdam: Edition Rodopi.

Haraway, D. (1991) "The actors are cyborg, nature is coyote, and the geography is elsewhere. Postscript to 'cyborgs at large'," in Penley and Ross (eds) *Technoculture*, Minneapolis: University of Minnesota Press.

Hebel, J. (1997) *Chinesische Staatsbetriebe zwischen Plan und Markt. Von der "Danwei" zum Wirtschaftsunternehmen*, Hamburg: Institut für Asienkunde.

Heintz, B. (2000) "Gemeinschaft ohne Nähe? Virtuelle Gruppen und reale Netze," in Udo Thiedeke (ed.) *Virtuelle Gruppen. Charakteristika und Problemdimensionen*, Wiesbaden: Westdeutscher Verlag.

Kiesler, S., Siegel, J., and McGuire, T. (1984) "Socio-psychological effects of computer-mediated communication," *American Psychologist*, 39: 1123–34.

Markus, H. and Wurf, E. (1986) "The dynamic self-concept. Social psychological perspective," *Annual Reviews Psychology*, 38: 299–337.

Ministry of Information Industry (2000) *2001 nian 12 yue zhuyao tongxin zhibiao zhaiyao biao* (December 2001 Summary of Important Communication Indices). Online. Available HTTP: http://www.mii.gov.cn/mii/hyzw/tongji/yb/tongjizil-iao200112.htm (accessed February 7, 2002).

National Bureau of Statistics (2000) *China Statistical Yearbook 2000.*

Oevermann, U., Allert, T., Konau, E., and Krambeck, J. (1983) "Die Methodologie einer 'objektiven Hermeneutik'," in P. Zedler and H. Moser (eds) *Aspekte qualitativer Sozialforschung. Studien zu Aktionsforschung, empirischer Hermeneutik und reflexiver Sozialtechnologie*, Opladen: Leske and Budrich.

Oldenburg, R. (1997) *The Great Good Place: Cafés, Coffee Shops, Bookstores, Bars, Hair Salons, and Other Hangouts at the Heart of a Community*, New York: Marlowe & Co.

Reid, E.M. (1994) "Cultural formations in text-based virtual realities," MA thesis. Online. Available HTTP: http://crosswinds.net/~aluluei/cult-form.htm (accessed December 16, 1999, no longer available).

Rheingold, H. (1994) *Virtuelle Gemeinschaft. Soziale Beziehungen im Zeitalter des Computers*, Bonn, Paris, and Reading, MA: Addison Wesley.

Sandbothe, M. (1998) "Theatrale Texte. Eine medienphilosophische Analyse von hypertextuellen Darstellungsformen im Internet," in H. Willems and M. Jurga (eds) *Inszenierungsgesellschaft. Ein einführendes Handbuch*, Opladen: Wesdeutscher Verlag.

Sautédé, E. (1996) "The Internet in China. Between the constable and the game-keeper," *China Perspectives*, 4: 6–8.

Shaw, V.N. (1996) *Social Control in China. A Study of Chinese Work Units*, Westport and London: Praeger.

Turkle, S. (1996a) *Life on the Screen: Identity in the Age of Internet*, London: Phoenix.

—— (1996b) "Virtuality and its discontents: searching for community in cyber-space," *The American Prospect*, 24: 50–7. Online. Available HTTP: http://www.prospect.org/print/V7/24/turkle-s.html (current as of February 12, 2003).

VirtualChina.Com (VC) (1999) *Falun Dafa and the Internet: A Marriage Made in Web Heaven*. Online. Available HTTP: http://www.virtualchina.com/archive/infotech/perspectives/perspective-073099.html (current as of February 12, 2003).

You, J. (1998) *China's Enterprise Reform. Changing State/Society Relations after Mao*, London and New York: Routledge.

Zeng, E. (2000) "Past, present and future of e-commerce in China." Online. Available HTTP: http://www.telecomn.com/english/china_comm (accessed November 15, 2000, no longer available).

13 Opening a Pandora's box

The cyber activism of Japanese women

Junko R. Onosaka

INTRODUCTION

> They [women] are trying to build real communication and relation-
> ships on the Internet, leaving behind "secure" and "soothing" conver-
> sations.... Women who were once confined at home to so-called
> issues of "privacy" such as child-rearing, care of the elderly, domestic
> violence, sexual harassment and other discrimination, are now step-
> ping out, as if a Pandora's box has been opened in Japanese society.
>
> (Matsuura, 1999, p. 20)

From May to September 2000, I took part in the Digital Asia Library
(DAL) project by cataloging Japanese websites at Ohio State University
library.[1] My work on the DAL project identified, evaluated, and cata-
logued Japanese materials available on the Internet. It gave me the
opportunity to analyze the Japanese women and women's groups most
active on the Web. It became clear, based on my study, that they have
begun to use the Internet for women's advancement; indeed, the number of
mailing news groups or websites established by them for that purpose has
increased exponentially in recent years. In fact, while a large bloc of Japanese women and their groups do not as yet use the Internet, it is clear that
the Internet has provided a tremendous opportunity for many Japanese
women to resist pressures in Japanese society for "harmony" and "silence."

Japan is the only non-Western society so far to have established itself as
an economic superpower, although it has suffered from a long economic
recession. The number of Internet users, moreover, has increased rapidly,
growing, for example, by 74 percent between 1999 and 2000, and, as of
December, 2001, 44 percent (55.93 million) of all Japanese use the Internet (The Ministry of Public Management, Home Affairs, Posts and
Telecommunications, 2002). According to September 2002 statistics provided by Global Reach (2003), Japanese is used by 9.7 percent of the
world online population (estimated at 619 million), more than European
languages such as Spanish (7.2 percent), French (3.5 percent), and German
(6.7 percent), constituting the third most widely used language after

English (36.5 percent) and Chinese (10.9 percent). Women in Japan are rapidly discovering the effectiveness of the Internet for accomplishing a variety of goals, and they are now a vital part of the Internet community. Indeed, the number of female users has increased dramatically: in 1997, 16.5 percent of users were women; however, as of 2001, 44.5 percent were women (The Ministry of Public Management, Home Affairs, Posts and Telecommunications, 2002). Furthermore, the explosive adoption of mobile Internet services, which make access to a PC unnecessary for Internet use – and are thus less expensive – promote women's participation on the Internet. For example, NTT DoCoMo launched i-Mode in February, 1999 as a limited 9.6 Kpbs mobile Internet service. Eventually, it converted NTT DoCoMo into the world's largest mobile ISP. The rapid adoption of such services is reflected in their use by at least fifty-one million subscribers as of March, 2002, and the fact that the number of mobile Internet users increased almost seven times between 2000 and 2002 (The Ministry of Public Management, Home Affairs, Posts and Telecommunications, 2002). Thus it would seem that many persons of comparatively lower income, including many women, have more access to the Internet than they did previously.

The DAL project revealed hundreds of websites operated by Japanese women and their groups. I analyzed about 200 Japanese language websites of individual women as well as non-governmental and non-profit women's groups divided by different functional types cut across subject areas. In particular, this study focuses on sites which: (1) are created by and primarily for Japanese women, (2) offer information on their current social conditions, (3) are relatively enduring (over one year), and (4) are structured to improve their situations and status. As will be shown below, these sites demonstrate the diversity of Japanese women as well as their determination to thereby improve their situations and status.

At the same time, we should also note here the importance of grass-root women's networking prior to the inception of Internet activism (Kinoshita, 1986). Using networks, women have made the most of the latest tools available to take action. From this standpoint, these same women now use the Internet as the most recent and crucial tool for disseminating information, communicating, and mobilizing. On the other hand, many women, especially housewives, have only started developing their networks through the use of the Internet. In this study, in addition to analyzing individuals and groups that use the Internet to pursue social change, I will also explore sites of housewives who are trying to change their situation. In doing so, I will analyze the ways in which they seized opportunities through using the Internet, and how they have changed as a result. This study highlights the powerful role of the Internet as a tool for expressing the multiplicity of women's voices. As a result, the diverse range of their activism on the Internet, as will be shown below, increases our understanding of Japanese women.

VARIETIES OF ACTION

Women as a marginalized group – the anonymity of the Internet

While noting the rapid increase in the number of female Internet users, these users complain about the lack of opportunities on the Internet to exchange information freely with other women. Unfortunately, Japanese female presence on the Net has often generated negative reactions. According to Kazuo Nomura, "some men seem to have an excessive reaction to women's opinions on a BBS or a mailing list – some male chauvinists think that men are superior to women and so barrage them with petty criticisms" (Nomura, 2000). Drost and Jorna (2000) also say in the Dutch context:

> Women were usually not welcomed as equal counterparts by the male-oriented online community. Especially in newsgroups, women were sometimes treated as an inferior species. As soon as the participating males discovered that the person asking a question was female, it was not at all uncommon for her to be made to understand that technology was too difficult for women, and that she should concentrate on other activities, such as cooking and sewing. This put off many women. Several left the Web for good.

On the other hand, network communication, insofar as it is not face-to-face communication, offers the written text as the only material available to judge the attributes of the other interlocutor. It is difficult to know what kind of person he or she is, and one can also pretend to be whatever one wants to be. At an interview conducted by Orita *et al.* (1999), one Japanese housewife said:

> As a housewife, I was always treated as subordinate to my husband. . . . My opinion was often treated not as mine, but as that of "my husband's wife." I think that the only place I was treated as an individual was on the Net – because I didn't indicate that I was someone's wife.

Moreover, she noted that if she mentioned on the Internet that she is a housewife, she would no longer be treated as an individual there either (Orita *et al.*, 1999). Besides, many Japanese men and women consider it inappropriate for women to talk about politics, sexuality, and family matters whether in a private or public setting. Given such social conditions, communication on the Internet enables women to take part in public discussions while preserving their privacy and attributes; that is, they have no need to engage in face-to-face debate, or otherwise to only use language or broach subjects "appropriate" to direct discourse. On the

Internet, one can select what attribute to show and what attribute to hide. That is, the Internet offers the Japanese woman as a marginalized member of society a novel avenue whereby to express herself in spite of coercive pressures that promote "harmony" and "silence." In this way, the anonymous character of the Internet provides a new horizon for marginalized members of Japanese society in general, including not only women but also gays and lesbians, the Ainu, Burakumin outcasts, Korean-Japanese, and so on.

Social support

The Internet provides a critical medium for home-bound people such as housewives who must care for small children and/or elderly parents. For example, according to Yuko Kitakaze (2001), the number of female Internet users who are 20 to 30 years old with children increased 190 percent between 1999 and 2000, while female Internet users without small children increased 140 percent within the same period. Seventy percent of female Internet users are housewives and 78 percent have children under 5 years of age. As a result, they have trouble working outside the home or even going shopping. Usually confined at home, they are hungry for information, especially on "child-rearing and the local community," and they find the Internet convenient (69.8 percent), an invaluable resource for information (65.1 percent), and useful for daily life (51.2 percent) (Kitakaze, 2001).

These users not only surf the Internet, but many also use BBS or mailing lists to have discussions and to exchange information with other users for various constructive purposes: 65.1 percent of housewives with children use the Internet to see homepages, 23.7 percent use it to read BBSs, and 12.2 percent use it to write their messages or opinions on the BBS (Kitakaze, 2001). Through these activities, they exchange not only information but also emotional "support." For example, "Reading messages by many mothers who have similar concerns about their children, they have feelings of relief and camaraderie" (Kitakaze, 2001). Furthermore, such activities on the Internet provide opportunities for them to increasingly appreciate their own "self-worth." Kitakaze (2001) says:

> From my own experience as a housewife, I rarely felt appreciated by anyone. My husband and my child never said "thank you" to me when I did things for them. But on the BBS, my very slight experience and advice were greatly appreciated, and I felt I had truly been helpful. Whenever I received a "thank you" from other users, I felt my existence was valuable.
>
> (Kitakaza, 2001)

Like housewives with small children, housewives who care for the physically challenged such as elderly parents also make the most of the Internet.

Sachiko Fujita, a 64-year-old housewife who has nursed her mother-in-law for eleven years, says, "The Internet is my 'rescuer'" (Fujita, 2001). She used to lead a very active social life, engaging in travel, climbing mountains, playing tennis, and was a member of a choir. However, she suddenly needed to move in order to take care of her mother-in-law – to a place where she had no friends with which to chat or to feel relaxed. Moreover, she had difficulty leaving her mother-in-law alone even for a short period. In response to the situation, she decided to start her homepage, "An ordinary housewife's Homepage," describing her daily care-giving experience primarily in Japanese, and partly in English and in French beginning in October, 1996 (Hashimoto *et al.*, 2001). She says, "I was exhausted due to caring for my mother-in-law all day long in an unfamiliar place, and the long-term nursing gave me continuous stress. It was the Internet that became a weapon to combat it." In this way, she found a voice on the Internet, and the Internet changed her life. She says:

> After creating my homepage, I was surprised to receive a number of encouraging email messages concerning my nursing experience. I was very glad to receive them. Some of them were from foreign countries such as the US, Australia, and Thailand, saying, "It has been very heart-warming for me to read your homepage." Such encouragement from unknown people really relieved me, and cheered me up. The Internet provided me with an unexpected experience and friends from around the world. From now on, I would like to continue sharing my experience with as many people as possible.
>
> (Fujita, 2003)

Currently in Japan, the number of bedridden elderly people is estimated at about 2.8 million. Thirty-three percent of the primary care-givers are their children's partners (usually the wife of the eldest son), 28 percent their partners, and 22 percent their children (*Asahi Shimbun*, 1997). Fujita's situation, in other words, is not at all rare.

Those who are home-bound tend to lose their connection to the larger society. Usually their social worlds become gradually constricted and withdrawn. However, the Internet becomes valuable for these people – not only housewives with small children or with elderly people, but also those who take care of children and other physically challenged people, and even physically challenged people themselves. Fujita, who later created a BBS on her homepage to exchange and share information on care-giving, said, "Information on nursing elderly people seems to be abundant, but in reality there is little that is useful. It is important for us who are actually taking care of elderly people at home to gather up-to-date information and exchange it." The Internet can thus enable people to exchange information in efforts to resolve or address social problems. Indeed, home-bound users thereby offer emotional support to each other. Fujita says:

Whenever we have problems or something sad or happy, we exchange mails and support each other on a BBS. It becomes a space to save, cure and heal us. . . . The Internet enables us to exchange mails whenever we have time. For home-bound people like us, the Internet is a site for healing.

(Fujita, 2001)

Financial independence

In addition, some housewives use the Internet to support them financially. For example, some of them start companies on the Internet. As of 2001, 90 percent of unmarried Japanese women between the ages of 25 to 35 work; while only 44.7 percent of married women from the same age group do so (Hataraku Joseino, 2001). Various factors, including the long work hours required in companies and insufficient childcare outside the home, discourage women with families from working outside the home. Mutsumi Okuyama says, "Most women with small children have a very difficult time maintaining both family and career, a condition that reflects the harsh working environment of Japanese women" (Tamura, 2000).

Noriko Teramoto of Shiga prefecture formed a group together with other acquaintances called "Dejimamu" (Digital Mom), which is for women who have small children, in January, 1996. More than half of Dejimamu members graduated from national universities and were previously employed in skilled professions such as system engineering and computer programming. All stopped working after having children. The inaugurators started Dejimamu saying, "While rearing our children, let's use the Internet and take part in society by using the Internet" (Teramoto, 1997). The group activities of Dejimamu include a monthly face-to-face meeting, group study, Internet counseling seminars for non-group members (twice a year), the publishing of textbooks about the Internet, the maintaining of a mailing list and a homepage, a year-end party, and so on. The group encourages mothers to broaden their world by using the Internet. In particular, it tries to help improve their interactive communication skills and abilities at self-expression as well as to promote information literacy by exchanging and sharing ideas on the Internet. In doing so, Dejimamu has begun to teach homepage creation. In October, 1999, it established its own company, Dejimamu Waakaazu (Digimom Workers) that contracts to perform jobs which can be done on the Internet at home. Later, the members of Digimom each started their own personal business on the Internet. Teramoto herself has developed Digimom Workers into a larger enterprise; others individually sell handmade crafts on the Internet, and one of the others has begun to publish community information using printed material as well as the Internet. In fact, in this connection, the activities of Digimom as a united group eventually came to an end. Teramoto (2003) says:

Originally, we were pushing baby cars, but now our children are going to elementary school.... We were very glad to meet friends on the Internet when we experienced the most difficult time in child-rearing.... We could live a fuller life because of the Internet. The Internet can definitely be a powerful friend for those who have small children.

In this way, the Internet has become not only a tool for improved communication, and increased knowledge and social supports, but has also contributed to the financial independence of women at home. "The Internet has become a weapon to empower women," says Mutsumi Okuyama. Okuyama used to be a career woman, but once she had a baby, her lifestyle completely changed. However, she now runs Ofisu Wiru (Office Will), an employment agency exclusively for housewives aged between 25 and 40 with children. The company, established in April, 1996, provides them with jobs that can be done only on the Internet at home. As of 2000, the number of registered members reached 700 (Okuyama, 2000). Okuyama says, "The Internet has become a tool to bridge between society and those women who have to be confined at home.... It will be a weapon to empower women" (Tamura, 2000). Furthermore, the Internet gave courage to women to resist pressures in Japanese society for "harmony" and "silence." As Teramoto says, "On the Internet, people who 'stand out from the crowd' do 'not invite trouble for themselves.'" Her statement evokes the famous Japanese saying "deru kui wa utareru," which means "when you stand out from the crowd you just invite trouble for yourself." Indeed, powerful social strictures tend to restrict Japanese women's interaction with others: they are especially expected to avoid distinguishing themselves from others and are encouraged to keep "silence" and not to disturb "harmony." However, Teramoto (2000) says:

On the Internet, if you do not stand out from the crowd, you will be buried. Usually women try not to stand out, but once they understand this, they try to show their abilities. They undertake work of their own accord and, in doing so, they have achieved something notable. What counts in business on the Internet is not whether one is a man or a woman or has children or not, but one's capability and one's ability to appeal to others.... The Internet requires the ability to design, market, and communicate – all of which women are good at. In this sense, the Internet becomes a weapon for women.

In acquiring access to the Internet, Japanese women have gained a weapon whereby they can challenge Japanese society and attempt to improve their situations and status.

Networking

The concept of Dejimamu is very similar to "Dutch Webgrrls" in the Netherlands. Dutch Webgrrls, founded in 1996, has several thousands of members today, constituting the largest organization of Internet female users in Europe. It provides a forum for women interested in using new media and technology to network, exchange job and business leads, form strategic alliances, mentor and teach, intern, and learn the skills to help themselves succeed in an increasingly technical workplace and world. For similar reasons, the number of Internet workshops for women offered by women's groups in Japan such as Dejimamu as well as women's community centers have increased lately. For example, in Akita prefecture in February, 1999, a women's group named "Mixed Salad" (*Mikkusu sarada*) held the "Internet Forum for women 99," which was attended by 150 women. Mixed Salad is a group of female Internet users who reside in Akita, which has extremely heavy snowfall and a long winter. The group's members used seventy computers to demonstrate to beginners how to use the Internet, and explained about "the possibilities of the Internet." Simultaneously, those who could not attend were able to watch the forum through live broadcasting, and could also ask questions. Preparations for the forum were conducted for three months prior to the event through exchanging opinions on a mailing list, along with face-to-face meetings (Shizuko, 1999).

The online newspaper *Akita News* was first published by a member of Mixed Salad in April 1997, and has since received almost 120,000 hits. *Akita News* includes daily news related to Akita, a map of Akita, recommended places to visit, special products of Akita, and so on. Through her involvement with *Akita News*, the founder discovered new opportunities to express herself and to better know the community. Furthermore, in doing so, she has continued to educate herself and broaden her horizons and feels she must be concerned about social issues. Through preparing the forum, she increasingly realized the potential of the Internet to promote empowerment:

> The Internet is a tool for sharing our knowledge and power with others. Beyond differences of the residence, occupation and so on, one's voice can be heard by people anywhere in the world, if one has a will to take part in the society and have access to the Internet.
>
> (Shizuko, 1999)

On the other hand, creating a homepage is not the only means to change one's situation. Takako Kinjō is a housewife living in Okinawa. Her "Kao no mienai ōensha" (cheerleaders whom I have never met) is a prize-winning article she wrote about her Internet experience (Kinjō, 1999). According to the piece, one day she found the homepage of a radio station, and thought it would be nice if it had a radio program for the mothers of small children. Based on what she had learned through joining a mailing list for mothers with small children, she proposed that the station begin such a program, and eventually the radio station asked her to create it. She reported this on the mailing list, and received many encouraging messages from other members of the mailing list around Japan. She noted that after she joined the list, she began to feel a stronger bond with other mothers on the list as well as a stronger sense of participation in society, although she mostly stays at home. The mailing list thus encouraged her to seize the opportunity to participate beyond the confines of her daily world. In this way, through the Internet, the women mentioned above improved their interactive communication skills as well as their abilities for self-expression, and boosted their confidence *vis-à-vis* others in society. The Internet provided women at home with confidence and encouragement to go outside, to meet people face to face, and to take action both as individuals and as groups of women.

Social service and collective action

In 1995, the Great Hanshin Earthquake hit Kobe, claiming more than 6000 lives. The emotional impact of the event changed the lives of numerous people, their surroundings, and even their ways of seeing the role of social organizations in daily life. The Kobe Earthquake made the public realize the significance of non-government organizations (NGOs) and of the Internet in reconstructing the lives of the people of Kobe. Soon after the catastrophe, many NGOs were formed and worked to help those in need. In particular, an NGO called "Inter V Net" drew the attention of many victims and their rescuers. Working with three large service providers, Inter V Net started to offer free Internet services to facilitate the provision of free service, information exchange related to the victims and the area, enabling the people involved to send and receive information easily. Inter V Net continued this project for more than three years, ending in July 1998. The Inter V Net project created awareness that the Internet can be used not only by people in business but also by people in need and by social service providers.

Haneko Inoue is one of those who was struck by the power of Inter V Net (Inoue, 1999). When she first opened her homepage in 1996, she put only her essays and the limited email messages she had received on the Web (Inoue, 1999). However, the homepage later came to reflect her interests in a broad range of issues such as love, marriage, divorce, domestic violence, child-rearing, work, and so on, and she received increasing numbers of e-communications. On June 21, 1998, she received a message from Papua New Guinea, where the sender, Koichi Hashimoto, resided. A member of Youth Co-op from Japan, he enjoyed her homepage because he had been thirsty for information on Japan. Soon after his message appeared on her website, a large earthquake struck Papua. Inoue proposed organizing a relief fund for victims in the area. She opened a bank account for this purpose, and used the Internet to make an appeal, eventually collecting 2,100,000 yen (US$16,200). Inoue said, "This was one of the best experiences that I've ever had since opening my homepage" (Inoue, 1999). Like women whom Takako Kinjō has known only on the Internet, the people in Papua New Guinea found in Haneko Inoue a cheerleader and supporter whom they had never met.

Mobilization for protest

The following case demonstrates how the Internet has the potential to immediately draw people's attention and cooperation, to reach people beyond their respective communities and eventually to encourage them to take action. After Japan's defeat in the Second World War, Okinawa became a United States possession, and, although it reverted to Japan, US military bases have remained.

When it was decided that the G8-Summit would take place in Okinawa from July 21 to 23, 2000, a woman in Okinawa named Hiroe Shimabukuro thought it would be the best opportunity for Okinawan people to demonstrate their opposition by proclaiming "No US military bases." She was aware that great attention would be paid to Okinawa from mainstream media around the world during the summit – a rare opportunity to capture Japanese and international attention. Shimabukuro, a 25-year-old Okinawan resident, decided to take action for a protest against US military bases in Okinawa; she put her site "Red Card Movement" on the Internet on June 9, 2000, just forty days before the summit. The site has a very detailed English language description of the history and problems suffered by the Okinawans, and begins with the following message written in English:

> It [The Red Card Movement] is a movement to show rejection towards the US military base presence in Okinawa. With dignity and undivided will, we raise the red card to both the US and Japanese governments, who unfairly place the burden of US military bases on the small island of Okinawa. We are also seeking to increase awareness of the Okinawan situation throughout the world.
>
> (Red Card Movement, 2000)

On the site, she asked people to show red-colored items including ribbons, badges, posters, stickers, or fliers at Kadena, the largest American airbase, on July 20, 2000. The color was a symbol of a rejection of the US base presence. The "red card" is used in soccer to indicate a serious violation and the suspension of the player from the game. After it went online, the site drew the attention of the media. Not only local newspapers such as

Okinawa Times and *Ryukyu Shinbun* but also national and foreign papers, including *Asahi Shinbun*, the *Boston Globe*, and the *New Observer*, covered the Red Card Movement's plans for the July 20 protest. She also sent emails in both English and Japanese to ask people concerned about the US base presence to take a look at her site. She wrote:

> In spite of the fact that I am an unknown person, one famous scholar decided to offer a link on his website, and then another professor in the US who saw his site sent a very encouraging email to me – and he promised to attend the July 20 protest! I was so impressed by them!
>
> (Shimabukuro, 2000)

Gradually the site attracted more attention, and received messages not only from within but also from outside Okinawa, including mainland Japan as well as foreign countries such as the US, Switzerland, Germany, Sweden, Indonesia, the Philippines, Korea, Mexico, and so on (Shimabukuro, 2000). Hundreds of emails, faxes, and letters were sent from individuals and groups such as citizens working in the airbases, survivors of the Second World War, US veterans, families of US military personnel, scholars, and journalists. The site included their messages, which often responded to messages from those who questioned or were hostile to the movement (and which are also included). It tried to convey the anti-base point of view by providing a variety of data, facts and historical background, and asked for their understanding and cooperation by telling them that the movement is not against Americans; nor is it intended to discriminate against any individuals.

The protest on July 20 drew over 27,000 people, who surrounded Kadena Airbase forming a 17-kilometer "red" human chain. The Red Card Movement played a major role in the protest activities coinciding with the G-8 meeting and received international media coverage including the BBC and CNN (*Newsweek*, 2000). The movement also spread to the mainland prefectures of Fukuoka, Hiroshima, Aichi (Nagoya), and Mie. The movement sponsored a mass demonstration on September 23, 2000 against the worldwide American military bases, which took place in Okinawa, the Philippines, Korea, Puerto Rico, as well as Portland (Oregon), Hawaii, Washington DC, and other cities in the US Thus, while the Japanese and US governments seem to have remained silent, a young Okinawan woman used the Internet to further her cause – thousands of red ribbons emerged, waving not only in Okinawa but also in mainland Japan and even in foreign countries, accompanied by the proclamation, "Take back our peaceful land! The military cannot bring peace!"

Women in rural prefectures

According to Makoto Konishi, the rate at which homepages are created is highest in Toyama, Ishikawa, Fukui, and Nagano, all rural prefectures subject to heavy snowfall. On the other hand, one of the lowest is in Tokyo (Konishi, 2001). In general, people in rural regions are said to be more restricted by stereotyped gender roles than people in metropolitan areas. To take part in public discussion is regarded as inappropriate for women in many rural areas. It is difficult for them to escape prejudice as well as to find like-minded acquaintances. However, as noted above, the nature of the Internet enables them to secure their privacy (through hiding their attributes) while they are enabled to communicate with others in similar straits; in doing so, it especially helps them to overcome the limitations that accrue to residence in many such rural communities.

Thus local women and other marginalized people, typically ignored in the mainstream media, are potentially empowered through access to the Internet. For example, Woman's Internet of Shizuoka (WISH) is a women's network established in 1997 in Shizuoka prefecture that provides information on women's issues such as healthcare, aging, child-rearing, peace, education, and environmental issues. The site started as an information navigator by collecting and arranging useful information on the web as a service for women in Shizuoka. Its mission is also to empower women through teaching them ways in which electronic media may be used to their benefit. The activities are carried out mainly via online conferences. The conference room of WISH on the Internet provides information on childcare, elderly women and working women's issues, and maintains lists of local women's groups that constitute an electronic bulletin board for women in the community to exchange information. As a result, the site has assisted in the creation and maintenance of a woman's network in Shizuoka. Such groups fill niches that national women's organizations cannot by enabling women to network in their own regions, and strengthen bonds with each other by providing platforms online for them to exchange ideas frequently.

Women have found that the Internet provides cheap and efficient communication and information exchange. Moreover, it empowers women so that they gradually expand female Internet communities and thereby begin to build significant relationships. It also increases women's capacity to make connections with each other including many that would otherwise have been virtually impossible. This factor is apparent especially in the case of women in outlying areas, who form local women's groups and exchange information on issues that are significant but overlooked by mainstream media. Although such groups do not necessarily mobilize women directly towards political activism, analysis of their activities demonstrates invisible but persistent efforts of Japanese women to effect social change. In this sense, these sites clearly form a women's cyber culture.

Acting locally and networking globally

As noted in the section on social service and collective action (above), many Japanese people noticed the power of the Internet in 1995. Their experiences of the Kobe Earthquake and of the United Nations Fourth World Conference on Women (UNWCW) in Beijing that year formed the immediate context for the establishment of some national networks for advancement of women on the Internet. This section considers the impact of the Beijing conference through analysis of the sites that came to be created for political action.

Over 30,000 women gathered at UNWCW, and the Non-Governmental Organization Forum held simultaneously in Beijing. The then Association for Progressive Communications Women's Networking Support Program (APCWNSP) implemented a women-led initiative to provide Internet access, electronic communications, and information services in addition to supporting the conference.[2] Over forty women, representing twenty-five countries, worked together to set up and manage a computer networking facility, and to provide training and user support to the women who used it. The project revealed and highlighted in greater depth women's relationship to and experience of working with computer communication technologies, and offered a useful corrective to conventional views of women and technology. Junko Yoshimura, who was one of the forty members and a member of the Japanese NGO, Women's Online Media (WOM), said, "This experience gave me tremendous confidence that we could support the Internet system in Beijing without any help from men" (Ikeuchi, 1996).

During the conference, 52,000 messages were exchanged, and the server received 100,000 hits (Taguchi, 1996). Furthermore, electronic information was repackaged into different formats such as newsletters, radio broadcasting, and faxes, translated into several languages, and disseminated worldwide. As women have become more active in ICT, they have become more aware of its diverse impact. With the spread of ICT came a new category of "have-nots" – the so-called "information-poor" communities and countries. Many organizations and volunteers responded by becoming involved in the so-called repackaging and translation of electronic information for the non-connected female majority. At that time WOM also translated information they received online and disseminated it via a Japanese newsletter, or put it directly on their homepage.

Haneko Inoue, mentioned in the section on social support and collective action (above), was one of many Japanese women who received the newsletter in Japan. She noted the broadcast power of new technologies in connecting people across continents:

> In 1985 I attended the Third World Conference on Women in Nairobi, Kenya, to hold the workshop "Working Women in Japan." I

sent some reports via airmail about the conference from Nairobi since I could not have access to fax there. My friend received them, and made photocopies of them to send people who raised funds to make my workshop in Nairobi possible. However, it took at least one week, and worse two weeks. Now I can read it in real time on the Internet, and the readers are infinite.

(Inoue, 1999)

Later, Inoue attended an Internet workshop offered by WOM, and also joined a mailing list of VCOM (formerly Inter V Com). Through exchanging information on the mailing list, she started to create her own homepage, as noted above. Thus the experience of exchanging information on the Internet was quite meaningful and significant not only for women who attended the conference, but also for those who did not. Interestingly, it is said that the mainstream media, governments, and even the UNWCW depended on information disseminated by APCWNSP via the Internet. In fact, it seems that information on the conference was more accessible for women who use the Internet than many non-users present in China; that is, people could receive information directly from the APCWNSP without being censored by the Chinese government. Therefore, such cooperation beyond national boundaries such as ATTAC implies the potential for "cyber internationalism" which would allow people to unite on the Internet to challenge a variety of officials and their institutions (ATTAC, 2003; Tsumura, 2001).

CONCLUSION

The Internet is, of course, not merely a tool for positive change. It tends to widen the gap between haves and have-nots, and is used to exploit women in various forms such as pornography or mail order bride sites. Japan is known as the world's greatest importer of trafficked Asian women, and may also be the world's greatest creator of child pornography websites (Matsui, 1999). The Internet can also work to reinforce damaging stereotypes (Sustein, 2001). Indeed, it is hardly surprising that a number of hate groups in Japan – including anti-feminist organizations and ultra-nationalist right-wing groups – found large audiences on the Web.

These reservations aside, this study has shown that the Internet offers a primary means to express the voices of Japanese women, to expand communications among women, and to make visible the diversity of Japanese women and their activism. Similarly, women and diverse minorities have wider latitude to speak out more freely on the Net than in most other social locations. In rural areas in particular there remain rigorous gender role expectations and implicit rules regarding social interaction, including non-verbal and face-to-face communication. Furthermore, compared to men, women (especially housewives) are forced to limit their relations outside the household. Residence in a rural area especially means one's networking is concentrated in kinship and local community ties. However, given the possibilities provided by the Internet, women can create, and indeed are creating, networks that transcend the limitations posed by rural or home-bound life, or social marginalization. It might be called an "information tie" – a new relationship among people. They can select the people and space for communication and, in doing so, can potentially expand their sphere of social activity. In this sense, for Japanese women, these websites host a dynamic cyberculture that both reflects and also enables change in Japanese society. The challenge is that as women increasingly gain access to the Internet, they must learn how to retrieve and organize relevant information in order to appropriate it for their efforts to end all forms of inequality.

NOTES

1 The Ohio State University, The University of Minnesota, and The University of Wisconsin-Madison began a joint effort to develop the Digital Asia Library (DAL) using the Cooperative Online Resource Catalog (CORC) system. DAL is a new model for organizing and providing access to intellectual content available on the World Wide Web, enhancing access to Internet resources relevant to Asian studies. I would like to thank Professor Maureen Donovan at the Ohio State University for giving me an opportunity to take part in the DAL project. Her encouragement, advice, and kindness enabled me to start this research. All translations, unless otherwise noted, are mine.
2 APCWNSP is organized to promote gender-aware Internet design, implementation, and use by the Association for Progressive Communications (APC), an internationally based electronic network NGO. Since 1990, APC advocates for and facilitates the use of information and communications technologies (ICTs) by civil society in various ways. Its members are from twenty-two countries, associate members from over fifty countries, and it has been admitted by 133 countries (see Ramilo, 2001).

BIBLIOGRAPHY

Asahi Shinbun (1997) "Kaigo Taiken (The experience of caring for elderly people)," October 7.

Association for the Taxation of financial Transactions for the Aid of Citizens (ATTAC) (2003). Online. Available HTTP: http://www.attac.org/index.htm (available as of January 20, 2003).

Drost, K. and Jorna, M. (2000) "Empowering women through the Internet: Dutch women unite." Online. Available HTTP: http://www.isoc.org/inet2000/cdproceedings/8a/8a_1.htm (available as of January 20, 2003).

Fujita, S. (2001) *Intaanetto ha Kaigoshufu no Sukuinushi* (The Internet is the rescuer for a nursing housewife), Tokyo: Aishobō.

—— (2003) "Aru heibon na shufu no hōmupeji (An ordinary housewife's home-page)," later "Yōkoso Sachiko no hōmupeji he (Welcome to Sachiko's home-page)." Online. Available HTTP: http://www.fuchu.or.jp/~sachiko3/profil.htm (available as of January 20, 2003).

Global Reach (2003) "Global Internet statistics by language." Online. Available HTTP: http://www.glreach.com/globstats/index.php3 (available as of January 20, 2003).

"Hataraku Joseino jitsujō/Josei rōdo hakusho (White Paper on Labor and Women)" (2001). Online. Available HTTP: http://www.mhlw.go.jp/wp/hakusyo/josei/01/ (available as of February 2, 2003).

Hashimoto, N., Hirata, T., Ikeda, Y., Mizusaki, H., Moriguchi, F. and Wada, S. (2001) *Women and Men in Japan: Gender Statistics*, Tokyo: Research Committee of Gender Equality and Education in Research Institute of Democracy and Education.

Ikeuchi, H. (1996) *Suteki na Josei ha Ima Intaanetto* (Now nice women are on the Internet), Tokyo: Japanmikkusu.

Inoue, H. (1999) *Josei ni yasashii Intaanetto no hon* (An easy Internet book for women), Tokyo: CQ Shuppan.

—— (2003) "E-sen jō no cha ya usagiya (Usagiya tea shop in E major)." Online. Available HTTP: http://www.osk.3web.ne.jp/~haneko/index.html (available as of January 20, 2003).

Kinjō, T. (1999) "Kao mo shiranai ōensha tachi (Cheerleaders whom I have never met)." Online. Available HTTP: http://www.ntt-west.co.jp/okinawfa/essay/bronze_05.html (available as of January 20, 2003).

Kinoshita, A. (1986) "Onna tachi no idobata kaigi (Women's chattering)," *Shakai kyôiku*, 30: 32.

Kitakaze, Y. (2001) *Intanetto suru mama shinai mama* (Mothers who are on the Internet and those who are not), Tokyo: Sofutobanku paburisshingu.

Konishi, M. (2001) "Kappatsuna shimin undō (Active citizen's movement)," *Saibaa Akushon*, Tokyo: Shakai Hihyōsha.

Matsui, Y. (1999) "Intaanetto o Josei no te ni (Put the Internet in women's hands)," *Onna tachi no 21 Seiki*, 20: 7.

Matsuura, S. (1999) "Josei tachi ga intaanetto de hajime te iru koto (What women are starting to do on the Internet)," *Onna tachi no 21 Seiki*, 20: 20.

Newsweek (2000) "So long, soldier," July 24.

Nomura, K. (2000) "Shakaigaku no Sahō: Nettowaku hen (Manners for sociology: networking." Online. Available HTTP: http://www.honya.co.jp/contents/knomura/on/on42.html (available as of January 20, 2003).

Okuyama, M. (2000) "Office Will." Online. Available HTTP: http://www.macnet.or.jp/co/o-will/ (available as of January 20, 2003).

Orita, A., Miyagawa, S. and Niimi, M. (1999) "Network communication brings opportunity for minority: identity of woman at home." Online. Available HTTP: http://www.isoc.org/isoc/conferences/inet/99/proceedings/3c/3c_4.htm (available as of January 20, 2003).

Ramilo, C.G. (2001) "Strengthening women's global networking for change," in *Global Networking of Women's Information – Searching for Enlargement of Women's Information*, Saitama: National Women's Education Center.

Red Card Movement (2000). Online. Available HTTP: http://www47.tok2.com/home/redcard/index-eng.htm (available as of January 20, 2003).

Shimabukuro, H. (2000) "Sando sha no wa kaigai made (Supporters' network reaches to foreign countries)," *Okinawa Times*, July 6.

Shizuko (1999) "Josei to Intaanetto (Women and the Internet)," *Akita News*, February 23. Online. Available HTTP: http://www4.ocn.ne.jp/~shizukot/essey7.html (available as of January 20, 2003).

Sustein, C. (2001) *Republic.com*, Princeton, NJ: Princeton University Press.

Taguchi, Y. (1996) "Pekin kaigi to Intaanetto (The Beijing Conference and the Internet)," *Josei shisetsu Jaanaru* No. 2, Tokyo: Gakuyō shobō.

Tamura, N. (2000) "Okuyama Mutsumi san ni kiku: pasokon ha josei ni totte fukuin (Asking Mutsumi Okuyama: the Internet is a blessing for women)," *Onna mo Otoko mo*, 32–4.

Teramoto, N. (1997) "Dejimamu (Digital mom)." Online. Available HTTP: http://www.biwako.ne.jp/~digimom/digimom.html (available as of January 20, 2003).

—— (2000) "Digimom workers diary 2000 February 10." Online. Available HTTP: http://www.digimomw.com/diary.html (available as of January 20, 2003).

—— (2003) "Intaanetto na Mama tachi, Dejimamu (Internet mothers, Dejimamu)." Online. Available HTTP: http://www.biwako.ne.jp/~digimom/index.html (available as of January 20, 2003).

The Ministry of Public Management, Home Affairs, Posts and Telecommunications (2001) *Information and Communication in Japan, the 2001 White Paper*, Tokyo: Gyōsei.

—— (2002) *Information and Communication in Japan, the 2002 White Paper*. Online. Available HTTP: http://www.johotsusintokei.soumu.go.jp/whitepaper/ja/h14/index.html (available as of January 20, 2003).

Tsumura, H. (2001) "Saibaa nashonarizumu e no hishō (Soaring towards cyber-nationalism)," *Saibaa Akushon*, Tokyo: Shakai Hihyōsha.

14 Support and spewing

Everyday activities of online Hindu groups

K.S. Arul Maragatha Muthu Selvan

INTRODUCTION

Because of its global reach and rich multilingual context, the Internet has the potential to influence different types of social relations. Unlike the traditional mass media, the Internet has an open architecture which has restricted efforts by authorities to regulate Net activities. This, in turn, has provided immense freedom and space for its users and members to express their feelings about their particular interests. The Internet provides a technological infrastructure for computer-mediated communication (CMC) across both time and space, creating a new group communication environment, a form of virtual co-presence established as a result of individuals' electronic interactions, creating a potential for virtual communities.

The interconnected computers do not by themselves provide congenial space for a group of people to float an online community in cyberspace. According to Baym (1995), the factors of temporal structure, external contexts, systems infrastructure, group purposes, and participant and group characteristics have been put forward as the most salient pre-existing forces on the development of computer-mediated community. Virtual community has its own advantages compared to the offline world. Computer-mediated communication will do by way of electronic pathways what cement roads were unable to do, namely connect rather than atomize us, put us at the controls of a "vehicle," and yet not detach us from the rest of the world.

Each online group exists in cyberspace with its own unique social setup and its affiliation with external social institutions. Kumiko Aoki (1994) divided the study of virtual communities into three separate groups:

1 Those that overlap totally with physical communities.
2 Those that overlap with these "real-life" communities to some degree.
3 Those that are separated totally from physical communities.

The rapid growth of personal computers, along with the popularity of cyber cafés, the rapidly expanding number of modems, and commercial sites are some of the factors that created the congenial atmosphere for the online groups to proliferate in the form of web-enabled Usenet access, BBS, mailing lists, and Internet relay chats (IRC). Correspondingly this has induced the rapid growth of online memberships in the wired environment.

Many scholars have defined the nature and functions of online communities. Harold Rheingold (1996), considered the father of virtual community studies, defines virtual communities as:

> Cultural aggregations that emerge when enough people bump into each other often enough in cyberspace. . . . It is a group of people who may or may not meet one another face to face, and who exchange words and ideas through the mediation of computer bulletin boards and networks. We do everything that people do when people get together, but we do it with words on computer screens leaving our bodies behind. . . . (Licklider and Taylor wrote in 1968) In most fields they will consist of geographically separated members, sometimes grouped in small clusters and sometimes working individually. There will be communities not of common location, but of common interest.

The ability to write the message or reply in a well-articulated manner is a crucial factor for a user to excel in an online discussion forum. Correspondingly, factors such as power and social status lose some of their meaningful role in online activities. As Oldenberg (1989) further explains, the virtual space in which people meet is neutral ground. Cyberspace is both available for everyone and at the same time it is owned by no one individual, corporation, or state. Conversation is clearly the primary activity, but this context favors people gifted in expression rather than just fast with their mouths. Online conversation is often much more thought out, and it is easier for everyone to get their say in and not be dominated by one or two loud people. In an online community, participants are in charge of their own involvement. Online communities are entirely participant driven, and the conversation is about what members initiate and react to.

Interactivity is an important element of new media. It eliminates time barriers for a user to access the contents conveniently at any time anywhere. The time-shifting facility enhances user involvement in the online environment. Lapachet (1994) explains that time is a crucial factor in the value of virtual communities. Virtual communities offer not only a multitude of topic areas, but also the ability to participate at a convenient time. There is no weekly meeting to catch after work. The meetings happen whenever the participants have time to log on and read the new postings. This time shifting allows participants leisure to ponder a particularly serious posting or article, and to write a coherent response. Time shifting enables people from many time zones to participate in a discussion, and allows users more control over their online experience so that they may participate at their leisure and convenience.

A group of human beings settled in a new environment tend to formulate norms and values for the smooth conduct of social processes of their new community. Likewise in the online environment, virtual members also establish their own group specific rules. Baym (1995) put forward the way in which the norms and values are being formulated by a news group. News group community members create shared social realities through interactive negotiation, and participants in CMC develop forms of expression which enable them to communicate social information and to create and codify group-specific meanings, socially negotiate group-specific identities, form relationships which span from the playfully antagonistic to the deeply romantic and which is more between the network and face-to-face interaction, and create norms which serve to organize interaction and to maintain desirable social climates. In CMC, as in real life, relationships take time to build. The social information unavailable in the immediacy of the face-to-face context may be gained verbally through computer-mediated interaction; the social penetration process just takes longer. People who meet online may then take that relationship offline if an opportunity arises. Many of the networks often have regional get-togethers.

There could be several reasons for a member to be associated with a virtual world. Oldenberg (1989) cites one reason as the loss of casual gathering places in our lives so that many people have turned to virtual spaces in which they can achieve some feeling of community. Lapachet (1994) also suggests that the virtual communities serve to fulfill a unique need for many people that they cannot find elsewhere in their lives. Although a multitude of special interest groups exist in the physical community, there is not always a forum located nearby to discuss the particular topic in which each person is interested. Virtual communities provide a forum for those discussions.

Those lacking a proper communication channel in real life are more dependent on computer-mediated communication. Lapachet (1994) raises the possibility that such participants could become so involved in virtual communities that it becomes their reality, thereby losing touch with physical reality.

Lockard (1997) cites several social impacts of online communities. The Cybersoc review on Lockard's article says:

> Cyberspace communities alienated people from the real world, a world that is largely unconnected (disconnected-disaffected) to the Internet, and provides us with a substitute reality where we believe that we are free, in control, and safe. But in reality, it is only diverting our dissatisfaction with the loss of community in real life, diverting it away from the social and political structures that have caused it and can still do something if we are lucky.

(Cybersoc, 1997)

However, the Internet also presents a potential threat to interpersonal relationships. Lapachet (1994) suggests that "It seems clear that there is a need for a good deal of responsibility and self control on the part of the participants, but there also seems to be a need for some group-nurturing from either administrators and/of particularly active members."

RELIGIOUS ACTIVITIES IN CYBERSPACE

Christian missionaries in the nineteenth century handled print medium for their religious propaganda. By the end of the twentieth century, there was a shift in using media channels for religious propaganda, and the popular electronic media have been used to spread religious messages. For millions of believers, the Internet has become a place where one can easily find God – or at least His followers. Churches and denominations worldwide have established websites in the hope of serving their members and converting non-believers. This is true even of the smallest faiths. For example, Zoroastrians, members of one of the oldest world religions, have embraced the Internet as a means of creating virtual communities for their frequently isolated believers and to preserve their faith. Sites often include sacred texts that can be downloaded or read online, in both modern translations and traditional languages.

The colonization of "cyberspace" by religious groups has been increasing, and there has been a growing study of religious behavior in virtual environments. In a study about communicating religions on computer networks, O'Leary (1996) found that, while online text-based ritual lacks physical presence, the interaction of text, graphics, video, and sound opens up a range of ritual possibilities that may have profound consequences for the symbolic expression of religiosity. Brenda Brasher, a theorist focusing on cyberspace and religion, believes that cyberspace religion prompts "new instances of convergences and cooperation" among religious groups. This is especially true in cyber-millennialism, where Christian millennial websites will often be linked to Jewish Zionist websites (Collette, 1999). Collette (1999) analyzed the possibilities of new media for religious activities. Religious groups, traditional or alternative, "have almost unanimously concurred that cyberspace is a place where they must be active" in order to grow and to survive.

A study by Schroeder and colleagues (1998) based on passive participant observation of the E-Church and on the analysis of text transcripts found that while relationships between participants in the E-Church are stronger than in other virtual worlds, it is inferior to a real church community. They have identified that social interaction is structured more tightly or formally in the E-Church than in other virtual worlds. Encounters are less haphazard, conversations are more focused and sustained, and the roles and structures within the group (E-Church) are more defined.

While giving reasons for the strength of relationship in comparison with other virtual worlds, the researchers point out that:

> The meeting has a beginning, a middle consisting of several parts, and end. Just as in the real world, there is some before and after church socializing. Importantly, this structure shapes the ebb and flow of emotional intensity of the meeting, as in any real-world ritual.
>
> (Schroeder *et al.*, 1998)

The researchers state that the non-availability of multifaceted face-to-face relations in the E-Church, which is common in a real church community, has reduced the online conversation into "small talk" which does not yield strong ties between the members.

INTRODUCTION TO HINDUISM

Hinduism has its origins in the Sanskrit work *Sanatana Dharma* which means everlasting religion. Hinduism was founded and has its greatest strength in India, although immigration and proselytism has spread the faith around the globe. Hinduism is one of the oldest religions in the world and is the faith of over four-fifths of the diverse peoples of the vast subcontinent of India, of the people of Nepal and Bali (Indonesia), and of millions of Indians who have migrated overseas. The purpose of this chapter is to examine the ways in which this ancient faith has migrated to cyberspace, and the ways in which the faith is enacted online.

GROUPS UNDER STUDY

The analysis of the Usenet news group field reveals that there are about thirty-four news groups dealing with India-related matters, among which are three news groups whose core theme is Hinduism. These news groups are *alt.religion.hindu*, *alt.religion.vaisnava*, and *uk.religion.hindu*. All three are open to public and non-moderated discussion forums. These three news groups have been selected for this study, as they are the three with the clearest focus on Hinduism:

1   *alt.religion.hindu* was established on April 26, 1996. As of January 16, 2003 this group had received about 35,100 threads (according to groups.google.com). The group is devoted mainly to the general principles of Hindu religion. It receives an average of seven messages per day.

2   *alt.religion.vaisnava* deals with all aspects of Vishnu[1] and Vaishnavism.[2] This group was originally called *soc.religion.vaishnava*, but later

it was re-established as *alt.religion.vaisnava* on March 30, 1995. This group has an archive of 21,300 threads as of January 16, 2003.

3   *uk.religion.hindu* was established during the same period – September 13, 1995 – with fewer users compared to the previous two Hindu online groups. As of January 16, 2003 it has 12,800 threads.

METHODOLOGY

A simple Internet search (December, 2002) through Google resulted in about 24,600,000 references to the word *Christian*, 4,350,000 to *Islam* and 1,970,000 to *Hindu*. This indirectly suggests strong growth and a presence of religion on the Web. It is not an exaggeration to say that almost every religion, no matter how small or unusual, has a presence online (Dawson, 2000). While comparing the quantity of religious presence on the Internet, Helland (2000) cites a reference from a Time Warner study: "There are almost three times as many WWW sites concerning God than there are sex."

In the context of an over-exposure of online presence of religion, it is crucial to map the religious cyberspace and purpose and use of the online environment for religious communication. There is a growing amount of literature available in the social science research arena that is pertinent to Christianity (see e.g. Horsfall, 2000) and Islam (Bunt, 2000). Since there is no reference in the academic circle to Hinduism and its role in cyberspace, to fill the gap this study has been undertaken in order to map the presence of Hindu religion in the terrain of computer-mediated communication.

The messages posted in the discussion room of selected news groups are the main data source for this study. There are two steps involved in the categorization of the messages in the two segments. In the first step, a cursory glance at the messages leads to the emergence of specified categories in each segment. In the second step, through close scrutiny, the messages are segregated according to their contextual and thematic nature. The theme and context of a message determines its location in the specified category.

The following examples indicate the process of classification at two levels – first, the general categories of "Flame Wars" and "Messages within Hindu VRCs" and second, the sub-levels within each of the general category. In the first example, a message with the subject line "Rama's mom has sex for a night w/horse" suggests a distorted story relating to a mythological event depicted in the Hindu epic *Ramayan*. This message highlights a minor detail (the epic *Ramayan* mentions that Rama's mother slept with the horse) and twists it (sex with a horse). The suggestion of bestiality reveals the author's intent to sensationalize and provoke a response from Hindus. It is categorized under the general category "Flame Wars," and within this, "criticizing Hindu religion." In the second example, a message entitled "Sivananda day-to-day" appears almost daily in *alt.religion.hindu*. It carries a small description of a passage on Hindu spiritual life by quoting verses from religious epics. The theme and its purpose of spreading Hindu ideals means that it is classified under the general category of "Hindu VRC Messages" and, within this, under "propaganda tool."

One final note is necessary before moving to the data analysis, and this is that the focus is primarily on Hindu news groups. If cross-postings are tracked to other sites, the direction of tracking starts from Hindu news groups. There has been no systematic attempt to do a comparative study of Islam-Pakistan news groups. As such, the reportage particularly of the flame war content is one-sided in the sense that the focus is on anti-India, anti-Hindu messages, and the reactions of Indians and Hindus to such messages. It is likely that Indians and Hindus also post highly negative messages in Pakistani and Islamic news groups, but these are not examined in this study and are outside the scope of this chapter.

DATA ANALYSIS

Email survey

Members of three non-moderated Hindu-based news groups, namely *alt.religion.hindu*, *alt.religion.vaisnava* and *uk.religion.hindu*, have become the subject of email survey. Through the initial analysis of three VRC[3] discussion forums in the study period from April 14, 2000 to April 13, 2001, a consolidated member list (614 numbers) was prepared. The intention in this survey is to identify the population of active members by using the number of postings in the study period as an indicator of activeness. A frequency distribution was constructed of members and the number of postings within the study period. Only a small number of members (thirty-five) posted ten messages or more during the study period. Although the web-based survey is cost-effective and has a global reach in comparison to traditional survey methods, the response rate for an online survey is lower compared to offline surveys (see a related discussion in Sheehan, 2001). Thus, in order to get a response from a larger number of members, the decision was made to use three postings or more during the study period as an indicator of active membership. This yielded a sample size of 154 members.

An open-ended questionnaire was prepared with the help of Survey Solution3.0 software and it was converted later into a HTML-based questionnaire form that was published on a website in the first week of May, 2001.

An invitation letter along with the URL of web questionnaires was mailed to 154 active members. However, eighty-two of the email addresses of active members were found to be invalid. The remaining seventy-two members received the invitation by email. Within three days, four responses were received. After one week, a first reminder was mailed to those active members who did not respond to the previous message. This yielded two more responses. A second and final reminder was mailed after another week. Finally, the total number of responses was only six, or a response rate of 8.3 percent.

Such a low response rate, despite the care and effort taken to increase the yield, may be reflective of the nature of cyber-communities described at the beginning of this chapter, namely that participants enter into communication primarily to meet the participant's individual needs in the areas of his or her interests. Within this orientation and in the context of the anonymity of the Internet, members are likely to first meet their own needs, and perhaps render assistance to those who profess similar interests, and less likely to support other interests (such as helping an Internet researcher). Unlike offline relationships, the lack of incentives other than text-based persuasion may also contribute to the low response. The small number of cases will not represent the true picture of Hindu VRC members' profile. Instead, the intention is to provide cases of motivations and profiles of members of the Hindu Net, which is presented along with a more systematic content analysis of message threads.

Demographic details

Table 14.1 provides a summary of the backgrounds of respondents. All the respondents are male and of different ages, varying between 23 and 55 years of age. The educational qualifications of respondents range from secondary or high school education to doctorates. The respondents have a technological background and they are associated with a skilled profession. All the respondents are practitioners of the Hindu religion to varying degrees, and some respondents also mention their affinity to other types of religious beliefs.

Even though these three VRCs are oriented towards Hinduism and India, it is significant that all six respondents are outside of India, with five

Table 14.1 Demographic details of respondents

Person	Age	Sex	Religion	Education	Place of residence	Place of birth
1	29	Male	Hindu	Bachelor's degree	USA	Malaysia
2	47	Male	Atheist*	Ph.D.	USA	USA
3	55	Male	Hare Krishna	High school	USA	USA
4	46	Male	Agnostic*	High school	USA	USA
5	23	Male	Hindu	Bachelor's degree	USA	India
6	24	Male	Hindu	High school	Indonesia	Indonesia

Note: *But profess leanings towards Hindu, Bahai, and Buddhist thoughts.

from the United States and the sixth from Indonesia. However, they all have a strong bond with or interest in the Hindu religion. This suggests that those far away from "home" are actually more likely to enter the Hindu Net because this reaffirms their identity, a sort of a substitute for the "real" "offline" experience which Indians can get at home with other Hindus.

Five out of the six respondents have had several years of presence in the online communities. Their association with virtual communities ranges from a few months to six years. Members' preference, profession, racial origin, and religious beliefs determine each individual's affiliation to his or her respective Usenet news groups.

When asked why they are involved in Hindu and India news groups, respondents cited strong inclinations towards Hinduism and the need to associate themselves with these religious forums to keep in touch with religious thought and sentiments, despite having migrated and settled in a different part of the world. Others may be committed to different religious systems but are involved in the profession that deals with Hinduism directly or indirectly (for example, one member cited that he is involved in the business of artifacts of India). They subscribe to these news groups in order to develop a better understanding of the country and its major religion.

The six respondents are all active in terms of their access and interaction with news groups. The respondents check new messages regularly, varying between daily access and once every three days. The interaction with online communities in terms of posting messages ranges from one message per day to thirty messages per week.

The majority of respondents said they would like to send their messages to various news groups for the sake of wider publicity, but the inclusion of the targeted news group depended on the nature of the messages or the preference of the member.

News groups serve as a public forum in which individuals find ways to express their feelings and to judge their opinions from others' point of view. Similarly it is a platform for members to propagate their personal religious works. Those rendering public service in the offline world are interested to extend their service in an online environment to spread religious beliefs which are important to them and to offer help (by way of information sharing and advice) to people of the same religious orientation.

CONTENT ANALYSIS

The messages of *alt.religion.hindu*, *alt.religion.vaisnava*, and *uk. religion.hindu*, which appeared between April 14, 2000 and April 13, 2001, formed the subject for the content analysis. In total, 6857 threads were posted on to three online Hindu groups during the study period. The majority of threads were cross-posted across three news groups. Cross-posted threads were removed from the population, leaving 4875 threads. From this base, 243 threads (5 percent of the population) have been selected for the analysis through a simple random sampling method. A total of 788 messages were posted under 243 threads in the given time period.

The 243 threads were divided further into two groups as messages appearing in Hindu and its closely related news groups, and messages appearing in Hindu online groups along with other non-Hindu-based news groups (see Table 14.2):

1 128 threads (52.7 percent) appeared on Hindu-based news groups only along with other related Hindu or Indian news groups (257 messages – 32.6 percent). These related news groups include *alt.yoga*, *alt.meditation, alt.fan.jai-maharaj*, and *soc.culture.indian*.

2 115 threads (47.3 percent) were posted on Hindu-based news groups along with other non-Hindu, non-Indian news groups. As will be shown in the following sections, the contents of such threads and messages are attacks on or criticisms of the Hindu religion (531 messages – 67.4 percent). These groups are of two types. The first category are religious groups (*alt.religion.islam* and *alt.religion.christian*), while the second category are geo-political/social cultural groupings (*soc. culture.pakistan, soc.culture.israel, soc.culture.usa*, and *soc. culture.british*). As the subsequent analysis will show, messages from Hindu news groups get cross-posted in both news group types because of complementary and conflictual interests.

Types of messages within Hindu VRCs

In this section, messages which appeared only in Hindu-related news groups (*alt.religion.hindu, alt.religion.vaisnava, uk.religion.hindu, alt.yoga, alt.meditation*, and *soc.culture.india*) have been included for the analysis. This allows the researcher to focus attention on postings within a primary Hindu environment. Members of three VRCs post messages to either inform or seek clarification about certain aspects of Hinduism and

Table 14.2 Threads and messages within the two news groups

	Threads		Messages	
	No.	%	No.	%
Hindu VRCs and related news groups	128	52.7	257	32.6
Hindu VRCs with non-related news groups	115	47.3	531	67.4
Total	243	100	788	100

Table 14.3 Type of messages posted in Hindu VRCs

Category	Threads		Messages	
	No.	%	No.	%
Announcements	22	17.2	27	10.5
Comments and opinions	32	25	90	35
Flame war	17	13.3	54	21
Propaganda tool	22	17.2	30	11.7
Sharing experiences	4	3.1	8	3.1
Questions	8	6.3	15	5.8
Unrelated	23	18	33	12.8
Total	128	100	257	100

matters related to India. Most of the respondents prefer to play a dual role as a questioner and as a mentor. The messages are categorized into announcements, comments, and opinions, flame war, propaganda tool, sharing experience, questions, and unrelated (see Table 14.3).

The flame war category of this segment is in distinctive contrast with the flame war discussed in the next section of the chapter where cross-posting in non-related Hindu sites is considered. The messages which appeared only in Hindu news groups, which are categorized as flaming, take mainly two approaches. The first is a reaction against anti-Hindu messages, with members expressing anguish and frustration. The second type of posting involves members criticizing feudalism in Hinduism.

Announcements

Members use the online Hindu groups as their publicity platform. The messages are posted in order to draw subscribers' attention to electronic web pages that deal with a specific area of the Hindu religion. In this online public platform, various offline activities are getting noticed in the web environment; for example, a message requests other users to denote funds for religious missions, and another gives detailed information about a popular television program on the Hare Krishna sect. On auspicious occasions, members exchange background stories about the relevant god or goddess and their role in Hindu religion. These announcement messages rarely elicit a reply or initiate any further discussion.

Comments and opinions

The uncensored online environment has provided immense freedom to the news group's members to raise comments and opinions on latest Hindu religion-oriented offline events. Most of the opinions were based on news reports that appeared in mass media in general and news portals in particular. There are three types of messages posted under this category. The first type gives additional information to a reported event. For example, there was a swimming competition in the Ganges; the message carried extensive details about the Ganges's role in the Hindu religion. Other examples include quotes from a newspaper report about the first Spanish translation of *Bagavad Geeta*.[4] The same message corrects the reported error and gives details about the very first *Bagavad Geeta*'s Spanish translation.

A second type of message involves commentary and analyses of reported events, and ongoing issues and concerns within India and Hinduism. For example, in a message, a member gives reasons behind the massacre of *dalits* in northern India. Some members discussed Brahmin domination, and the discrimination of the caste system in the Hindu religion. The third type of message acknowledges events that mark the development of the religion; for example, the messages carried notes on the establishment of Hindu mission groups in India and abroad, the role taken by the Hindu temples in Western countries, and religious leaders' spiritual itinerary in other continents.

The level of discussion depends on the nature of the content, and the more opinion-driven nature of the second type of message as opposed to the informational nature of the first and third type of message means that those messages involving commentary and discussion will generate more discussion.

Flame war

These are messages posted by Hindu news group members reacting to the flame messages. Written from a Hindu perspective, these postings criticize the flame war messages that are posted in diverse news groups including non-Hindu-oriented online groups. These messages blame flame messages for taking an antagonistic approach to Hinduism, for being critical, and attempting to spread misinformation about Hinduism. Some messages are posted in Hindu VRCs with the intention to criticize the Islam religion. Other messages also involve attacks on Hindu subsects, exposing the fragmentations within Hinduism. There is also criticism of India's feudal and caste system.

Given that these are Hindu news groups, Hinduism and India-based sensitive matters attracted more attention, while anti-Islam-based matters were totally neglected. The level of religious predisposition towards members' respective religion or subsect or religious leaders could have been the driving force for the flame war posting. The flaming content of this category targets mainly either religious leaders of Hindu religion or Islam. The nature of such messages will be analyzed in greater detail in the next section where flame messages in non-Hindu VRCs are considered.

Propaganda tool

Quoting from various Hindu-based religious literatures, these messages provide interpretations of the practice of Hindu religion from a variety of angles. The ultimate aim of the interpretation centers on truth and peace, and these messages suggest the way in which to attain truth and peace in real life by practicing the Hindu religion. Some messages analyze communal harmony and some narrate the integration of science and religion. Some members post Sanskrit phrases from religious literatures, such as the *Bagavad Geeta*, along with an elaborate explanation. Members use these Hindu online groups as a platform to propagate ideals of Hinduism.

Sharing experiences

Those who have recently started to practice Hinduism or a subsect of religion share their new religious experiences. For example, a Christian girl married to a Hindu shares her encounter with a new, combined religious practice. Another member reveals his new experience with the Hare Krishna sect.

Questions

People from Western countries and Hindus settled in foreign countries frequently raise questions about Hinduism. They have used these news groups to expand their understanding of the Hindu religion. Considerable numbers of messages were posted to request fellow members to answer certain queries, which arise out of an interest to know more about a religious leader or Hinduism itself, or cows or garuda purana,[5] or temples in Germany. Question-based messages are quite likely to receive answers from fellow members, indicating the usefulness of such a medium.

Unrelated

A comparatively large number of threads – twenty-three (18 percent) – appeared in this segment with thirty-three messages (12.8 percent). Some messages are religious in content but do not concern Hinduism directly or indirectly (e.g. Islam and Christian postings). Other, unrelated messages cover a variety of topics (for example, details on computer viruses, the nature and role of communism, information on cancer, and jobs in the IT field).

The unrelated category also includes flame war postings which are unrelated to Hinduism. These unrelated flame postings end up in Hindu VRCs because flame postings are posted in a wide variety of non-Hindu online communities. These flames appearing in Hindu VRCs are classified as unrelated when the flames target the wrong audience. These are of two types: (1) messages which bear no relation to the Hindu religion since they deal mainly with Islam and Christianity, and (2) response messages which target Hindu communities when the originator of the flame is from another online group.

Messages with flame war content

A determined anti-Hindu propaganda campaign is being carried out in the Hindu-based news groups. For the sake of wider publicity, the anti-Hindu propaganda-laden flame war messages targets various news groups which deal with broad areas of Islam, Christian, and Western countries along with Hindus; for example, *soc.culture.usa*, *soc.culture.israel*, and *soc.culture.british*. The primary intention of these messages is to attack Hindu religious sentiments and India. The messages are segmented into seven categories.

The messages of this segment appeared in Hindu news groups and, through cross-posting, include the wide variety of non-Hindu news groups, namely *alt.religion.islam*, *alt.religion.christian*, *soc.culture.pakistan*, *soc.culture.israel*, *soc.culture.usa*, and *soc.culture.british*. The messages are divided into seven categories: (1) comparing Hindu vs. Islam, (2) comparing India vs. Pakistan, (3) criticizing Hindu religion, (4) criticizing the Islam religion, (5) praising Islam, (6) censuring fellow members, and (7) unrelated (see Table 14.4).

In the first two categories, messages compare two entities (religion and nation); each entity is weighted in comparison with the opponent. The third and fourth categories of message specifically target and criticize the individual religion. There is a marked difference between "comparison" (first and second category) and "individual attack" (third and fourth). The fifth category deals with the Islam religion in order to propagate its ideals in an unreached area. The sixth category of messages attacks fellow members, particularly those who are engaged in flaming (anti-Hindu)

Table 14.4 Types of message with flame war content

Category	Threads		Messages	
	No.	*%*	*No.*	*%*
Comparing Hindu vs. Islam	7	6.1	125	23.5
Comparing India vs. Pakistan	11	9.6	26	4.9
Criticizing Hindu religion	36	31.3	162	30.5
Criticizing Islam religion	9	7.8	26	4.9
Praising Islam	6	5.2	28	5.3
Censuring fellow members	14	12.2	71	13.4
Unrelated	32	27.8	93	17.5
Total	115	100	531	100

activities. In the seventh category, messages carried information which is irrelevant to Hinduism in either a positive or negative way.

The reader should note again the comment made in the methodology section above, namely that in the analysis presented below, the focus is primarily on Hindu news groups and, as such, the direction of flames is likely to be a one-sided analysis since no attempt is made to see how postings and, in particular, flames, appear in Islam-Pakistani news groups.

Comparing Hinduism vs. Islam

Based on real-life situations, messages made comparisons between the Hindu and Islam religions, for example, social status of women. Messages abuse their opponent at the same time as they support their own religion. The unique characteristics of respective religions became the bone of contention. Each message weighs its religion's positive characteristics and its equivalent treatment in the counterpart religion. Women's role and their status and way of worship are some of the examples. In general, there is no boundary to attacking rival religions, though, at a comparative level, the Hindu religion is the main focal point of criticism rather than Islam.

Comparing Pakistan vs. India

Day-to-day news events trigger a comparison between India and Pakistan, particularly in terms of the strength of each nation. Quoting news clippings from web portals, these messages contrast the nation's performance in the field of the arms race, or in regional sports meetings. Analysis of India and its related events were always discussed in a negative way. Political leaders from both countries invariably end up being dragged into such discussions. While it is tempting to suggest the origins of these postings, given their anonymity, it is impossible to verify if the postings originate from India, Pakistan, or indeed from a third country.

Criticizing the Hindu religion

While the first category involves a comparison between Hinduism and Islam, this category contains postings attacking Hinduism without reference to Islam or other religions. Different ways have been adopted to denounce Hindu religion. Intentionally, original Hindu mythology stories were twisted for the convenience of maligning the religion. Three main social practices of the Hindu religion were highlighted in most of the instances such as the *Devadashi*[6] system, women's role in the religion, and free sex. Depiction and incarnation of Hindu gods and goddesses were questioned. Unlawful social events and existing social evils in India are being identified as the consequence of practicing the Hindu religion.

Criticizing Islam religion

The founder of the Islam religion, Mohammed and his life with his wives, was dragged into the flame war discussion. Some messages relate the internal contradiction in the holy book of Islam, the Qur'ān. While the anonymity of postings means that the sender's identity cannot be established, these messages may have been posted by Hindu believers out of irritation against flame war on Hinduism.

Praising Islam

People who recently converted to Islam share their new way of life. Interestingly, other messages similar to the conversion experience were crafted, way of writing and method of presentation, verbatim. The importance of the Qur'ān and its interpretation and code of conduct for Muslims were other examples in this category.

Censuring fellow members

Given the anonymity of news groups, attackers of Hinduism and India have taken to using different Hindu names to post their flame messages. The use of Hindu names marks these attackers as a "fellow" member of the community, thus masking their identity. A handful of people are involved in the practice of spreading flame wars against the Hindu religion. Those affected by the flame war on Hindu religion take revenge by way of attacking those people personally. The people responsible for the flame war on Hinduism never responded to any of the criticism posted against them. The members who have received criticism are involved extensively in the message propagation that falls within the context of previous categories (except for (4)); such propagation activities include anti-Hindu, anti-India propaganda and carry out pro-Islamic dissemination.

Unrelated

For the sake of wider publicity, out-of-context messages used to appear in online Hindu groups. Other religious materials were also posted here, for example, messages about Christianity and Buddhism.

DISCUSSION

All the news groups of the present study, namely *alt.religion.hindu*, *alt. religion.vaisnava*, and *uk.religion.hindu*, are open to the public, without moderators or controllers of messages. This prevailing situation is conducive for members to express their opinions without any inhibitions, and almost every Hindu believer shares his or her voluntary responsibility for the smooth running of the discussion forum. In the course of time, the framework for the discussion has settled into certain categories according to the principles from which these news groups originated. On the whole (apart from flame war contents), the online Hindu groups function for two important reasons: popularizing Hinduism and sharing individual religious thoughts.

The main discussion centers on matters related to Hinduism and its birthplace, India, but the point of reference in most instances orients towards offline activities of Western countries. The reason could be the composition of online Hindu groups; the members of three news groups are mostly Indians settled in foreign countries and foreigners interested in Hinduism with marginal representation of people from India. The reasons may be that the level of Internet penetration and knowledge about Usenet is comparatively lower in India than in Western countries.

Geographically dispersed Hindu believers come under the electronic umbrella to share the various materials available in different places, particularly the effort of integrating electronically available Hinduism-based resources by way of posting announcement messages. Most Hindu online group members are outside India, where it is difficult to find a place in the offline environment to express or to share or to participate in any religious activities that might have forced them to associate with the Hindu-based virtual religious communities. Interest in Hinduism binds them electronically, cutting across geographical barriers. Hindus outside India are more likely to use such a medium because of the relative unavailability of other sources of religious advice and information. Perhaps having such resources in English is also a contributing factor, along with the relative availability of home computers and Internet connections. Taken together, such forums may play a vital role in keeping primordial identities alive in a transplanted world of the migrant, performing the functions of ethnic enclaves in a previous era.

The content analysis of the 128 threads posted in Hindu VRCs suggests that members are participating constructively in the discussion in terms of adding facts to the existing pool of information in order to increase understanding of the Hindu religion. The way the topics are discussed indicates that members potentially use online Hindu news groups as a tool to propagate popular Hindu religious themes. Members who have converted recently to the Hindu religion share their experience and delight with others. Hinduism-based queries are raised in order to broaden knowledge about the Hindu religion. Unlike other religions where there is a commandment or responsibility to convert non-believers, there is no reference in the Hindu epics to propagate religious ideals. However, dispersed and migrated Hindus and sympathizers of Hinduism from different parts of the world have identified the advantage provided by the online platform to unite together to enhance their identity and understanding of the religion.

This global level of integration, being relatively cheaper and faster is not possible through any other form of communication method.

However, the "alt" group's enormous freedom has also allowed for flaming. The analysis of 115 threads cross-posted on Hindu and non-Hindu news groups indicated the nature of such postings. The handiwork of a few people's outrageous postings maligns the constructive effort of online Hindu groups to popularize Hinduism. The number of members involved in this flame war work is very few compared to the strength of Hindu believers, but the quantity of flame war messages overcomes the numbers of messages that deal positively with Hinduism. The method of message construction, focus of flaming, and inclusion of target news groups are meticulously planned to counteract the main activities of Hindu-based virtual religious communities. Their main target news groups are all other major religions and prominent society and culture-based discussion forums such as *soc.culture.usa*, *soc.culture.british*, *soc.culture.israel*, and so on. The aim of the flame war is to attack Hinduism, thereby disrupting the online Hindu community's integrative functions.

Judging by the reactions of members of Hindu news groups, the content of the flame war has quite clearly created frustration and irritation among Hindu believers. Once in a while members discuss in great detail how to find a method to overcome the flame war menace. Since it is an unregulated discussion forum, members advise other members to totally ignore the flame war content. Angry protesters in turn post messages to counteract the flame war and even, in some instances, postings carry malicious content about Islam. Both types of flamers end up being severely criticized by others.

The findings about the structure and conduct of three news groups in the present study parallel major findings of similar studies, and in some cases contradict the existing literature. The three VRCs have provided a platform in which geographically separated people banded together on the basis of common interest to conduct broad-based discussion on the nature and functions of the Hindu religion. The formation of these news groups goes along with Harold Rheingold's (1996) definition of virtual communities.

Even though the sample size is very small, the result of the survey conducted by this researcher among the members of Hindu-based news groups is suggestive of non-availability of space for intimate relationships. The three VRCs have been in existence for over five years. Most of the respondents have been associated with VRCs for the past five years but did not demonstrate any meaningful relationship with fellow members. The overall set-up of these news groups does provide a qualification to the principles of Nancy Baym on norm and value formation for the online groups in the sense that, while news groups do possess some of the characteristics of online communities, a number of features conspire to weaken the identity and solidarity of their members.

In comparison to the major seven news group hierarchy (comp, misc, news, rec, sci, soc, and talk) the category "alt" is easy to create. News groups have left it open to anyone to read and post messages without any restrictions. This advantage exposes "alt" news groups to flaming. Thus, while the majority of Hindu news group regulars share a common religious identity, the severity of flame war messages works against the function of the news group to share religious information and propagates ideals of Hinduism. An examination of the postings indicates that there is evidence of support and identity building but the venomous environment of flaming and the inability of news groups to prevent such attacks hinder identity and value building, since flames by their very nature are corrosive to such efforts. Thus, despite advice from members to ignore such flamers, their presence is counter-productive. Other factors also come into play, such as the community being spatially dispersed. While it is impossible to make any claims based on a very small unrepresentative sample of news group regulars, it is possible to venture an opinion that the situation is probably that members share in this news group because of their beliefs, but perhaps they do not see the need to move beyond a common identification and sharing to develop closer relations.

Certainly, the results of this research support the concepts of Oldenberg (1989) and Lapachet (1994) on members' role in online communities. Hindu-based news groups are an assembly of Hindus and others with a strong inclination towards Hinduism from different parts of the world. Technological advancement and the level of accessibility have determined the formation of these online groups. Outside of India, Nepal and Bali (Indonesia), Hindus and believers are a minority, and this makes it difficult to nurture the religion and share the interpretation of ideals of religion. This situation is a strong impetus for the dynamism of these news groups. The electronic discussion forums under this study act as a potential tool for Hindu believers to share and popularize the Hindu religion. Segregated people have been integrated through these virtual communities on topics of common interest.

Believers or practitioners contribute reliable interpretations or quotes from original sources with the aim of expanding the Hindu religion into new areas. Senior members advise others to ignore flame war contents with reference to hot discussion on the flame war. Members of online Hindu groups are quite serious about message inflow, apart from the flame war materials and members involved in the flaming business.

In summary, the findings indicate that the online Hindu groups are mechanisms to support and popularize the Hindu religion. It integrates geographically segregated people into a common interest group for the sake of sharing intellectual thoughts in order to broaden understanding of the vast area of Hinduism. This is particularly important for the Hindu diasporic community, since the ability of such forums to transcend geographic limits means that Hindus overseas have access to the knowledge and support of other Hindus, making the adjustment in another country easier. In the case of the Hindu Net, existing identities and beliefs are mapped on to a new cyberspace. Such primordial sentiments thereby allow for a quick adjustment to a Hindu cyber-community. The sentiments within religious communities may also lead to negative attitudes towards what is seen as competing faiths. However, the numbers are small, although these involve an extensive and quantitatively high amount of anti-Hinduism propaganda. Comparing various religious news groups and their structure and functions in the future will give a better understanding of online religious communities.

NOTES

1 Vishnu, major god of Hinduism and Indian mythology, popularly regarded by Hindus as the preserver of the universe. In the ancient body of literature called the *Veda*, the sacred literature of the Aryan invaders, Vishnu ranks with the numerous lesser gods and is usually associated with the major Vedic god Indra in battles against demonic forces.
2 Vaishnavism, also called Vishnuism or Vis nuism, or in Sanskrit Vais navism, is the worship of the god Vishnu and of his incarnations, principally as Rama and as Krishna. It is one of the major forms of modern Hinduism – with Saivism and Shaktism (S aktism). A major characteristic of Vaishnavism is the strong role played by *bhakti*, or religious devotion. The ultimate goal of the devotee is to escape from the cycle of birth and death so as to enjoy the presence.
3 Virtual religious communities are defined by this study as "a community gathering in the wired environment for the purpose of religious discourse."
4 A holy book of the Hindu religion. Its composition is based on dialog between Lord Krishna and the Arjuna, the character of Mahabaratha (Hindu epic).
5 Garuda Purana: it is named after Garuda, the vulture vehicle, of Lord Vishnu. It deals with the rites held over the dying, the death moment, the funeral ceremonies, the ritual building up of a new body for the preta or deceased, the judgment, the various after-death states until rebirth. It also deals with sun-worship and astrology and is probably Indo-Zoroastrian in origin.
6 Hindu girls hypothetically consider desired gods as their husbands and devote their entire life to religious service.

BIBLIOGRAPHY

Aoki, K. (1994) "Virtual communities in Japan," Paper presented to the Pacific Telecommunications Council. Online. Available HTTP: http://www.vcn.bc. ca/sig/comm-nets/aoki.txt (accessed June 10, 2001).

Baym, N.K. (1995) "The emergence of community in computer-mediated communication," in S. Jones (ed.) *CyberSociety: Computer-Mediated Communication and Community*, Thousand Oaks, CA: Sage Publications.

Bunt, G. (2000) "Surfing Islam: Ayatollahs, Shayks and Hajjs on the superhighway," in J.K. Hadden and D.E. Cowan (eds) *Religion on the Internet: Research Prospects and Promises*, Amsterdam: JAI Press.

Collette, L. (1999) "Cyberspace: the new frontier for religion," *Cybersociology*, 7. Online. Available HTTP: http://www.socio.demon.co.uk/magazine/7/lin.html (accessed June 10, 2001).

Cybersoc (1997) "The Cybersoc Bibliography Project – Online and Virtual Communities Page." Online. Available HTTP: http://www.socio.demon.co.uk/topicVC.html (accessed January 2001).

Dawson, L. (2000) "Researching religion in cyberspace: issues and strategies from the sociology of the Internet," in J.K. Hadden and D.E. Cowan (eds) *Religion on the Internet: Research Prospects and Promises*, Amsterdam: JAI Press.

Helland, C. (2000) "Online-religion/religion-online: virtual communitas," in J.K. Hadden and D.E. Cowan (eds) *Religion on the Internet: Research Prospects and Promises*, Amsterdam: JAI Press.

Horsfall, S. (2000) "Toward understanding how religious organizations use the Internet," in J.K. Hadden and D.E. Cowan (eds) *Religion on the Internet: Research Prospects and Promises*, Amsterdam: JAI Press.

Lapachet, J.A.H. (1994) "Virtual communities: the 90's mind altering drug or facilitator of human interaction?" School of Library and Information Studies, University of California, Berkeley, CA. Online. Available HTTP: http://bliss.SIMS. Berkeley.EDU:80/impact/students/jaye/jaye_asis.html (accessed June 10, 2001).

Lockard, J. (1997) "Progressive politics, electronic individualism and the myth of virtual community," in D. Porter (ed.) *Internet Culture*, London: Routledge.

O'Leary, S. (1996) "Cyberspace as sacred space: communicating religion on computer networks," *Journal of the American Academy of Religion*, 44, 4: 781–808.

Oldenberg, R. (1989) *The Great Good Place: Cafes, Coffee Shops, Community Centers, Beauty Parlors, General Stores, Bars, Hangouts and How They got You Through the Day*, New York: Paragon House.

Rheingold, H. (1996) "A slice of my life in my virtual community," in P. Ludlow (ed.) *High Noon on the Electronic Frontier: Conceptual Issues in Cyberspace*, Cambridge, MA: MIT Press.

Schroeder, R., Heather, N., and Lee, R.M. (1998) "The sacred and the virtual: religion in multi-user virtual reality," *Journal of Computer Mediated Communication*, 4, 2. Online. Available HTTP: http://www.ascusc.org/jcmc/vol4/issue2/schroeder.html (accessed June 10, 2001).

Sheehan, K. (2001) "Email survey response rate: a review," *Journal of Computer Mediated Communication*, 6, 2. Online. Available HTTP: http://www.ascusc.org/jcmc/vol6/issue2/sheehan.html (accessed November 23, 2002).

15 Communication and relationships in online and offline worlds

A study of Singapore youths

Waipeng Lee and Brenda Chan

INTRODUCTION

By any measure of information technology (IT) development, Singapore is a success – and way ahead of many of its Asian neighbors. Singapore is among the world's fifteen leading information societies (World Times, 2002), and more than half of its workforce is engaged in information-related professions (Low and Kuo, 1999). The Singapore government – motivated to build a nation and to attain a competitive economy – has put forth several plans since the 1980s to make IT omnipresent at every sector and level of society. Major plans include the Civil Service Computerization Program (1981), the National IT Plan (1986), the A Vision of an Intelligent Island (1992), and Masterplan for IT in Education (1997). Children, heirs to the country and members of the future workforce, are certainly part of the scheme. The 1997 Masterplan for IT in Education, which demands curricula to include 30 percent IT skills and computer training for teachers, has ushered the schools along the information superhighway. More recently, the 2002 Masterplan II for IT in Education continues to promote IT actively in schools.

Under the spurs of the government, the impact is evident. Although the general public had no access to the Internet until 1994, the penetration rate has reached 46 percent among adults aged 18 and over, and 71 percent among 13-year-olds in 1999 (Kuo *et al.*, 2002). Follow-up surveys by the Singapore Internet Project which tracked Singapore students' Internet usage patterns in 1999, 2000, and 2001 show that more than 90 percent of 13 to 15-year-olds were regular Internet users by 2001, spending an average of 9.8 hours a week on email and online chats, information search, and cyber entertainment. As the Internet swiftly becomes an integral part of life, there are concerns over its influence, especially on the post-MTV Net-surfing generation. Many of these concerns, such as pornography, are not peculiar to the Internet; but, unlike newspapers, radio or television, the Internet has a unique characteristic – that is, interactivity, which allows online interaction and transaction, and the formation of cyber or virtual communities. Furthermore, these virtual communities can be free of geographical boundaries; and the Internet permits speedy one-to-many, as well as many-to-many communication. Potentially, members of virtual communities can influence each other in a manner unrivaled by telephones and facsimile machines. This adds new concerns to modern information societies, such as Singapore, where technology-mediated communication prevails. Perhaps what is more unsettling to some in Singapore is that schoolchildren have access to such a potentially powerful medium.

Certainly, the media, new or otherwise, are not the only conduits for "unwholesome" values and practices, deemed detrimental to Singapore society. Singapore is a cosmopolitan city-state, which promotes globalization. It has a widely traveled populace, and one out of five people who live within its borders are non-citizens. All these factors can affect Singapore's identity and sense of community. To forge a common bond among its people, the government has been advocating the adoption of a national ideology that consists of five collectivistic values – nation, family, community, consensus, and harmony – as a means to "safeguard against undesirable values permeating from developed countries" (Ministry of Information, Communications, and the Arts, 2002). Despite Singapore's modernity and urbanization, local scholars do not believe that it has lost its sense of community (Chua, 1997; Ho, 1988; Wong *et al.*, 1997). According to them, the resettlement of people from shop houses, squatter settlements, and villages to multi-story, high-density public housing has not eroded ethnic, neighborhood, and religious communities. Singapore's diminutive size, ethnic mix, and public policies may have saved itself from fragmentation (Ho, 1988). The country's collectivistic nature may have also played a part, as the social fabric places a heavier emphasis on groups (Gudykunst, 1998; Markus and Kitayama, 1991, 1994; Triandis, 1989). As such, individuals' self-identity intertwines with the collective.

While culture is relatively stable, it is not static. Because of this, widespread use of the Internet theoretically opens up the floodgates for cultures to interact. In comparison to traditional media, the Net is difficult to control and regulate. Children and teenagers, often described as impressionable and immature, are in the midst of this cultural vortex. The younger generation has embraced the new medium due to the catalytic push from the government and schools. Parents are concerned over the Internet's impact, but they are also aware that their children will not succeed in school without IT. In fact, according to a *Strait Times* survey, one in three Singapore parents reported to have spent an average of S$1020 per year on computers and software for their pre-school children (Ariff, 2002). We know young Singaporeans spend a considerable amount of time on email, online chats and discussion, surfing, and playing online games. According to the Singapore Internet Project, more than one-third of their online time is spent on communication. However, there is little research examining the nature of their social interaction over the Internet. Theoretically, this time may be spent on absorbing cultural elements of other societies, or even "undesirable values." Imaginably, they can also instigate a radically different lifestyle and be associated with an "unapproved" culture over the Internet right under the noses of their parents and teachers.

The literature has pointed out consistently that meaningful relationships are especially important among adolescents (Berndt, 1992; Buhrmester, 1996), and it is through social interaction that they acquire social competence crucial to the smooth operation of a community (Buhrmester, 1990; Caplan and Weissberg, 1989; Duck, 1989). A failure in peer relationship may result in mal-adaptation and they will have difficulty being part of a society (Berndt, 1992; Hartup, 1996). Moreover, peer relationships underlie communities (Chua, 1997; Wong *et al.*, 1997), and it is through social interaction and communication that people form common bonds and a sense of belonging (Rheingold, 1993). Optimists seem to think that it is possible to form genuine relationships in cyberspace (Katz and Aspden, 1997; Parks and Floyd, 1996; Utz, 2000). Critics, however, have wondered if virtual communities are "communities" at all. After all, a community has to be self-sufficient. A traditional community, as Havighurst and Jansen (1967) have pointed out, requires people to interact within a particular space; and to share economic and social institutions, values and norms, and a common life.

INTERNET AND FRIENDSHIP

In 2001, young Singaporeans were spending about four hours a week on computer-mediated communication, specifically online chats and email messaging, according to the Singapore Internet Project data; and for the most part, this communication is with their peers. This is not surprising since adolescents need friends with whom they share experiences, explore identities, and discuss problems that range from conflict with parents to emerging sexuality (Buhrmester, 1996; Hartup, 1996). Traditionally, friendship occurs typically among people with shared characteristics, such as ethnicity, age, class, and education (Allan, 1979; Lazarsfeld and Merton, 1954; Verbrugge, 1977); and attribute homogeneity in peer relations has been observed among Singapore schoolchildren (Foo, 1989; Sim, 1990). Rapid developments in IT are challenging the traditional conceptualization of friendship, which assumes physical proximity as a necessary condition in the initial establishment of friendship (Adams, 1998; Festinger *et al.*, 1950), and geographical co-location of a community (Havighurst and Jansen, 1967). Equipped with new technology, especially the Internet, this new generation of Singaporeans is no longer limited by distance, speed, and cost of communication to make, develop, or maintain friendships.

It is possible, therefore, that "friendship" will move into cyberspace, and render face-to-face interaction redundant. Attribute homogeneity will be less important, since the Internet is borderless and real identities can be easily concealed. Pessimists allege that the new technology will cause social isolation and erode the community (Kraut *et al.*, 1998). After all, friendship and community are based on commonalities. Optimists, however, argue that the Internet has the potential to promote "new forms of solidarity and cooperation" (Slevin, 2000); and fragmented societies that have lost their sense of community in the process of modernization, industrialization, and urbanization may recover their collective identity (Rheingold, 1993). As Jones (1995) suggests, computer-mediated communication is not only a technology and a medium, it is also an "engine of social relations." Thus, highly urbanized and modern Singapore adolescents should provide an indication of the role of the Internet on relationships, which, as in many other Asian nations, are highly valued.

The purpose of this project was to examine the impact of Internet communication on friendship development and maintenance among the "most wired" of youths, those in Singapore. Given the high diffusion and extensive use of the Internet in communication, as well as the "globalized" nature of the city, it is an ideal test case to examine the role of information technology in these issues. To examine these questions, we invited twenty-four adolescents aged between 13 and 14 to participate in a focus group study with parental consent in November, 2000. The fifteen female and nine male participants were divided into three discussion groups. Each participant was given a $10 incentive and taxi fare. A separate room was set up to host their parents and guardians.

At the beginning of each focus group discussion, participants were asked to talk about friendship, specifically the qualities of friends. This served two purposes – as a means to understand the adolescents' definition of friends, as well as to serve as a warm-up. Subsequently, they were each given a piece of paper with four colored boxes. The four boxes represented four different types of friends. In the yellow box, participants wrote down names of friends whom they first met face-to-face, but the Internet had later become a means of communication with them. In the pink box, they wrote down friends whom they first met online, but some time later they had seen each other face-to-face. The green box was for online friends with whom they had no other means (e.g. face-to-face) of interaction. Finally, the blue box was for friends with whom they had never communicated via the Internet. This exercise forced the participants to associate actual people with each category of friends, which made the discussion more concrete and meaningful. It also provided a visual aid for participants, since keeping track of four types of friends could be confusing. For each category of friends, participants talked about how they met, their characteristics, communication topics and activities, and quality of their friendship.

Since the data reported here are part of a much larger project examining friendship formation and maintenance among Singapore youth, we will not attempt to provide definitive answers to the many provocative questions arising from this brief literature review. We will, however, report the general tone of the responses, which give some meaningful indication of how Singaporean youths use the Internet in relationship maintenance, and have some relevance to the impact of the Internet in Asia more generally.

The findings of these focus group discussions tended to downplay the impact of the Internet in relationship formation. The majority of the participants said that they have many friends whom they first met face-to-face, such as at school and camps (e.g. leadership and holiday), and through extra-curricular activities. Subsequently, the friendship moved on to cyberspace. However, this did not replace face-to-face interaction or other forms of mediated communication, such as using the telephone. In fact, the adolescents said they often use the Internet to organize themselves and arrange for face-to-face get-togethers.

In fact, the role of the Internet in some ways serves a purely utilitarian function. Moving a face-to-face relationship online is a matter of convenience and efficiency. Compared to telephone calls or face-to-face meetings, the Internet allows effective, one-to-many communication. For the most part, the adolescents use the Internet for arranging outings, discussing friendships and problems, and trading gossip. Instead of repeating the same message or gossip to different people, it is simply easier to broadcast it to their friends via the Internet. Furthermore, they can send materials, such as popular songs and pictures, to each other online.

Since computer-mediated communication is private and conducive to disclosure, it provides a good opportunity to share sensitive information or opinions. Normally, 13 to 14-year-olds in Singapore hang out as a group. In such a group setting, discussion of sensitive and private matters can be rather awkward since not all friends are equally trustworthy and understanding. The Internet, however, allows them to share thoughts and feelings with selected friends. Of course, telephone calls are another option. Unfortunately, they are less private as family members can overhear the conversations, and often parents and siblings are not happy when the calls are too long.

Furthermore, the Internet seems to help those with difficulties in verbalizing their thoughts and feelings. As one adolescent, Karanjit, said, "They tend to tell you certain things that they don't dare to tell you over the phone or face-to-face. When they type ... they just find it better." Because of this, it is not surprising that some adolescents find that they know their friends better after they include the Internet as a channel for communication.

The Internet gives the adolescents a means not only to maintain their current relationships but also to seek out new friends. However, the data from the 2000 Singapore Internet Project survey of Secondary-One students show that close to 60 percent of the 871 respondents do not have online "pen pals"; and for the remaining 40 percent, most managed to

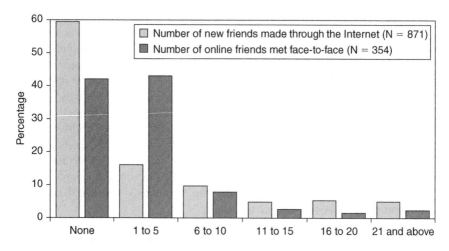

Figure 15.1 Online and offline friendship formation
Source: The Singapore Internet Project, year 2000 survey data

befriend only a handful of people via the Internet. Furthermore, as shown in Figure 15.1, adolescents do not actually meet these online friends face-to-face. This is consistent with another study of Singaporeans aged between 15 and 30, which reveals that they hardly ever form close online relationships and that making new friends over the Internet is rare (Goby, 2000). Similar to the survey respondents, our focus group participants do not have an overwhelming pool of online friends.

Although proximity is no longer a prerequisite for friendship in this Internet age, the face-to-face element remains important. Adolescents' close friends are typically people within their immediate environment and whom they first get to know face-to-face. They continue to meet, but also use a variety of communication channels, including the Internet, to maintain their relationship. In times of trouble, they turn to these close friends, who understand them and whom they can trust. As participant Xiaojia said, "They will understand the situation you're in. But online friends, I don't think they really understand." In fact, online friends are ineffective and unhelpful. Another participant Ferene echoed this sentiment: "Online friends just tell you to cheer up. They won't help you solve your problems anyway. So, there is no point in telling them."

This suggests that virtual relationship cannot fulfill entirely the functions of traditional peer relationships and meet the needs of young Singaporeans. To the few exceptions, however, virtual friendship has its occasional advantage; that is, their secrets are safe with online friends, who have no direct contact with their social network. Perhaps this shows that adolescents value their social network and are concerned about what people within their immediate life space think of them. According to these few adolescents, it is possible to build up trust with online friends, but it takes a long time.

Contrary to what adults believe, adolescents' online friends – that is, people whom they first meet over the Internet and may or may not have interacted through other communication channels – are mostly local. Besides, they often "meet" these online friends through their schools' online channels. In other words, their cyber-pals are often schoolmates whom they have not met. Moreover, they have not expressed strong inclination or interest in seeking foreign online friends. This is consistent with the Singapore Internet Project 2000 and 2001 survey findings that most adolescents' email communication and online discussion are with local people. In the 2001 Singapore Internet Project Student Survey, 79.6 percent of the 794 Secondary-One Internet users said their email communication was mostly with local friends, 4.7 percent said it was mostly with foreign friends, and 15.7 percent said the numbers of locals and foreigners were about the same. Both the 2000 and 2001 surveys revealed that the students' online discussion about relationships, hobbies, entertainment, and sports was predominantly with local people. Although the adolescents do not consciously pick online friends based on socio-demographic characteristics, they inevitably end up befriending people similar to them. They prefer people whom they can talk with and who share their interests, such as computer games. Even though Singapore is a small country and the Internet provides opportunities for borderless, global relationships, our findings suggest that adolescents communicate primarily with other teenagers within their own culture.

There are some exceptions to this trend. Although most of their friends are local, a few have ventured into a foreign world. For example, a couple of the focus group participants do communicate with teenagers from Indonesia and Malaysia, two neighbors that are both geographically and culturally proximate. They talk about their schools and learn about in what ways the education systems are different. One specific individual has been learning Japanese as her third language, and to her it is beneficial to discuss the language with people who are competent speakers.

Thus, it is helpful to delineate the distinction between the impact of the Internet on prior relationship maintenance and on relationship formation. In the Singapore context, the Internet presents an alternative and convenient venue for young Singaporeans to interact with friends from their immediate social environment. Some scholars have argued that Internet-based exchanges may be detrimental to social relationships because they are shallow, and lack the richness of context and visual-aural cues (Perse and Courtright, 1993; Rice, 1993). However, the Internet, like telephone and face-to-face meetings, has both positive and negative features. Adolescents simply choose the medium that best serves their needs. For example, our focus group participants do have a few friends who are not interested in using the Internet or do not have easy Internet access. They do not terminate the friendship; instead, they make telephone calls or see these friends face-to-face.

As Kendall (1999) argues, people do not make the distinction between online and offline worlds. The so-called virtual community is merely an extension of the physical world, and the dichotomy is often unnecessary. Meeting people online is quite common. However, it takes months for adolescents to transform an online encounter into friendship; and more often than not, the interaction will be terminated before it reaches a meaningful stage. According to the adolescents' own definition, friends must be willing to talk and share problems. In addition, friends must be trustworthy, reliable, helpful, and understanding. Frequency of contact and how long they have known each other are not criteria for defining friendship. Online friends have difficulties in reaching some of these standards, especially in being helpful and understanding. This is imaginable since adolescents and their online friends do not share an immediate social network.

Overall, the Internet facilitates existing face-to-face friendship. Meeting people is easy on the Internet, but turning online acquaintances into friends is not easy. In the Singapore context, the Internet is binding adolescents to other young people within their homogeneous world; and the Internet is part of their real world.

INTERNET AND SOCIAL COMPETENCE

Besides relationship formation and maintenance, other significant issues have relevance to the ways in which relationships are mediated through the Internet. For example, as with family and school, peer groups are an important and influential socialization force during adolescence; and although adolescents have fewer rights than adults, they are expected to engage in genuine social interaction (Cahill, 1986). Traditionally, peer groups function as a microcosmic community where adolescents acquire and hone social skills, including the art of negotiation and impression management (Buhrmester, 1990; Caplan and Weissberg, 1989). Thus, peer socialization is important, as it helps adolescents to become socially competent.

As increased attention has been given to the role of the Internet in social interaction, a question arises as to whether the Internet will enhance or cripple young people's social competency. Some Singapore-based researchers have suggested that as children become more reliant on impersonal machines for communication and entertainment, their social skills will suffer and social isolation will increase (Low *et al.*, 1999). This certainly does not bode well, since it implies the disintegration of a community. However, if the Internet is an extension of adolescents' real world, then it can also be a venue for them to acquire social competence.

From our focus group discussions, we learn that the Internet does present another platform for developing social skills, specifically in networking and making introductions, and handling awkward situations and negative emotions. As mentioned above, adolescents use the Internet to stay in touch with their friends, especially those who share their interests or who are from other schools. "I don't really meet them very frequently," said one focus group participant. "So through the Internet, we can just talk to each other." Furthermore, it is common for adolescents to introduce a friend (or a group of friends) to other friends via the Internet. This typically happens when they think both parties share certain characteristics (for example, have common interests) and may like each other. Sometimes this can happen with or without the consent of either party. Online self-introduction is common too. A focus group participant has provided a description about how she sometimes notices familiar faces at school. Unfortunately, they have never been formally introduced. She will go through the school yearbook on the Internet and find out more about them. Then she will go online and initiate contact.

Unfortunately, friendship may not flourish despite enthusiastic introductions. In addition to disappointments, adolescents will have to learn how to deal with their own as well as their friends' negative reactions. For example, young people often pull pranks on each other over the Internet. They may pretend to be someone else and chat with their friends online. However, their friends may not necessarily appreciate these behaviors and become angry.

One difficult transition is that of meeting online friends for the first time. Since adolescents assume that the encounter will be awkward, they strategize to minimize this awkwardness. Thus, these meetings usually take place in a public arena (e.g. an Internet café) and adolescents typically invite other friends to go along. This method seems to work in at least two favorable ways. First, it provides them with protection. For example, new online friends will not dare to engage in sexually explicit discussion in public and in front of other people. Second, if the encounter is excessively awkward, their offline friends can help extricate them. Similarly, new online friends also come with a group of friends. In the end, it is two groups of adolescents meeting in a public place. Almost all focus group participants who have attempted to meet their online friends have experienced disappointment, nervousness, shyness, and regret. "They turn out to be very different from what you know about them from the Net," advised Ferene. "So, at least you should bring along your friends and maybe you can talk to your friends instead." Together, they learn to cope with the psychological discomfort.

The second type of social competence that may be observed through adolescents' interaction on the Internet is organizing skills. As mentioned above, young Singaporeans regard the Internet as an efficient channel for planning face-to-face meetings. For example, they discuss where they should meet, what they should do, and whom they should invite. These arrangements may be private or related to the school's extra-curricular activities.

A second significant area of socialization is helping to establish the appropriate boundaries for interaction. Adolescents often gossip about friends and teachers at school, swap stories about extra-curricular activities, and chat about gender and friendship. At this age, adolescents are still in the process of forming their identities. Although they do not have a problem interacting with the opposite gender, the topics of discussion are not necessarily the same. Just as in the physical world, boy–girl conflict and mutual teasing exist at this age. As Audrey described, "When the girls of our class see the boys of our class, they'll try to quit the channel.... Then when the guys know it is us, they'll start to make fun of us."

The third type of social competence that adolescents can glean from the Internet is on disclosure and lie detection. In fact, the Internet provides perhaps an ideal context to develop these skills. As expected, disguise is a norm in adolescents' online interaction. We described above how adolescents pretend to be someone else in order to fool their friends over the Internet. This type of disguise is set up for pranks and fun. The deceived party may get upset. Since they know they may be targets of pranks, they do not immediately believe. Pranks and teasing are part of the adolescent world. However, adults are worried about deception and disguise on the Internet. For example, individuals can adopt different personas and even assume the opposite gender – a difficult feat in the physical world. However, adolescents seem to think it is purely for pleasure and fun. Amanda's story may perhaps illustrate how adolescents can coordinate themselves to fool a friend:

> A whole group of us went to my friend's house. We had nothing to do, so we went online. Then we saw this friend online. So, we messaged her, and pretended to be a guy. We asked her to go steady (to go on a date or be in a dating relationship), and used all kinds of romantic phrases.

In contrast to the perceptions of adults, disguise and deception seem rather innocuous to adolescents. Identity is an important criterion to judge a relationship and interaction (Donath, 1999). However, the lack of visual and aural cues in computer-mediated communication makes it difficult for individuals to detect disguise. To some, this is a pitfall of online communication. Individuals will not know if they have been cheated. However, adolescents are learning from this presumably negative aspect of online communication.

Another type of disguise occurs when meeting strangers online. The deception is mutual, and they do not get angry when they discover the truth. Adolescents are fully aware that people whom they meet online may not be telling the truth, and therefore they, too, hide their identities. Since both parties are presumably lying they are even, and there is no need for negative sentiments. In fact, after discovering the truth, the relationship continues. This resonates with Clark's (2000) findings that dishonesty does not result in termination of friendships among American teenagers.

They typically distort two characteristics – gender and age. During the interaction with an online stranger, they usually try to match the other party's characteristics. Masquerading is a norm and it is not "wrong." In fact, they think it is beneficial in three ways. First, it protects them. They seem to understand the need to be careful. Second, they believe a success-ful match of identity will result in greater acceptance and smoother inter-action. Third, disguise allows them to have fun. Disclosure is incremental. Some form of negotiation will take place, and as one party reveals a little truth, the other will follow suit. However, before the disclosure process begins, adolescents will attempt to determine what is true and what is not. Participants in our focus group sessions revealed a number of fairly sophisticated strategies for cheat detection, such as seeking confirmation from friends. Since many of their online friends are students in their own schools, checking with their friends may help to piece together the puzzle as to who these online friends are and if they are telling the truth. Other strategies include an attempt to identify their online friends' IP addresses, which may tell them from where they are sending their messages. Asking for an exchange of photographs, and trying to find clues in the tone and use of language, may also help.

CONCLUSION

It is problematic to pitch online communication against face-to-face com-munication or to separate virtual and physical worlds. Computer-mediated communication is a lean channel (Walther, 1992); that is, it has fewer cues and is more suitable for simple, equivocal messages. Compared with face-to-face communication, it is lower in social presence, which means there is less involvement in the joint process of communication (Short *et al.*, 1976). Taken out of context, computer-mediated communication seems inferior (Jones, 2000; Rheingold, 1993). However, it has advantages that are unmatched by other channels for interaction. As scholars have pointed out, face-to-face communication can be dysfunctional and unpleasant – such as quarrels and verbal abuses (Hamman, 1998). It is perhaps more apt to view online communication, not by itself, but to examine it within an individual's entire repertoire of communication channels.

In the case of young Singaporeans, the Internet has become part of life, although it is by no means their only, or even primary, communication channel. Convenience, practicality, and efficiency determine their choice of communication channel. Similarly, there is no evidence of a virtual community that is disengaged from the real world. Although young Singaporeans have transferred some of their time and activities online, they remain connected to their society. Peer relationship is rooted in their community, especially the school. Interaction beyond the borders is limited. Adolescents want people who will listen to them and understand them. Therefore, it is not surprising that their online communication is directed mainly at local teenagers whom they already know. It is obvious that the Internet allows adolescents to extend their peer interaction into cyberspace. If indeed there is infiltration of foreign, unacceptable elements, it is less likely to be through computer-mediated communication. Furthermore, this type of peer interaction, as in the real world, continues to help them acquire certain social competence. This example from Singapore indicates that there is no evidence to show that the Internet will cripple young people's social skills or lead them towards isolation.

BIBLIOGRAPHY

Adams, R.G. (1998) "The demise of territorial determinism: online friendships," in R.G. Adams and G. Allan (eds) *Placing Friendship in Context*, Cambridge: Cambridge University Press.

Allan, G.A. (1979) *A Sociology of Friendship and Kinship*, London: George Allen & Unwin.

Ariff, S. (2002) "Parents willing to spend on kids' PCs," *Straits Times (Singapore)*, October 5. Online. Available Lexis-Nexis Database.

Berndt, T. (1992) "Friendship and friends' influence in adolescence," *Current Directions in Psychological Science*, 1: 156–9.

Buhrmester, D. (1990) "Intimacy of friendship, interpersonal competence, and adjustment during preadolescence and adolescence," *Child Development*, 61: 1101–11.

—— (1996) "Need fulfillment, interpersonal competence, and the development contexts of early adolescent friendship," in W.M. Bukowski, A.F. Newcomb and W.W. Hartup (eds) *The Company They Keep: Friendship in Childhood and Adolescence*, Cambridge: Cambridge University Press.

Cahill, S.E. (1986) "Childhood socialization as a recruitment process: some lessons from the study of gender development," in P. Adler and P. Adler (eds) *Sociological Studies of Child Development*, Greenwich, CT: JAI Press Inc.

Caplan, M.Z. and Weissberg, R.P. (1989) "Promoting social competence in early adolescence: developmental considerations," in B.H. Schneider, G. Attili, J. Nadel and R.P. Weissberg (eds) *Social Competence in Development Perspective*, Drodrecht, The Netherlands: Kluwer Academic.

Chua, B.H. (1997) "Modernism and the vernacular: transformation of public spaces and social life in Singapore," in J.H. Ong, C.K. Tong and E.S. Tan (eds) *Understanding Singapore Society*, Singapore: Times Academic Press.

Clark, L.S. (2000) "Dating on the Net: teens and the rise of 'pure' relationships," in S.G. Jones (ed.) *Cybersociety 2.0: Revisiting Computer-Mediated Communication and Community*, Thousand Oaks, CA: Sage.

Donath, J.S. (1999) "Identity and deception in the virtual community," in M. Smith and P. Kollock (eds) *Communities in Cyberspace*, New York: Routledge.

Duck, S. (1989) "Social competent communication and relationship development," in B.H. Schneider, G. Attili, J. Nadel, and R.P. Weissberg (eds) *Social Competence in Development Perspective*, Drodrecht, The Netherlands: Kluwer Academic.

Festinger, L., Schacter, S., and Back, K. (1950) *Social Pressures in Informal Groups*, New York: Harper.

Foo, C.M. (1989) *Patterns of Friendship Formation in the School Setting*, unpublished academic exercise, Department of Sociology, Singapore: National University of Singapore.

Gegas, V. (1981) "Contexts of socialization," in M. Rosenberg and R.H. Turner (eds) *Social Psychology: Sociological Perspectives*, New York: Basic Books.

Goby, V.P. (2000) "Social interaction and the Internet in Asia: A study of young Singaporeans," *Australian Journal of Communication*, 27 (3): 79–90.

Gudykunst, W.B. (1998) "Individualistic and collectivistic perspectives on communication: an introduction," *International Journal of Intercultural Relations*, 22 (2): 107–34.

Hamman, R. (1998) "The online/offline dichotomy: debunking some myths about AOL users and the effects of their being online upon offline friendships and offline community," unpublished M.Phil. thesis, Department of Communication Studies, University of Liverpool. Online. Available HTTP: http://www.socio. demon.co.uk/mphil/index.html.

Hartup, W.W. (1996) "The company they keep: friendships and their developmental significance," *Child Development*, 67: 1–13.

Havighurst, R.J. and Jansen, A.J. (eds) (1967) "Community research: trend report and bibliography," special issue, *Current Sociology*, 15 (2).

Ho, K.C. (1984) "Networks of interpersonal relations: a comparative study of friendship, kinship and neighbourhood relationships," unpublished MA thesis, Department of Sociology, National University of Singapore.

—— (1988) "The community study: a discussion of the method with modifications for research in Singapore," working paper no. 96, Department of Sociology, National University of Singapore.

Jones, S.G. (1995) "Understanding community in the information age," in S.G. Jones (ed.) *CyberSociety: Computer-Mediated Communication and Community*, Thousand Oaks, CA: Sage.

—— (2000) "Information, Internet and community: notes toward an understanding of community in the information age," in S.G. Jones (ed.) *Cybersociety 2.0: Revisiting Computer-Mediated Communication and Community*, Thousand Oaks, CA: Sage.

Katz, J. and Aspden, P. (1997) *Friendship Formation in Cyberspace: Analysis of a National Survey of Users*, project report for The Markle Foundation. Online. Available HTTP: http://www.nicoladoering.net/Hogrefe/katz.htm.

Kendall, L. (1999) "Recontextualizing "cyberspace": methodological considerations for online research," in S. Jones (ed.) *Doing Internet Research: Critical Issues and Methods for Examining the Net*, Thousand Oaks, CA: Sage.

Kraut, R., Lundmark, V., Patterson, M., Kisler, S., Mukopadhyay, T., and Scherlis, W. (1998) "Internet paradox: a social technology that reduces social involvement and psychological well-being?" *American Psychologist*, 53: 1017–31.

Kuo, E.C.Y., Choi, A., Arun, M., Lee, W., and Soh, C. (2002) *Internet in Singapore: A Study on Usage and Impact*, Singapore: Times Academic Press.

Lazarsfeld, P. and Merton, R. (1954) "Friendship as social process," in M. Berger, T. Abel and C.H. Page (eds) *Freedom and Control in Modern Society*, New Jersey: Van Nostrand.

Low, G.T., Quah, M.L., and Yeap, L.L. (1999) "Loneliness among adolescents," in A. Chang, S. Gopinathan and W.K. Ho (eds) *Growing up in Singapore*, Singapore: Prentice Hall.

Low, L. and Kuo, E.C.Y. (1999) "Towards an information society in a developed nation," in L. Low (ed.) *Singapore: Towards a Developed Status*, Singapore: Oxford University Press/Centre for Advanced Studies.

Markus, H.R. and Kitayama, S. (1991) "Culture and the self: implications for cognition, emotion, and motivation," *Psychological Review*, 98 (2): 224–53.

—— (1994) "A collective fear of the collective: implications for selves and theories of selves," *Psychology and Social Psychological Bulletin*, 20 (5): 568–79.

Ministry of Information, Communications, and the Arts (2002) *Our Shared Values*. Online. Available HTTP: http://www.sg/flavour/value.asp.

Parks, M.R. and Floyd, K. (1996) "Making friends in cyberspace," *Journal of Communication*, 46: 80–4.

Perse, E.M. and Courtright, J.A. (1993) "Normative images of communication media: mass and interpersonal channels in the new media environment," *Human Communication Research*, 19: 485–503.

Rheingold, H. (1993) *The Virtual Community: Homesteading on the Electronic Frontier*, Reading, MA: Addison-Wesley.

Rice, R.E. (1993) "Media appropriateness: using social presence theory to compare traditional and new organizational media," *Human Communication Research*, 19: 451–84.

Short, J., Williams, E., and Christie, B. (1976) *The Social Psychology of Telecommunications*, New York: John Wiley.

Sim, T.N. (1990) "An investigation of friendship patterns and maternal attitudes and practices in children with conduct problems," unpublished academic exercise, Department of Social Work and Psychology, National University of Singapore.

Slevin, J. (2000) *The Internet and Society*, Cambridge: Polity Press.

Triandis, H.C. (1989) "The self and social behavior in differing cultural contexts," *Psychological Review*, 96 (3): 506–20.

Utz, S. (2000) "Social information processing in MUDs: the development of friendships in virtual worlds," *Journal of Online Behavior*. Online. Available HTTP: http://www.behavior.net/JOB/v1n1/utz.html.

Verbrugge, L.M. (1977) "The structure of adult friendship choices," *Social Forces*, 56: 576–97.

Walther, J.B. (1992) "Interpersonal effects in computer-mediated interaction: a relational perspective," *Communication Research*, 19 (1): 52–90.

Wong, A.K., Ooi, G.L., and Ponniah, R.S. (1997) "Dimensions of HDB community," in J.H. Ong, C.K. Tong, and E.S. Tan (eds) *Understanding Singapore Society*, Singapore: Times Academic Press.

World Times (2002) *The 2002 Information Society Index*, Boston, MA: World Times Inc. Online. Available HTTP: http://www.worldpaper.com/2002/feb02/isi.jpg.

Index

Printed and bound by CPI Group (UK) Ltd, Croydon, CR0 4YY

01/11/2024

01782632-0017